Author: Thomas A. Ellis

Copyright © 2020 Thomas Ellis

First Edition June 2020

Edited by Dr. Victor A. Streeby

Cover Art by Jeff Walters

Layout by Jeff Walters

Photographs by Thomas Ellis

Printed by Hott off the Press in the USA

Hott off the Press

1330 Keosauqua Way

Des Moines, IA 50309

hottoffthepress.com

Christina's Story:
Behind the Glass

Author: Thomas A. Ellis

Edited by Dr. Victor A. Streeby

To my wife, Christina:

I miss you every day. The minutes seem like years passing and my heart yearns to be with you again. I know I wasn't the best husband during our marriage, but I always loved you and I know you loved me. You always smiled and made the best out of life that you could, and I am forever proud of you. With all my heart, I can say that you, my lady, are an angel and always have been. The memories you have given me I will treasure throughout all of my days, as each one was a gift from God. Without fail, you always loved me, listened to me, and gave me strength. I thank you for being my wife and for loving me all these years. Mostly, I thank you for being you. Not a day goes by that I don't miss you and think about the love that was in your heart for me. Christina, as I raise my head to Heaven, I know you are looking down at me. Your heart is my heart, and my heart is your heart, forever. Life isn't the same without you. My heart is broken and half of my soul is gone.

With all my love to you,

Thomas

In Loving Memory

Of

Christina Lorraine Ellis.

1970-2018

Dedicated

to

Christina Lorraine Ellis

Acknowledgements

Our Lord Jesus Christ

Our God of Abraham

Most Holy Mother Mary

Donna Ellis (Mother)

Trenton Ellis (Son)

Charlotte Harter (Aunt)

Marsha Vincent (Aunt)

Dr. Victor A. Streeby, Ph.D. English – Creative Writing

Dr. Ronald Berges, DO Psychiatry

Dr. Russell England, DO Psychiatry

Dr. Stephan Zella,, DO Psychiatry

Dr. Jean-Marie Stephan, MD Oncology

Dr. Lonnie L. Lanferman, MD

Cindy Millard (Department of Human Services)

Mark Williams (Department of Human Services)

James Mancilla-Ruiz (Department of Human Services)

Ray Bigham

Tru Howard

Jaimee Smith

Justin Thomas

Janice Mason

Friends at Camelot Towers

Nucara Pharmacy (Staff)

University of Iowa Hospitals and Clinics

Mary Margaret

Bryan Kinnaird

William Echols (LandShark Scuba & Snorkel Center)

Rick Wemer (Patterson Monument)

Hawkeye Caramazza (Patterson Monument)

Bob Rajchel (Photography, Video and Designs)

Preface

Sometimes, in one's life, the Devil finds his way in, takes hold, and a life is wounded and the soul is on the brink of annihilation. Just as the lady who lives in the darkness and dwells in a shaft with no light around silently screams out for help, for no one to hear. But, then a man, walking in the wilderness, in the darkness, hears the cries of the lady deep within the well she fights to get out of, and stops and listens. He uncovers the well that the lady has been in for so long. He extends his right arm into the depths of Hell she was forced into at such a young age. Reaching deep within the blackened abyss, he feels her hand. With all his strength, faith and courage, he pulls her into the light. Laying her upon the ground he whispers, "You are safe and it's okay to cry." He tells the lady, "You will hurt, and you will feel pain, but with faith in God the Father, you, my lady, will heal." Wrapping his arms around her, he comforts her and the seeds of life begins to grow within her again. I told this story to Nicole almost every day. For this story is, and was, her actual life from the age of five years old until the day she passed away. From the torment of evil spirits to eventually learning faith, she was a survivor of the sins of society, and the tortures of the Devil in human and beyond-human forms. Nicole lived, loved, hurt, cried, and finally found her savior in Jesus Christ, becoming free for the first time in her life, upon her death.

Contents

Chapter One
Behind the Glass

The strings of the cello play a soft melody in my head as I walk to the front door. What once was beautiful is now gone from my heart, but lives for all eternity in my soul. I raise my head to the heavens. The clouds roll in from the heavy winds and the thunder begins to shake the ground below. Lightning networks across the sky, lighting the dimmed world. The rain slams against Mother Earth and upon my flesh. I stand in the downpour, looking for my wife, but she is gone to my Lord in Heaven. I turn and walk through the ruins of what was once a temple. The walls are cracked, our pictures have fallen, and our house I do not recognize. I no longer have any direction in life but to fulfill the promises I made to my wife. I look around and try to pick up the pieces of our life together, just fragments, but still precious to me. I reach the bedroom and enter. My body is cleaved, my soul bleeds, and my shoulders are heavy with sorrow. I disrobe and stand naked, gazing at my wounded body. I didn't even have time to feel anything.

I walk to the altar and kneel before my Lord in Heaven, kiss his feet and light the candle. Struggling to hold myself up, my eyes fill and my chamber rages with pain. The emotions pour out and I feel this hurt of immense magnitude overtaking my body. The tears stream down my naked flesh. I fall from the altar as I fell from grace, with my thoughts filled with anger and rage. I stand and move to the bed, reach for my bible and begin reading. The light is dim, but the words are illuminated. I stop and exclaim to my Lord in Heaven, "Help me understand why I was shown a great many things by your hand, my Lord, and some I wish I could un-see, but I can't. My wife was plagued by the Devil and I was shown the face of Lucifer and his demons. I know now, my Lord, that no one is safe."

Lucifer snatches souls like a thief and enters the unseen when our love has been reduced to its lowest point. He ravages our bodies in the darkness of day and in the light of the night. He injects a euphoric feeling of power into our veins that rushes in and takes over our better judgment. Our minds are filled with an intense lust for pleasures of the senses. He rapes the souls of everything good, without warning, stealing the drops of goodness – one by one by one. And yet we are unaware that Lucifer and his demons are there, destroying our will and our faith without mercy. He tortures our soul with man-made instruments, those of every fleshly desire, laid out on a platter for us to devour. Yet, we are blind to the hidden poisons that the platter of pure gold possesses: hatred, deception, greed, isolation, destruction, desecration, anger, and arrogance.

My Lord, Lucifer hides in the shadows of every corner of the earth, annihilating tens of thousands of men, women and children every day. He murders our souls and we, like lost sheep, congregate to his feet, oblivious to the notion that we are there feeding him. Pride is Lucifer's power and he is eternally hungry. When, my Lord, did we allow ourselves to become weakened by material pursuits, lust and greed, that render our souls bereft of your Divine guidance? How has it come to pass that we have forgotten your Word, my Lord, and the praise you deserve? Every day, Father, I see Satan, and he is subtle and smooth in his methods of stealing our hearts and minds. We all seem lost and the weight of the silver in our purses weighs heavy within. The droplets from our tongues are the seeds that fill our baskets. Satan clouds our minds with lies, sins of the flesh, alcohol, drugs, and hatred. He masks himself behind the glass, pretending to be good, falsely claiming he can give us all we need. My Lord, the Devil cuts down the trees and skins the bark until damnation is successful. Even now, he is watching me as I bleed with sorrow. Lucifer forced my hand, and my wife's hand, into:

The Devil's House

The house marked by the Dove

remains in the light for all to see.

What is believed to be the light of God

is sullied and tainted by Satan.

Blood stains the hands of the living demons

that scour the earth to collect, ravage, neglect and euthanize

all who enter. The sounds of those crying for help,

in pain, and those who become sedated

into the netherworld become silent

for no one to hear. Nicole and I

were cast into the fire. Alone, I fight

to protect the one in the house of the Dove.

But I couldn't even protect her…

Why did you leave us, my God of Abraham?

Where were the angels? Why couldn't I feel you,

my Father in Heaven? Abandoned, I felt, my Lord.

I asked You, when would it be over?

When can my wife and I leave

the fiery Hell of Satan's house?

When will my Father's daughter go to Heaven?

My veins bleed from the jagged razors

slowly cutting away at my soul.

I cannot hold them off forever.

My blade is dull, my heart is weak, and I am tired.

The mocking, whispering and laughter penetrates

my mind. I scream out in pain.

I fall to my knees. My blade is breaking,

my mind shattering. Help me, Father,

stop this war, stop her suffering and mine.

Please, take her to be at your side.

I beg of you, allow us to rest.

My Lord, I am now living day by day, and my eyes see beyond the glass where the angels and demons fight constantly. My Lord, Jesus, I did not know my eyes would be shown the afterlives of Heaven, Hell, and the multitude of demons scouring the earth. I am tired, Father, weary and weak, and even as I pray to you, the Devil is listening. I know now that Heaven is always at war with Satan, and many angels have died fighting to save us from the depths of Hell. We are not safe until we follow the light in the darkness and heed your Word as gospel. Humility, faith, and your Word make the sword that will fight the Devil and drain the iniquities from your creation. Help me understand why the illusory perceptions between falsehood and truth lie in the rivers that run dry in the shadows of light. Help me understand why a life becomes the rock that bellows into the night of day, to be seen when the ears of men and women hear without sight.

My Lord in Heaven, for decades the Devil ravaged, cleaved and maimed my wife, and without fail he destroyed her life through the hands of many people. Yet, she found faith and love through You and Your works, my Lord, and believed and kept her faith until the end. But, Father, the Devil kept coming and found new ways to hurt us both. I am sorry, Lord, for I failed you and my wife. My sword was broken, my shield fell, and my armor was nearly destroyed. My horse, named "Faithful," is exhausted and lays within the dust. I am tired, my Lord, and my eyes grow heavy from the pain and sorrow. I must tend to these wounds and stop the bleeding, Father. My bed is broken, and the war continues, inwardly and outwardly. My heart longs to know that, one day, the Devil will meet the sword which will be forged again and laid upon my hand. Along with my brothers who protect the kingdom of Heaven, I am with you, my heavenly Father.

My Lord God, I know you did not leave my wife and me. Please hear me, Father, and show me the way home. Lead me to your Word. With my bible in my hands, and my cross around my neck, I lay down and rest my head upon the pillow my wife once used. The quilt covers my body and you, my Jesus, comfort me in my hour of need. I cry out and call my wife's name, hoping she can hear me through the storm. Laying in the rubble upon my broken bed, darkness is about me and the cold settles inward. My wounds still bleed as I lay on the mattress. I begin to hear a peaceful melody playing. A lady's voice cries out in the wind, "I love you, honey. Come home soon, my husband." I embrace her words with love. I close my eyes, and with the bible in my hands, her picture on my chest and tears running down my cheek, I drift in and out of the worlds we live and die in. I see my brothers, the archangels, standing watch over me as I begin to fade into the night. Finally, I sleep, and my heart beats slowly as my battle-torn body marks the war that has passed.

I begin to dream of the time when my wife and I lived together. Memories fill the place where I sleep. As the night moves on, the storm subsides and the archangels watch over me. The Devil stands in the distance, contemplating his next move. He tells his demons, as I sleep under the protection of the angels, "He is broken and the time to strike is coming. We will devour him like the water that surges upon the mountains. Yet, we must wait until the time is right and the angels have gone." The archangels turn and face the Devil and his demons, drawing their swords as each angel takes form around me. Tossing and turning from the pain, my soul cries deep within. One archangel whispers softly in my ear, "My brother, we are all proud of you, for your wife is with our Lord Jesus in Heaven. Her torment is no more." The archangel kisses my forehead and says, "Aaron, go and see the beauty upon the land."

Deep within my mind, I dream of a place I've never been before. When I awaken, I look around and see beauty everywhere. I think to myself that this place seems to be untouched by the Devil. I look down at my once-cleaved body and, to my amazement, it has been healed. How can this be? Where am I? Looking up to the sky, I pray to Father in Heaven. "My Lord, where am I? Have I died? Is this Heaven, or am I dreaming?" His voice returns, "I am here, my son, and you must heal, Aaron. My angels will protect you now, my son, as the Devil will come for you in your tormented and weakened state. You will know, feel and see him, and your eyes will not be blind. I have shown you a great many things in this world, even where the Devil sits and watches."

"But, my Lord, why *me*? Why am I the one to know how a soul can be snatched like the thief that takes the sheep from the Shepherd?"

Hearing no answer, with faith I walk into the new land that has been brought before me.

Chapter Two
The Light

*A*s I walk along the green-meadowed trail below the mountainside, I slowly look down and watch each step. I think to myself, with each mark I make against the flesh of Mother Earth, how long will it be before she consumes my worldly existence? In the distance I hear the Mute Swans upon the glacier waters that cascade down from the snow caps above. Stopped in my tracks, I see the swans' snow-white plumage, orange bills and black markings above me. The frozen moment appears to be a painting from the angels in Heaven. The green reeds, blue waters, and the backdrop of the Alps take my breath away. I continue to gaze at the beauty before me and make my way to a huge, multi-colored stone, impossible to miss in the distance.

I perch my body high on the granite as the waters stretch far behind it. The swans move, the sun shines down and the breeze caresses my flesh. Softly, I lay back and rest. Mother Earth wraps warmth, comfort and peace around my body. My eyes close and the magnificent sensory perceptions continue as I hear the air-splitting cries of white-tailed eagles soaring in the heavens. I feel so at peace, like I know this place, but do not know why or how. Laying upon the granite, I am surprised at its comfort and my body molds to every contour. Sinking deep within myself, my mind drifts and my flesh is momentarily absent as time slips into the night. Suddenly, I become aware of the presence of another, and when I awaken a white-tailed eagle is perched inches from me, her eyes fix on mine. For what feels like an eternity we seem as one.

I wonder what she is thinking, as I am doing the same. I notice her raise her head and stare into the heavens. I follow suit and look up – there is no moon, but the stars glow like lanterns in the sky. We both watch and finally the eagle takes flight and I sit up. I slide down off the granite and my impressions take hold once again upon the breast of Mother Earth. I continue to move forward in the darkness of night. The air is cooler than it was during the day, but still very soothing. The night is beautiful as I gaze at the crystal-clear lake in the distance where the Mute Swans reside. The stars sparkle on the water like diamonds dancing on a ballroom stage.

In the distance a remote light catches the corner of my eye. I stop and wonder who else could be out here in this wilderness that feels like a forgotten home. My curiosity has peaked as if I was a twelve-year-old child waiting for Christmas to come. The anticipation inside of my mind brings forth so many questions. Through the meadows I walk toward the light and remind myself to take my time and not let the excitement grip every ounce of my being. The lake grows closer and I can smell the water as if it had rained with no clouds in the sky. Continuing on, I approach the lake with my eyes still fixed on the light, but I am suddenly stricken with amazement.

The lake is larger than I expected, and the Mute Swans are many and sleep peacefully on the water. I spot a family of deer all nestled in the womb of Mother Nature. Out of the corner of my eye, I see a wooden bench sitting on a marble patch about fifteen feet away from the water. How can this be when it seems I am alone here, in this place that has no name? As I approach the bench, I observe that it has the craftsmanship of a skilled carpenter. My hand softly grazes the wood and I realize the bench is made from oak and dogwood. I press down on the seat and kneel to view the structure in its entirety.

I rise and then sit facing the water. The sound of the waterfall feeding the lake is soothing and I find myself falling asleep where I sit, relaxed, and filled with peace. Morning sets in and, after a big yawn and a few stretches of my body, I rise. I cannot believe I am the only one around to enjoy the beauty of all God has to offer here. Yet, I still wonder if I am truly alone. I remember the light I had gazed upon. Although I do not see it now, in the daylight. I still remember the direction it was coming from. I set out to walk around the lake and enjoy every moment of the morning sun.

Watching, I see a bear cub splashing around, playing with his mother in the water. I smile when I see the momma bear pushing her bear cub over. Some of the Mute Swans take flight and look back at me. Even the momma bear stops and looks, but I keep going, as instinct compels me to do. The morning sky bears colors of blue, auburn and orange. The white, billowing clouds float in the oceans of blue. I begin to thirst and find myself drinking the cold lake water and cannot believe how pure it tastes. I look out and wonder if I will make it to the light I had seen last night. In my mind I am hopeful, but the light seemed so far away.

Pushing on, I finally arrive on the other side of the lake and now find myself standing on a trail that should not be here. I ask myself, how did it get here and who made this trail? I know I am alone in this place. I just know it. I look, and the road that goes up the mountainside appears to be well-maintained, with flowers on both sides, lilies, and rose bushes planted every thirty feet. It smells divine, combined with the other fragrances in the air. As beautiful as everything is, I know something is missing, but what could it be? I walk the trail and notice more wildlife coming out into the warmth of the sun. Dew blankets the ground and clings to my boots, moistening the leather.

The sun is now high above in the sky and my journey up the mountainside has extended for miles. I wonder if I was mistaken and the light was just a reflection from something. I take a few moments and sit next to a rose bush and enjoy the scenery. My right hand softly pulls a stem down with a partially open rosebud and I breathe in deeply. Instantly, I am taken back to the time when I tended to my own garden…but, as the day moves on, so must I. The sun is on the downward slide and the wind is picking up. I raise my head and look to see if rain is coming, but the cloudless sky reassures me that the night will be quiet.

Suddenly, stronger winds push against my body and I stand like an anchor seated deep within the ground. Through the blustering I hear a lady's voice call my name. Chills run down my body. Again, I hear the same voice calling my name…"Aaron, Aaron."

I yell out into the evening winds, "Who are you? Where are you?"

But the lady's voice is gone. The wind has stopped. I do not understand what is happening. Am I losing my mind? Are things not as they appear?

At the top of my voice I cry out to our Father in Heaven, "Help me understand what is going on. Please, Father!"

I kneel and close my eyes, trying to grasp what is happening. Then I hear a man's voice ask, "Are you all right?"

I look up and see a man standing before me, wearing a white T-shirt, his face covered in a brown beard with some gray. His build is slim as he wears brown work boots. His voice is captivating and very deep. I ask, "Who are you?"

"My name is Johnathon. What is your name?"

"I am Aaron. Where did you come from, Johnathon?"

"I was walking down the trail when I heard your voice crying out to someone, but I couldn't make out who you were talking to."

"I wasn't calling on anyone…it was nothing."

"It sure sounded like you were in some sort of distress, Aaron."

"It really was nothing, but if you would like to sit with me, I could use the company."

"I would like that, Aaron, thank you. If I may ask, how long have you been here?"

"I don't know where 'here' is, nor do I know how long. It feels like I have been here for years, though."

"How long have *you* been in this place, Johnathon?"

"Oh, I come and go when I am needed."

"What do you mean? Who needs you?"

"It's complicated, Aaron, but the point is I am here now. This sure is a beautiful place you have."

"This is not my place!"

"Are you sure about that, Aaron?"

"Quite sure, Johnathon. I have never been here before. It's like I woke up in a dream and can't remember how I got here, or what I am supposed to be doing. In my confused state I heard a lady's voice call my name twice through the strong winds. That's when I cried out to Father in Heaven to help me understand what is going on."

"So, I did hear you crying out to someone."

"Yes, you did. I didn't want to admit that one minute I was enjoying the scenery, and smelling these beautiful roses, and then, in another, I heard a lady's voice in the wind. And, by the way, I have seen absolutely no one the entire time I have been here and then you appear after I cry out to Father in Heaven. How do you explain that?"

Smiling, Johnathon replies, "I guess you might say that I am a traveler and the wind takes me where I am needed."

"What about you, Aaron? What's your story?"

"Again, I don't remember how I got here. Before this I was resting in bed, with the angels watching over me, and my thoughts flourishing of the first time I met the love of my life."

"That sounds like a very peaceful setting."

"It was far from peaceful, Johnathon. But times like those always have a way of taking me back to the memories of my wife and all we shared together."

"I must say, Aaron, this is the first time I have seen you smile since I met you."

"Johnathon, she made me smile like no one else could."

"Aaron, if you don't mind, I would like to hear about you and your wife."

"Well, it's a long story Johnathon, and I am not sure you would believe half of the things I would tell you."

"Aaron, you might be surprised..."

With night approaching, and the air beginning to chill, Aaron gathers materials for a camp fire. He finds two sticks and strips them of their bark before working them against each other with rapid force. When smoke first appears, he blows on it gently to kindle the flames, and then adds some brush to allow the small fire to spread. The growing flames begin to give warmth.

"I see you found an old log to sit on, Jonathon," Aaron observes from his comfortable bed of meadow grass near the fire.

"Are you comfortable, Aaron, laying on the meadow floor?"

"I am, Johnathon."

As the night grows deeper the stars begin to shine, the padding from the tall grass feels like a soft, pillow-top mattress. The softer sounds of nature are all around, and the crackling of the fire adds to the ambiance.

"Johnathon, in the distance last night, I saw a light to the west on the mountainside. Was it coming from your place?"

"No, I don't have a place here, Aaron. I just pass through every so often. I would still like to hear about you and your wife sometime.

"If you're sure, Johnathon, but it will take some time."

"Well, I've got time and the fire is young."

Chapter Three

Impressions

"Johnathon, I grew up in a town with about thirty-thousand people. My parents had strong faith and they instilled every ounce of the church's beliefs in my brothers, sisters and me. We always went to church every Sunday and religion classes on Wednesday nights. My father was a factory worker building farm equipment and my mother worked in retail. Our house was simple and, with three other brothers and two sisters, sometimes the house seemed small, but we managed. We boys slept downstairs, my two sisters shared a room upstairs, and of course mom and dad had their own room. By no means were we rich. In fact we were very poor, especially when dad was laid off from work."

"You're smiling, Aaron. What were you thinking about?"

"I remember it was Christmas time and my parents didn't have any money for the six of us. Mom and dad put the Christmas tree in front of the picture window in the living room. There were lights on the tree with ornaments and dad always made sure the angel stood perfectly on the treetop. It was Christmas Eve and mom told me I better go to bed because Santa was coming. I asked my mother what Santa was bringing me for Christmas."

Mom replied, "We will just have to wait and see, Aaron."

"I don't remember what time it was when I woke up that night, or Christmas morning, but I do remember getting up and moving my blankets. I stumbled out of bed and made my way to the stairs. I grabbed onto the railing and with each step I took the stairs creaked a little. I opened the basement door that led to the kitchen. As I turned the corner and walked into the living room, I saw my mother sewing on the sewing machine. Mom looked at me and I asked her what she was doing."

Mom replied, "Never you mind, Aaron. Hurry up and do what you're going to do and get back to bed because Santa won't come if you're still awake."

"After I went to the bathroom I went straight to bed."

"How old were you, Aaron?"

"I was seven or eight years old, I think. That morning we kids woke up and Santa had been there. I grabbed my present and opened it. I got a stuffed animal. It took years for me to realize that mom went without sleep that night so each of us kids had a present to open Christmas morning. Dad made a fine Christmas dinner with what we had in the house and, as a family, we sat together and enjoyed the birth of Christ."

"That sounds beautiful, Aaron."

"Johnathon, it was, and to this day I still have the orange plaid bear my mother made for me."

"Aaron, a mothers love lasts forever."

"Yes, it does Johnathon."

"Aaron, tell me more."

"There were times when dad would walk my sister and I home from grade school. Sometimes he would buy us soft-serve ice cream from the filling station on the way home before we walked through the cemetery. As we would walk we would look at the different stones that had been placed to mark those who have gone to our Lord in Heaven. Some of the roads in the cemetery were paved and others were gravel. The trees, I remember, seemed like they had been there for centuries and some of the stones were so weathered we could barely read the names. Dad would tell my sister and I about the Bible and how Father in Heaven has prepared a place for us when it's our time to go. He would even quote scripture, and the one I always hung onto was 'where two or more are gathered in his name, I am there with you.' But, as strong as my faith was, there were moments that I would get scared of the unknown."

"What do you mean, Aaron?"

"I remember one time when I was thirteen or fourteen years old and fell asleep downstairs in my bed. I had a bad dream. I remember I heard a voice coming from the northeast corner of the basement. The man speaking was chanting, over and over, 'the Devil is your friend, the Devil is good, come to me.' I tried getting up out of bed, but it was a struggle. I felt fear and it was like something was holding me down. I crawled out of bed and made it to the staircase leading upstairs. I used my arms to pull me up, but it still felt as if someone or something had me and would not let go. I fought hard to make it up the stairs. When I made it out of my room, my father was sitting on the couch that sat below the picture window in the living room on the south wall, reading the newspaper. He asked me what was wrong, and I told him about my dream. Dad explained that the Devil is always looking and preying upon people to try to destroy them, young and old, through deception and invasion – and that I must remember God the Father is always watching over us."

"Your father seems like a very spiritual man."

"He is, Johnathon, and after he talked with me about the bad dream I went back to sleep. When I woke up dad was still there reading the paper. I told him thank you for talking to me about the man speaking of the Devil. Dad stated that we never had any conversation about that and I had been sleeping the whole time. It was very odd, and I did not understand what happened, but I was also very young."

"Aaron, sometimes things happen for a reason and they cannot be explained, but having your father in the dream gave you strength and courage."

"I know, but through the years there were other strange things that happened. When I was in third grade, I knew I had to go to Arizona. I was sitting at my desk in school looking at the map of the United States and pointed at the state not knowing why, but I knew I must go one day. Another strange occurrence happened when I was seventeen years old. A friend and I went to grab something to eat at a local restaurant. He ordered a drink and asked me if I wanted one. I said sure, and when the waitress brought us our drinks she sat both glasses in front of us. I remember my friend moved the glasses to the side and grabbed my wrist. As he held my wrist tight he asked me, 'Are you ready to fight?' I replied, 'Yes, I am,' and he said 'No, you're not, but when the time is right you will know it.'"

"What kind of fighting was your friend talking about, Aaron?"

"He wouldn't tell me…he just said I would know when the time came."

"I have to say Aaron, that doesn't happen every day. It sounds like you were following a path you were always destined to travel."

"There were many times Johnathon, when I was younger and still living at home, that I would smoke a cigarette late at night, leaning on my old 1979 pick-up truck asking Father in Heaven to reveal more to me. I would say, 'Father, please guide me and show me the way.' It was as if I knew of, and could feel, another plane of existence just beyond this life."

"What do you mean, Aaron? Are you talking about Heaven?"

"Yes, and also about Hell. There are many planes of existence, Johnathon, and I believe one must look behind the glass in order to truly see beyond the boundaries that bind our flesh and souls. Do you mind if I recite something I wrote? It might help you understand what I mean regarding the different planes of existence."

"I am all ears, Aaron."

Thoughts of the Unseen

I ask, what are we, and who are we as people? Are we a blank soul floating on the winds

of chance? Are we the formation of a society that gleams in the eyes of the sun? What if the reality of the illusion that people manifest is the screen we, as people, can't see because we are all blind to the existence of the soul created that is bound in the flesh? What if we are the rock that stands silently upon the dirt and serves a purpose beyond the wall? If man or woman delivers true nature within the heavens above the plains, then the rock does not fall silent but becomes the symbol of the unseen. What if the rock spoke to the air, wind and rain in a voice that moved through time, speaking of the waters that surged in one's life?

The rock may stand on a blade of grass and hold true for some time, but it may tilt upona whisper. Even as the rock tilts, it remains stone and breathes within the unseen. The stone is around the picture, behind the glass, behind the screen that gives birth to the essence of the flesh written on the pages of the canvasses of white. The stone chapters of the new beginnings that rest below and above the senses of the ticking of the clock are stained by the ink that bleeds in the rivers of falsehood and truth.

"What do you think of that, Johnathon?"

"I cannot say I understand fully what that means, but it invokes thought. If I was to speculate, I would say you were talking about being mindful and that life is not one-dimensional. Or, it might mean that we, as humans, have overlooked the true nature of our existence because we, as a society, have stopped communicating effectively and forgotten our true origin. But, Aaron, if I may say so, it sounds like you're a little different than most."

"Johnathon, that isn't the first time I have heard that…."

"Hang on, Aaron, I am going to get another log to put on the fire."

"Johnathon, all I could find is twigs and brush to keep the fire going. Where are you getting these logs for the fire from? I did not cut any trees down, nor have you, since we met."

"Oh, the logs were off in the distance. I spotted them and set a few off to the side while you were starting the fire earlier."

"I see Johnathon." I said, not sure about anything. I look up at the stars from the meadow floor. They shine brightly, and I again began to wonder about the light I had seen earlier. Sitting up, I turn westward and look for the light on the mountain. The excitement once again takes hold of my flesh. The light shines from what looks like the side of a cliff, and it's closer than I expected.

"Johnathon, do you see the light sitting on the cliff-side?!"

"I see it, Aaron."

"You said earlier Johnathon that you pass through here every so often. Do you know what that light is, or where it's coming from?"

"I can't say that I do, but the night is getting late. We need our sleep, but in the morning we can set out together to search for the light if you want."

"I would like that, Johnathon."

After Johnathon lays one last log on the fire, he begins to rest on Mother Nature's lush surface. I bed down, anxiously waiting for morning to come. Knowing that I have a friend to walk with me on this journey gives me peace, and my eyes grow heavy as a calmness takes hold.

Chapter Four

Cliff-side

*S*lowly, the burnt auburn sky breaks through, and I open my eyes to see the sun rising in the east. I turn my head and, in the distance, the wildlife rustles, bringing a smile to my face. In the heavens above, white-tailed eagles soar proudly. The smell of lilies and roses perfume the land. Stretching my arms, sitting up now, I look for Johnathon. I call out for him, but he's nowhere. I notice the log is gone that he was sitting on. The fire is out and where he was laying there are no impressions upon the land. I walk over to the path and call his name. Nothing. I wonder where he went, and if last night was just a dream. Is this all a dream?

Standing on the path that leads up the mountain, I decide to move on with my journey toward the light that resides on the cliff-side. With each step I gaze at the cliff. The higher I climb up the mountainside, I cannot help but look out at the land. As far as my eyes can see the beauty is miraculous and words cannot fully describe this place I am in. The sky is clear, the birds are many, and the lilies and rose bushes never end on this path. I turn back around and begin walking up the trail. With each step I take I know I am getting closer to the light. As mid-day approaches I come to a fork in the road – one continuing up the mountainside and one veering to the left.

I stop and ask myself, which way should I go? My mind says to go higher on the mountain, but my heart says to go left. I decide to take the path that veers to the left, thinking to myself that this must be the way to the light. The trail twists and turns and I stop to rest a moment and sip on the water I drew from the crystal-clear lake below. The anticipation is killing me inside, so I move forward. The trail leads me through a canyon and, as I walk around the bend, I cannot believe what I am seeing. I fall to my knees. How can this be? I pray, "Dear heavenly Father, please help me understand what is going on and why I am in this place. I feel like I am losing my mind. I need your guidance." Suddenly, I feel comfort and a warm breeze blows against my flesh. Inside of my mind I hear a voice: *"It's going to be okay, Aaron. Have faith."*

The sun is high, and the rays coming from the supreme orb burst through the clouds, lighting certain areas of God's creation. Slowly, I rise and collect my thoughts. I walk to the cliff's edge, and faintly I can see the lake below and the trail winding back down the mountain. The pine trees are green and orchestrate a melody as the wind blows through each needle. Turning back around, I stride to a fountain that flows with crisp, clean water. An angel beautifully stands on the water fountain's base. Made from white marble stone, each piece appears to be chiseled by the hands of a stone cutter. Her wings are spread, and the details of the statue are flawless.

Behind the fountain I see a cabin with pine trees in the back and one on each side. There are steps placed in the middle, leading up to a deck that stretches from one side to the other with railing wrapped around it. In front of the porch on each side there are three rose bushes and lilies spaced perfectly between them. I call out and ask if anyone is home. With no reply, I walk up the stairs and look through the glass in the door. I knock loudly and again ask if anyone is home. I move to the window on the left side of the cabin and peek to see if anyone is stirring around, but I do not see a soul.

I try the door latch and it opens. This cabin belongs to someone, and I think to myself that it's wrong to enter this home and that I wouldn't like someone coming into the place where I live. But I know I was led here by the light and there must be a reason why I am in this place. My mind hears a voice inside my head telling me that it's okay to enter. My hand reaches for the latch and I crack the door again.

In my heart I know it will be okay and whoever owns this place will understand. I hope. As the door opens, it creaks softly.

Walking in, I see a rug that says *"Home Sweet Home."* On the left of me there is a place to hang coats, and a bench to sit on and take off one's shoes or boots. I sit and take my boots off and begin to look around. As I leave the entryway I see the downstairs is open. The dining room, living room and sitting room are together and I can see the archway to the kitchen in the southwest corner of the cabin. The furniture is remarkable and has the mark of a craftsman. I ask myself why anyone would leave a place this beautiful empty. Is this cabin meant for me? Am I supposed to be here? Again, I hear the voice inside my head reassure me. Slowly, I make my way through the cabin.

In the living room, the fireplace is made from stone with a wooden mantle above. The entire cabin seems to be fully furnished. A staircase leading up to the loft turns in circles. I call out in a deep loud voice. "My name is Aaron. Is anyone here?" but there is no answer. I move towards the staircase and walk up to the loft. At the top of the stairs, I see it's all open – a king-sized bed, another fireplace, and furniture all around. Everything looks handcrafted. Even the bedding appears to be hand-sewn, with the stitching across the top of the comforter reading, "*I Love You.*" There's a rocking chair by the bed and a book called *A Love Story* sits on the end table by the oil lamp. I turn back around and head downstairs. The sitting room has a baby grand piano that is gloss black. I run my fingers across the piano and realize there is no dust. Someone must be maintaining this home.

My thoughts again flourish and I wonder who owns this magnificent place I am in and why I am here. Despite the splendor of this cabin, my anxiety is high and I need a release. I open the housing and the fallboard of the piano. I sit on the bench and stretch my fingers. I press down on the ivory keys and check to see if the piano is in tune. I close my eyes and begin to play Beethoven's *Moonlight Sonata*. The sound is amazing, and I am surprised by the music echoing throughout the cabin as if somebody else was playing it. After I finish, I rise and close the fallboard and housing. The fireplace is enticing, and I take a few logs sitting by the fireplace and light the fire before making my way to the dining room table as the cabin warms.

Through the window I see the rushing water flowing down the mountain. The muted sound is relaxing. Evening has come on, and I decide to stay in the cabin and get some rest. If someone does come home, I hope he or she will not be upset that I am here. The water flowing from outside and the crackling of the fireplace cause my eyes to grow heavy. I move to the couch, lay down and use my coat for a blanket. The arm of the couch is soft and makes a great pillow. I close my eyes and slowly drift off to sleep, thinking about the lady's voice in the wind, Jonathan, and this place that has no name.

Chapter Five
A Heart Stolen

As the morning slowly creeps in, I sit up and think to myself I sure could use a cigarette. Walking to the front door, I look over at the china hutch buffet and see a pack of cigarettes. I know those were not there last night. Picking up the pack, I take one out and smell the freshness of the tobacco. With a smile on my face I bring the pack with me. In the entryway I put my boots on and step outside, making sure to close the door behind me. I sit in the chair and relax. Looking out above the cliffs, I notice the clouds are getting darker in the distance. I can see lightning and hear the thunder. When I was young my mother always said thunder was the crashing of potato wagons in Heaven. I smile and enjoy the cigarette as the storm sets in for the day. My mind wonders what happened to Johnathon. I hope I will see him again. Weeks have passed, and I feel so alone.

I have not heard the lady's voice since the first time and I still wonder what this place is and where I am at. On the porch in the rocker I hear a white-tailed eagle in the sky. I stand and walk to the railing, look up and see her descending toward me from the darkening clouds. In a matter of moments, she lands on the railing within arm's reach of me. The eagle does not seem to fear me, nor do I fear the eagle. I extend my arm before God's creation and to my surprise the eagle steps up on my forearm. Our eyes meet once again, but as the rain sets in the eagle takes flight toward the heavens and disappears. Lost in the awe of what just happened, I begin to hear a faint voice in the distance. It grows louder, and I hear someone calling my name.

I stand and yell out, "I am here at the cabin!" and walk down off the porch into the rain and look in the direction of the trail. It's Johnathon! After greeting him and shaking his hand, I ask, "Where did you go, Johnathon?"

"I remembered I had some things to do. I apologize for leaving, Aaron. Is this the beautiful place you were looking for?"

"This is where the light was coming from Johnathon."

"Is anyone home, Aaron?"

"No, no one has been here Johnathon, and I have been staying in the cabin for weeks now. Has this place always been here?"

"Not that I ever remember, Aaron, but I have to say it's amazing. The view, the angel water fountain, and the cabin all feel relaxing and peaceful. Shall we get out of the rain Aaron?"

"We seem to be of one mind, Johnathon."

The two step back into the cabin and dry themselves off before Johnathon, seeing the piano in the sitting room, asks "By any chance do you play, Aaron, and would you show me?"

"I can play most anything. How about if I play 'The Rose' by Bette Midler'?"

"That sounds good to me Aaron."

I open the housing and the fallboard and sit on the bench. I stretch my hands and fingers to prepare as I always do. Johnathon takes a seat by the fireplace and I begin to play. With every stroke of the ivory keys, my thoughts flood with old memories. I look over and see Johnathon smiling and enjoying the moment.

"That was excellent, Aaron. Have you been playing long?"

"Yes, I have been playing for years. But I want to show you something in the dining room, if you would please come with me."

"Of course, Aaron. This place is full of wonder."

Sitting at the table, I tell Johnathon to gaze through the window and look at the river running down the mountain. The water rushing is now the only sound we can hear for who knows how many miles.

"Aaron, one could say this place is like Heaven."

"In the mornings, I have been getting up and staring out the window, just listening to every sound that Mother Nature has to offer. It is the perfect opportunity to spend some time in thought.

"What do you think about, Aaron?"

"With no one around, it's hard not to think about everything – my life, poetry, where I'm at, and my wife. This place reminds me of a poem I wrote, called 'Memories.' Even though it's not winter time, this place still reminds me of the poem."

"Could you recite the poem, Aaron?"

"If you would like me to, Johnathon. Here it is…

Memories

Softly I sit and gaze through the glass –

Slowly, I sip my coffee and watch

the blanket of white fall

from the morning sky. We embrace

each other's silence as our thoughts together

haunt the halls of this old cabin.

The newly painted timber

from the snow and ice sparkles

in the distance like diamonds.

When I was a child her heart became my heart

and loving her is all I have

ever known and loving me is all she needs.

She gives me inspiration and listens

to my every word without fail.

Passing years seem like yesterday,

Remembering back to when I was young

playing in the woods. An old relic

is all that remains and a part of me understands

that my time is coming to an end.

I gently reach over to crack the window,

and blissfully the coolness

rushes in, whispering

I love you.

"Thank you for sharing that with me. Do you write like that all the time, Aaron?"

"I mostly write about love, loss, the traveler, happiness and sadness. I like to project raw emotions on the canvasses of white."

"If you don't mind me asking, Aaron, was that poem about your wife?"

"Yes, it was Johnathon, and she passed away not too long ago. I blame myself every day."

"What causes you to blame yourself for her death?"

"It doesn't matter, Johnathon?"

"Well, Aaron, maybe sometime you can tell me about it, if you want to."

"Maybe some time."

"I would like some coffee, would you like a cup Johnathon? The coffee will be straight because I haven't been able to find any cream or sugar since I have been at the cabin."

"Aaron, I prefer something to dilute the coffee, but I understand."

Aaron enters the kitchen and with each step the floor squeaks a little. Aaron starts the percolator on the wood stove. Johnathon enters the kitchen and opens the cupboard doors.

"Aaron, I thought you said there was no cream and sugar."

"Since I have been here at the cabin, I have not seen any cream and sugar as I told you."

"But Aaron, I have some right here."

"Johnathon, this doesn't make any sense.! I have looked in that cabinet a hundred times and the cream and sugar were never there."

"Aaron, it was all the way in the back and would be easily missed if not looking carefully enough."

"Except that I took everything out of the cupboard, Johnathon. Don't you find that odd? Strange things seem to happen in this place that I can't for the life of me understand. The other day I woke up and was thinking I would love to have a cigarette. As I got up, I looked over and a pack was sitting on the china hutch buffet and I know the cigarettes were not there before."

"Sometimes, Aaron, we don't have to understand why things happen…we just need to embrace the good."

"I suppose you're right. The coffee is ready and here is your glass. Spoons are in the top drawer on the left-hand side of the cabinet."

The two move back into the sitting room, find their chairs and enjoy the coffee. As the fire burns, the light reflects off of the piano and the warmth coming from the fire fills the cabin.

"Johnathon, I would like to know about you. Don't take this the wrong way, but whenever I ask you a question I get simple but vague answers."

"What would you like to know?"

"You have said you pass through here from time to time and you go where you are needed. What does that mean?" I don't understand, Johnathon.!"

"Aaron, I live far away, but closer than you think. I pass through here so I can make sure everything is okay. I have been told by others I am like the watchman. In every situation, whether it's good or bad, there are things we should be thankful for. In this case, you made a new friend. At least I think we are friends."

"We are friends, Johnathon, but why are you like the watchman?"

"I am not sure why people call me that. But back to your story, the last time we were talking on the trail you were telling me a little bit about yourself? Could I hear about your wife?"

"Yes, you can, Johnathon, but I am going to need more coffee."

Walking into the kitchen I make my way to the wood stove that heats the percolator. I am still trying to figure it all out – the stove, the temperature, the cabin, the unexplainable. Back in my rocking chair I notice the rain has stopped and the clouds have cleared. Moonlight shines through the window, aiding the oil lamps in giving light.

"Okay, Johnathon, we have the fire, the coffee and I'm ready to talk if you are willing to listen."

"If you are comfortable, Aaron, I am ready."

"My wife, Nicole, was an amazing lady. We first met in a local bar in the downtown area of Fairview, Iowa. It had two levels – the top one a mix of 80s, 90s and country music, and the downstairs level played hip hop. Being able to have two separate crowds in the bar made it a nice place to hang out. I had been divorced from my first marriage for almost two years and was enjoying life."

"If I may, Aaron, why did you get divorced from your first wife?"

"The strain of losing a child had taken its toll on us both and we went our separate ways."

"I am sorry to hear that you lost your child, Aaron. What happened?"

"My son was just a baby and went to sleep."

"You emphasized *my son*. What do you mean?"

"After the separation and burying Anthony, my ex-wife didn't want his baby book, pictures or anything that belonged to him. She wouldn't even help with the purchasing of his headstone after the divorce. So, for all of these years, I have held on to Anthony's pictures and baby book."

"Again, I am so sorry to hear that, Aaron."

"It's okay, because I know Anthony is in Heaven," I said, fighting back the emotions that are always just behind a thin veil.

"But back to my Nicole, my beautiful lady. I remember I was standing at the north corner of the bar when she came out of the ladies' bathroom wearing a silver Adidas t-shirt, white Adidas pants and K-Swiss shoes. Her black hair, which shimmered in the light, went down to the middle of her back. She looked gorgeous! When our eyes met, we both smiled at each other and she went to her table. She stood about six feet tall and weighed about one hundred and thirty-five pounds."

"She sounds beautiful, Aaron."

"Johnathon, she was stunning.!"

"As I finished my drink, I set the bottle down on the bar and decided to leave. As I was walking toward the back door, it was like my eyes closed and someone took my hand and led me to her table.

Finding myself standing in front of her, I looked at her and saw she was looking back at me. With confidence, I asked her if she would like to go to dinner and a movie. She asked me if we could meet the following Saturday at the bar instead of going to dinner? I told her that would be fine and the rest, as they say, is history."

"Aaron, it sounds like you both were attracted to each other from the first moment your eyes met."

"There is no doubt about it. Now, Nicole and I had a rough time through the years, but I always loved her, and she loved me."

"What do you mean 'a rough time through the years,' Aaron? Do you mean just like what most couples have?"

"No, these I would argue were not like anything other couples experienced. There were a lot of unexplainable things that happened. Do you remember when we first met, Johnathon, and I told you it was a long story and you might not believe everything I told you."

"Yes, I remember and I replied that you might be surprised. I like to keep an open mind about things."

"It will likely take all you can handle if you want me to continue, Johnathon."

"Please do, Aaron."

"After a few weeks of dating Nicole, she told me that she had a meeting coming up with Child Protective Services (CPS) concerning the removal of her two children. She had three children, but the oldest daughter lived with their dad. So, there were three daughters altogether. Nicole was scared that she would lose her kids, but I reassured her it would be okay. I asked her if she wanted me to go to the meeting with her. Nicole was surprised that I cared, and she said that would make her feel a lot better about it. As Nicole and I walked into the meeting together, one of the CPS workers asked who I was. I explained that my name was Aaron and I am here for the meeting. The CPS worker stood up and said, 'this does not concern you.' I replied very boldly that Nicole was my fiancé. Although, I had not asked her to marry me yet, the CPS workers did not know any different. Nicole was a good woman Johnathon, but because of her past she struggled her entire life with psychiatric, drug and alcohol disorders."

"If you don't mind me asking, Aaron, what was her childhood like?"

"Nicole became a ward of the state at a young age. When she was a little girl, her father was shot in front of her mother, her sisters, her brother and her over a bad drug deal. Nicole's mother took the loss extremely hard and had a mental breakdown. She locked all the children in the basement of their house, boarded up the basement windows and left them there for four days before CPS showed up and removed them."

"Did they have food or water, Aaron?"

"Nicole, her sisters and her brother had water from the basement spigots, but there was no food. So the trauma of seeing her father gunned down was followed by more trauma of being locked in a basement with her siblings. But it didn't stop there. Nicole was the youngest of the children and the state separated her from the rest of her family. She found herself completely alone."

"Aaron, why would the CPS workers do such a thing as separating Nicole from her brother and sisters?"

"I can't fathom their reasoning, but that's what happened – and she was only five or six years old."

"That's unbelievable, Aaron, that a series of events so tragic could happen to anyone at such a young age. Tell me things got better after that."

"I wish I could, Johnathon."

Nicole was finally adopted around the age of seven by a lady and her husband with no children of their own. The adoptive father retired from the United States Navy as an officer and the adoptive mother was a home maker. In the beginning Nicole thought it would be okay in her new home with new, loving parents. She had her own room filled with toys, new clothes and nice furniture. They owned a three-bedroom house with a garage in the back. The back yard was very large and Nicole had room to play. But after six months or so, unspeakable things started happening."

Chapter Six
A Little Girl's Tears

"What happened to Nicole, Aaron?"

"The adoptive father began abusing her physically, mentally, and sexually. But that doesn't come close to saying anything about what she went through. It started out slow, with the adoptive father sneaking into her bedroom late at night in a clown costume that looked evil.

"Aaron, did Nicole ever tell you what the clown costume looked like that he wore when he would frighten her at night in the bedroom?"

"Yes, Johnathon, she did. She said that, on those nights, he wore a red-and-white striped clown jumpsuit. His face had white paint fading into a grey color that flowed down to his neck and the front of his chest where the jumpsuit was partially unbuttoned. His eyes were painted black in the shape of diamonds that blended. On his forehead, Nicole talked about a pentagram being in a blood-red color that had what appeared to be drops of blood running down his face onto the jumpsuit. She described his lips being painted black. He wore fake, sharpened teeth in his mouth and a hat that had horns coming out of each side, curling down to his shoulders. He would paint his hands to match his face paint and his nails were jagged. The clown jumpsuit was a button down the front, so he could take it off with ease, and he always had a knife with him when he performed this hellish, unnatural act.

He always made sure she was sleeping when he went into her bedroom. Then he would scare, torment and hurt her.

"Aaron, what would he do to Nicole?"

He would hide in the closet and make noises until Nicole would wake in fear. That's when he would jump out of the closet and act like a demon. Nicole always said he played a recording with the sounds of people screaming in pain, as if each person was being tortured in Hell. She would wake in fear, and described this glowing red light that shined through the door jambs. That's when the adoptive father would jump out of the closet and act like a demon with his butchers' knife in hand. Then he would begin violently acting out his abusive sexual tendencies upon her.

Needless to say, she became terrified of the night. There were times he would slide under the bed and be that monster repeatedly. Nicole told me that, when he would hide under the bed, she would be woken up by these hands reaching out and grabbing her as he would make the bed shake. She would be sleeping and feel these hands grabbing her so hard she would scream with pain as his claws would scratch her body.

"Aaron, that is sickening to hear. I cannot imagine how scared Nicole must have been to go through that kind of abuse from someone who was supposed to love and protect her."

"He always made Nicole wear Barbie doll pajamas to sleep in because that's what he wanted her to wear to bed and that's what he liked. When she told Samael that she didn't want to wear the pajamas, he would force her to wear them anyway…after torturing Nicole with the clown costume, he would have his way with her. As she laid there, crying, and begging him to stop, he would finish on the pajamas she was wearing. Sometimes, late at night, the adoptive mother would walk by the room and peek in and tell her husband he had 'been in there long enough.' When he finally left, Nicole would cry and pray to Father in Heaven, asking him to send someone to help her. But no one came to save her. Her heart was breaking every single day she endured that horror. The memories of what Samael did to her induced fear in her as a child and that fear stayed with her into adulthood. Through the years, I would stay up and watch over her as she slept. She always said it was nice to finally be able to rest."

"You were right before when you said my limits would be stretched, Aaron. As sorry as I am for you losing your child, I am more filled with sorrow about Nicole."

"Johnathon, I wish I could tell you that was the extent of her abuse. As a little girl, she was lost in a nightmare that she couldn't escape from. She called me her guardian, or the watcher, and I was, but not back in those days when she lived in a constant Hell on earth."

"My heart breaks for Nicole, Aaron."

"As did mine Johnathon, every time I listened to what she would reluctantly remember."

"If you don't feel like telling me more about her, it's okay, Aaron."

"I can go on. I just find it hard every time I think of how miserable she must have been."

"Aaron, when you were with Nicole, did the fear of clowns ever go away?"

"Never. She always told me she hated clowns and I understand now why she did. As time progressed, he found other ways to project his evil onto her. He would take her by the hand and walk her to the garage in the evenings and force her to play Russian roulette. Before he would walk out of the house he would grab his gun out of the safe. Once he and Nicole were in the garage, he made sure to shut the garage doors, so no one could see what he was doing to her. He also wanted to make sure no one could hear her if she cried out. Once he shut the garage doors and windows, his demonic actions came out in force, much like they did at night-time. He would take the gun out from behind his back and put a bullet in the chamber of his Smith & Wesson .38-special handgun. He would tell her if she wet herself after he pulled the trigger, there would be consequences.

"What were the consequences, Aaron, if she wet herself?"

"Oftentimes he would beat Nicole and do things to her sexually. In the garage, he also made her perform other acts that didn't include him."

"What do you mean, Aaron?"

"He was sick, or possessed, because he would force Nicole to do things to animals."

"That is just wrong, Aaron!"

"I know, but it happened. I don't know how she ever survived. The only thing I can say is God was watching over her and gave her strength. I remember Nicole telling me she would sit by the tree in the back yard and cry for hours."

"Would any of the neighbors see her crying, Aaron?"

"No, because they had a fenced-in backyard."

"Did the adoptive mother aide her husband in abusing Nicole, other than allowing it to happen?"

"Nicole talked about the numerous times her adoptive mother Jezebeth took her into the bathroom and would undress her and tell her to get in the water. Jezebeth would bathe her, wash her hair, dry her off and put make-up on her and style her hair. When the adoptive mother was done dressing Nicole up, she would call for her husband Samael, who would come into the bathroom with a smile on his face and take Nicole into the bedroom..."

"Why would Jezebeth allow that to happen, Aaron?!" Johnathon interrupted, his once-calm demeanor now visibly rattled.

"I can only guess, Johnathon, but I would say that living with the monster that was her husband forced her to want to make him happy – for fear of what he was capable of doing to another human being. Throughout the years when we were married, I listened to the horrific and terrifying stories of how Samael would continue the abuse. And it just kept getting worse...he would chain Nicole up in the basement and beat her to the point she would pass out. But before he would beat her and after he would bind her in chains, he would slip his hands under the clothing Nicole wore and started his satanic rituals of sexual deviance.

When Samael wasn't abusing her, Jezebeth would grind her fingernails into Nicole's arm, or slap her around out of spite to punish her further. Jezebeth would, at times, get jealous because her husband was spending more time with Nicole than her. She would get rewarded for helping him abuse Nicole. Samael would allow his wife to go shopping, or buy jewelry, when his wife made him happy. Every time Nicole saw a new brooch or bracelet on Jezebeth, it made her sick to her stomach because she remembered what Samael did to her for that piece of jewelry."

"Johnathon, I need to stretch my legs for a few minutes before I go on."

Walking into the dining room Aaron cracks the window and the rushing water from the river sounds beautiful. A cool breeze brushes against him and, in the night, an owl hoots three times. Johnathon looks at Aaron and sees a tear flail against his flesh. Johnathon can see Aaron's heart hurting and the sadness surfacing, but Aaron holds back.

"Are you okay, Aaron?"

"I am now. I was getting ready to tell you about the adoptive parents feeding Nicole. She was only allowed to eat when they told her she could. Sometimes, she would sneak food and hide it, so they wouldn't know she had something for later. She would get hungry because they didn't care if she was hungry or not. There was a padlock on the fridge to keep her out.

For seven years Nicole endured constant abuse. As the abuse went on, she started losing her faith in God and worshiping the devil. She told me the state came in and investigated the matter, but when it was all said and done the case was dropped. She talked about how Jezebeth and Samael walked out of the state office with their check book in hand. Nicole was devastated that she had to return home with them. Those few brushes with the authorities fueled even worse abuse for her when they got home…"

"Please tell me she got away from those people, Aaron."

"Eventually she did, but not until after she gave birth twice at home."

"My God, that poor child!"

"I know, Johnathon, it saddened my heart when she told me what happened. Both times Nicole gave birth the adoptive parents took her into her bedroom and tied her hands to the bed. They forced her to endure the pain of child birth each time without the aid of any medical help. After Nicole gave birth each time the adoptive father killed her two children."

"That man was evil, Aaron, and a murderer!"

"Johnathon, he was much more than a murderer."

"He put Nicole's first baby in a cardboard shoebox and buried her. The second child she gave birth too, he took from her right after he was born. Nicole always said one minute her babies would be crying and then there was silence…"

"How old was she when she gave birth, Aaron?"

"She was twelve when her first child was born and fourteen when the second child was born."

"So, she has five children?"

"Yes, she does, and she knows those two are in Heaven."

"Do you know where the adoptive father buried Nicole's two babies?"

"I do, Johnathon. Do you remember me telling you how Nicole would sit by the tree in the backyard and cry for hours?

"I remember Aaron."

"Once she and I were sitting at home on the couch, watching a movie together, and something in the movie reminded her of her children. She started crying and I held her in my arms. With tears running down her face, she told me that Samael buried her babies under the tree in the back yard. She always said when we were together her babies were always in her heart, even though she couldn't save them. She loved them always and, even when I told Nicole there wasn't anything she could have done, she still blamed herself for their death through the years."

"If I may ask, Aaron, what were the two babies' names?"

"Nicole named the babies Mathew, or as she called him, Mattie, and she named her daughter Amber."

"Those are beautiful names, Aaron."

"Thank you, Johnathon, they are beautiful names and I have also held Mattie and Amber in my heart. Nicole finally ran away after the years of abuse from the adoptive parents. The state eventually found her and took her back. That's when the adoptive parents gave up their rights to her and told the CPS worker they didn't want her any more. They said she was uncontrollable and violent."

"Aaron, I can understand how Nicole would be angry and hurt, and why she lost her faith."

"The torment of the abuse left Nicole broken inside and she tried getting help. But, unfortunately, during those years there wasn't much help for her and the abuse didn't stop there. She was then placed in another foster home and was sexually abused by the foster parent's son, who was much older. Nicole would run away, and the state would just take her back to the home. Ultimately, after months of abuse, more children started coming forward and then CPS believed Nicole. The foster home was shut down after that happened and Nicole was placed yet again."

"I have no words, Aaron. It's a lot to take in and digest."

"Johnathon, I am going to grab another cup of coffee and step outside for some fresh air."

Chapter Seven
Hope Shadowed by Darkness

*S*tepping outside, I listen to the sounds of Mother Nature getting louder. I sit in the rocker and smoke the cigarette I just lit. With each drag I take I embrace the silence, save the wind blowing in the trees. Animals begin rustling around as I stare at the angel water fountain. Relaxed, I finish the cigarette and head back into the sitting room where Johnathon awaits with coffee.

"You were telling me, Aaron, that Nicole's abuses didn't stop there. Do you want to continue?"

"Yes, Johnathon, I can. Growing up, people always labeled Nicole as a 'trash bag' kid because the foster homes would keep her for a while and then want the state to place her in another foster home. Sometimes, the foster parents would kick Nicole out for one reason or another, which made her feel like garbage. Nicole was always told by the people running the foster homes that she was no good and would never amount to anything. Everything was building up in her, and her anger and violent behaviors became more predominant. So, most of the time, Nicole ran away from the homes. She would stay on the streets until she was picked up and taken back by the authorities."

"How did Nicole adapt to the streets, Aaron?"

"She told me living on the streets was better than being rejected all the time."

"Aaron, where did she live when she was growing up?"

"She lived in Arizona, Johnathon."

"Didn't you say when you were in grade school something inside of you said you should go to Arizona?"

"It was a feeling I had deep in my gut."

"That doesn't sound like a coincidence, Aaron. Was there ever any light that shined in Nicole's life amid all that darkness?"

"There was, eventually, when Nicole was placed in a foster home that was monitored very closely by the state. The husband, Ernie, and the wife, Savanna, owned several businesses in the metro area and worked with the children as much as they could. As Nicole stayed in their foster home, she met a lot of people and one of the girls she met was a girl named Cherry. They became good friends at the home and Nicole and Cherry did *everything* together. She talked about Cherry all the time."

"That had to provide some help for Nicole, Aaron."

"It did, to a degree, but her pain was still running through her mind, body, and soul. Ernie and Savanna tried to find every avenue they could to help the children succeed. The older children living in the foster home were able to work at Ernie and Savanna's businesses when they weren't in school. And they made sure the children were fed and protected from abuse. They talked with the children and made sure – to the best of their ability – to raise the children right. During the time Nicole stayed with Ernie and Savanna, they took a liking to her and worked with her all the time. But they had challenges to overcome because Nicole was still very angry, and she didn't trust anyone.

There were times when Nicole would black out and she wouldn't remember what she had done for hours at a time. Because she was so frustrated with everything going on inside her, she would run away from the foster home. Ernie would take the time to go find her and bring her back, and he and Savanna would sit her down and reassure her it would be okay. But Nicole wouldn't, or, more likely because of her abuse, *couldn't* believe them. She told me she constantly expected that, at any moment, the tides would turn against her. After Nicole was there for a while, Ernie and Savanna decided to help Nicole the best way they knew how. They asked their attorney to petition the courts for information on her brother and sisters. They also talked with the CPS worker and were able to get some information that led to them finding her sisters and her brother. Ernie and Savanna, once notified of their whereabouts, pulled Nicole into the living room and handed her a piece of paper with the information they had received from the attorney and the state. Nicole was excited, and she smiled for the first time she could remember. Ernie, Savanna and Nicole embraced, and she told me she cried that night.

A plan was put together for everyone to meet. It was a few weeks later when Nicole, after years of separation and no knowledge of her siblings since their separation, re-united with her sisters and her brother. Ernie and Savanna rented a hall and prepped it with balloons, signs, food and drinks for everyone. Nicole stood under the sign that said 'I have missed you.' She met her sisters – Sandy, Angie, and Cathy – and her brother, Luciano. They all embraced and talked all night long. As she and her family laughed and cried, Ernie and Savanna felt happy for Nicole. It was a joyous occasion for all."

"Aaron, I would say God the Father was present that night."

"I believe in my heart that God was protecting her and shining light into Nicole's life as best as He could. Sometimes, Johnathon, I think about the spiritual warfare between God and the Devil that took place in her life."

"Aaron, many times I have asked myself why people ask, 'Why did God allow this to happen?' when I believe blame should be placed on the Devil and he should be confronted always."

"I agree, Johnathon, but the Devil is a coward and he hides behind every lie that he can."

"If you don't mind me asking, Aaron, have you ever met the Devil?"

"I have Johnathon, many times, but I don't want to talk about that right now."

"It's okay Aaron. If you want we can talk about that later."

"Yes, some other time."

"What ended up happening with Nicole's family, Aaron?"

"She and her family stayed in touch for quite some time, but eventually lost contact with each other. But I would like to revisit the reasons why after I throw another log on the fire and top off our coffees."

I stop for a minute after adding wood to the fire. A cool breeze from inside the cabin flows against my body and thoughts of Nicole flourish in my mind. Softly, I whisper "I love you, Nicole." I hear this voice inside of my mind saying, "I love you, too, Aaron." I smile and look at the fire dancing.

"Aaron! Aaron! Are you okay?"

"Yes, I was just thinking about Nicole. It's getting late. How about we talk more in the morning..."

Aaron makes his way to the oil lamps and turns the dial until the light slowly burns out. Johnathon finds a comfortable place on the floor and Aaron heads for the couch. He pulls the blanket over him and tries to quiet his mind as he begins praying for guidance to Father in Heaven.

"Aaron, always remember Father loves you and you are special."

"I am just me, Johnathon. Nothing more and nothing less."

"Good night. I look forward to hearing more about Nicole tomorrow."

"Good night to you, too, Johnathon."

As dawn approaches, light begins to engulf the cabin. Johnathon and Aaron wake, make coffee, and gather in the kitchen of the place that is not theirs. Shortly after good mornings are exchanged, the smell of fresh coffee fills the cabin.

"Aaron, if you are feeling up to it, I would like to hear more about Nicole."

"What would you like to know?"

"Well, last night you mentioned that she found some light in all the darkness she faced by finding her siblings, but it sounded like that didn't last long."

"Yes, Johnathon, you are right about that. But a second light came into her life after she lost touch with her family – a guy named Jacob, who came from a good family and was raised with a strong religious foundation. Nicole was still a ward of the state and having a hard time dealing with life. She began self-harming by cutting and sometimes would black out and have no memories of what she had done for periods of time. When Jacob began dating her, he soon fell in love with her. He would take Nicole out for ice cream and then he would drive to South Mountain that overlooked the cityscapes near Apache Junction, Arizona."

Their dates were simple, but she enjoyed the moments when they were together. Not long into their dating, things started to happen. Jacob would get calls from Nicole needing help, after she would run away from the foster home and walk the streets. Sometimes Jacob would find her passed out with a bottle of booze, sleeping behind gas stations or by a dumpster. Through the years they dated he was always there for her, though. He told me that being with Nicole was amazing, but there were also hard times. He never knew about the abuse she had endured in her life. He didn't even know she had a brother or sisters. So she held back a lot of things from Jacob, and I can only figure it was some form of safety measure."

"You said Nicole would run away from the foster home. What happened to Ernie and Savanna, Aaron?"

"Nicole was struggling and she began pushing them away. I guess you might say she built a barrier to keep people out from the scars she held deep within. That is why she started leaning on Jacob for help instead of them."

"Why didn't Nicole call her brother or sisters?"

"That, too, was a struggle for Nicole. As much as their reunion was joyous, it also brought up the memories of her father getting shot and her and her siblings being locked in the basement by her mother."

"I can understand that, Aaron. Even the people she considered as 'home' were unknowing causes of torment to her."

"From her earliest days, Nicole's idea of what 'love' meant always included a lot of pain and anguish. It affected all of her relationships. Jacob would tell me that one minute Nicole could be an angel and the next minute she was like a demon filled with hate. She would hit him and cuss him out, and then act like nothing had happened. Despite her mood swings, he stayed with her and always believed in her. As time went on, though, Jacob's parents didn't approve of them dating, but he always stood his ground and continued to help Nicole."

"Why did Jacob's parents disapprove, Aaron?"

"They said Nicole was not good for him. She had dropped out of school in eighth grade and they didn't feel Jacob would succeed in life if he was with her. But he ignored their disregard and held on to the love he had for her. Jacob's parents were good people Johnathon. They cared and loved Jacob and were just concerned for their son as any parent would be."

"They sound like very loving people Aaron."

"They were Johnathon."

"So, what happened next Aaron?"

He took Nicole to her first prom and tried showing her that life can be good. But, as hard as he tried, she would always just back away."

Chapter Eight
Trying to Survive

"Aaron, it sounds like no matter what Nicole did, or where she went, or how hard she tried enjoying certain moments of her life, the Devil just kept knocking her down."

"There is no doubt that the Devil was present in Nicole's life. Her pain was horrendous, as you can now imagine after listening to what happened to her, and she was forced into survival mode. I remember her telling me one time about this old woman she met. She was walking down a gravel alley that ran behind a quick shop in Arizona. Nicole said this old lady, who appeared from nowhere, was just standing there looking at her. She had long, grey, ratty hair, was in her seventies or eighties, wore ragged clothes, and her eyes seemed black. After ten minutes or so Nicole said the old lady started throwing rocks at her and began speaking in a language she didn't understand. Nicole started running down the alley in fear, and the old lady followed, but before she could get away she heard her scream out, 'you're mine!' When Nicole stopped and turned around, the old lady was gone, and she was in disbelief. The rocks had hit her many times and she was bleeding from the face."

"Did that really happen, Aaron?"

"Yes, and I believe that the old woman was a demon from Hell, as the Devil has many servants."

"Have you ever met anyone with black eyes?"

"Johnathon, later I will tell you about an old man named James that came to me after I met Nicole, but for now I'd like to finish telling you about Jacob and Nicole."

"Okay, Aaron, I am listening."

"The harder Jacob tried to show Nicole that life could be good, he and Nicole were fighting what I call 'the unseen' – the Devil, the streets, the pain and the anguish. The unseen is around us all and it's everywhere. Do you remember the piece I wrote called: "Thoughts of the Unseen?"

"Yes I do, Aaron, and I have thought of it many times since you read it to me."

"I am certain that there is always a war going on between the angels and demons and it's behind the glass."

"I believe you Aaron, but how do you know this?"

"Johnathon, the war between good and evil rages on in Heaven, in Hell, and on Earth because I have seen behind the vail…but that is for another time, Johnathon. Sorry I went off on a tangent."

"You're fine, Aaron. So what happened to Nicole?"

"Even when Nicole was with Jacob, she would do things that no teenage girl should ever have to do. Sometimes she would prostitute herself for money and would steal food to eat. She did what she felt she had to do to survive. Nicole didn't rely on anyone for very long, and isolating herself from those who cared for her had its share of consequences. One night when she was walking the streets alone, four men dragged her into a poorly-lit, abandoned lot and gang-raped her. After they had their way with her, they beat her and pounded her head against the concrete. She ended up in the hospital and the only person she wanted there was Jacob."

"Please tell me he went to see her, Aaron."

"He did, and sat by Nicole's side the whole time, holding her hand and trying to reassure her that it would be okay. A week passed, and when the hospital finally released her, Jacob was there to pick her up from the hospital. Since she had left Ernie and Savanna's home, and didn't really have a place, Jacob made sure she had a roof over her head. He got Nicole a motel room that rented by the month, provided food for her, and checked in on her all the time. Jacob talked to her about getting a job, and it wasn't too long after that she began working in a restaurant, taking care of buffet tables. She knew Jacob was proud of her, but her mind just couldn't handle it and she quit after a few months."

"What do you mean when you say her mind couldn't handle it, Aaron?"

"Nicole had a hard time focusing, due to the recent head trauma and the years of abuse she re-lived every day. So the discipline of working clashed with her like two storms colliding, and she built her own domain with barriers all around her – to keep herself safe and others out. After she quit her job, she went back on the streets and was drinking more than ever to block out the memories of what happened. Jacob tried with all his heart to help her, but she left him and started seeing someone else."

"How long did they date?"

"On and off for three years. Nicole was seventeen and Jacob had just turned eighteen. At the end of their relationship, he went to her after receiving a call. She said she needed to talk to him, and when he met her in a parking lot in Mesa, Arizona, her face was black and blue, her eyes were bloodshot, and she was crying. The new boyfriend had beaten Nicole. Jacob told her that he was going into the military, and if she could just hang on until basic training was over, he would take her from this life. He wanted her to get the help she needed so she would never be hurt again. But she was still addicted to drugs, and alcohol, and her psychiatric disorders were consuming every ounce of her existence. She told Jacob that she was sorry, opened the door of his truck, said I love you and then went back to the man who had beaten her.

That was the last time Jacob saw Nicole. He went into the military and started his life. When he got out, though, he looked for her for six months, but never found her. He told me he always kept her pictures to remind him of the lady who stole his heart. There was something about her that kept him going back whenever she called. He said she wasn't like any other lady he had ever met before in his life."

"He sounds like a good man, Aaron."

"He is, and Nicole always talked about him in a positive way. She even tattooed his name on her right ankle as a remembrance of the young teenage man who tried to help her."

"When is the last time you and Jacob spoke to each other, Aaron?"

"Jacob and I talked a month after she passed away. I apologized for not calling him sooner, but I had a hard time finding his number. He told me it was okay. He was deeply saddened by her passing and said if he would have known she was dying he would have been on the next flight out to see her."

"Now, that is a special kind of love, Aaron."

"Jacob was thankful that she found someone who was by her side, loved her through the years and was there in the end for her. He loved Nicole and never forgot her. I am thankful to him for everything he did to try to help her."

"If I may ask, Aaron, what was the new boyfriend's name?"

"His name was Richard, but everyone called him Dick."

"What happened while they were together?"

"Johnathon, I would like to stretch my legs before I go on."

"Okay, Aaron. If you don't mind, I would like to see more of what's here in the cabin."

Johnathon enters the downstairs bedroom and lights the oil lamp. He is surprised at the full-size bed with log frame before him, as well as a curio cabinet in the corner with a nightstand by the bed. The bedding is beautiful, with hand stitching across the top that says, *"My Rose, My Heart, My Love."* Aaron walks back into the cabin to find Johnathon and his discoveries.

"Did you know this room was here, Aaron?"

"I was aware of it, but I never paid it much attention."

"There are a lot of beautiful things in this room, especially in this curio cabinet."

Aaron turns to view what has been placed on the glass shelves of the curio, and stares in disbelief. "These things *can't* be here, Johnathon."

"What's the matter, Aaron?"

"On the first and second shelf there are three of the five items that I placed on Nicole's resting place. This isn't possible!"

"Which items are those, Aaron?"

"The two red roses that stand wrapped around the angels – that light up blue in color. The Irish blessing rock with the shamrock lays on the ground in front of the cross that says 'God bless this amazing woman,' and the brown and white bears I have in my home. It just doesn't make any sense, Johnathon. What is this place and how can it be!?"

"Aaron, why don't we turn out the oil lamp and go back into the sitting room and we can talk about it."

Returning to the sitting room, Johnathon sees the confusion on Aaron's face. "Are you okay?"

"No, Johnathon, I am not. I have been in this place for who knows how long, things have been appearing, and disappearing, and I've been hearing a lady's voice in the wind. Even you seem to appear out of the heavens."

Chapter Nine
Another Lost Child

"Johnathon, I have walked and witnessed so much beauty in this place, and I am thankful, but I want to know what's going on."

"Aaron, it's okay. Sometimes in one's life people are given an opportunity to experience certain things, whether they be good or bad. These gifts, such as our dreams, or being able to walk in another plane of existence, are rare and we should embrace the moments. Even in the worst situations, Father in Heaven watches out for us, or He sends someone to help us make it through."

"I believe in what you are telling me, Johnathon, I just wish I could make sense of all of this. I remember about a week before Nicole passed away she told me it was like she was being pushed and pulled from one world to another. Now I feel like I've been pulled from my world into this one and I am beyond confused."

"Aaron, I am telling you it's okay. If you can put your trust in me, in my hands, all will be all right in the end. Do you trust me?"

"I have no reason not to, Johnathon."

"Then let's drink our coffee and continue our talk. And

remember, Aaron, in time Father will reveal to us why all things happen. I know it's hard to be patient when all around you is a mystery…"

"I am trying, Johnathon. I think I just need some sleep."

"Aaron, we can resume our discussion tomorrow, and I will turn off the oil lamps and add to the fire."

"Thank you, Johnathon."

Johnathon walks through the cabin and tends to the lamps and the fire, wondering, as he performs his tasks, if Aaron is okay. He can't imagine all that Nicole went through and how Aaron must be feeling right now. His heart is heavy with sadness at the suffering of his brethren.

Aaron's mind, unable to shut down, tells Johnathon, upon his return, "Earlier this evening, you talked about how God sends someone to help us through tough times. When Nicole got sick, there was a lady who stood by our side the whole time."

"Who was she, Aaron?"

"Nicole and I always said she was our Guardian Angel. Her name was Heather. She stood six feet tall, weighed only one-hundred and fifteen pounds and had long, blonde hair. She always smiled and helped with anything she could."

"God has many angels on Earth. It sounds like Heather was sent by God to help you and Nicole during that time."

"Johnathon, are you going to be here in the morning when I wake?"

"Yes, Aaron, I will be here. Why do you ask?"

I just don't want to be alone right now."

"You're never alone, Aaron," Johnathon says in almost a whisper.

The crackling of the fire is the last voice they hear before slumber, and the darkness of night once again is overtaken by the morning light.

Slowly, Aaron opens his eyes and turns his head to see if Johnathon stayed. He smiles as he sees his friend laying on the floor.

"Johnathon, hey, we need to get up."

"All right, Aaron, I am getting up."

Aaron sits up and makes his way into the kitchen to start the wood stove that will heat the percolator. He remembers the cream and sugar that were never there before Johnathon showed up. After grabbing two freshly brewed cups of coffee, he asks Johnathon, "How about if we sit outside and enjoy the morning sun?"

"I would like that Aaron."

Walking through the threshold of the door, they feel the sun's rays against their flesh. The morning sky features a palette of red, orange and blue and the sun shines brightly above the cliffs. The wind blows softly and bird songs echo through the trees. The coffee steams as they take their first sip.

"Aaron, did Jacob ever marry?"

"He did, twice. His first marriage didn't last, and I don't know why, but Jacob and his second wife have been married for twenty-five years."

"That makes me happy to know that he found someone. How are you holding up today, Aaron?"

"I am still confused about everything that I don't understand, but I have faith."

"I am glad to hear that, Aaron. Before we continue on about your wife, or Dick, can I hear more about you? Will you tell me about your son, Anthony?"

"When I met my first wife, I was in my early twenties and she was also young. We both wanted a child and I remember we were living on the west end of town. We were waiting for the results from the at home pregnancy test. When the test was done, we were happy it showed positive. Through the months she carried our son, I would read to Anthony every night. I let him know how much I loved him. I revered Anthony because he was my heritage and my legacy. I even got him his own Bible."

"Do you have a favorite Bible verse, Aaron?"

"I actually do, Johnathon. Samuel Two, verse Twenty-Two – Song of David."

"Aaron, I enjoy that verse as well. It gives strength to those in need of the Lord."

"My first wife and I finally made it to the last month and I was ready to hold my son. I remember I had finished my day servicing vending machines and was at the warehouse unloading when my wife, her mother and sister showed up. They were crying. My wife got out of the car and told me she had not felt Anthony move for three days."

"Why would she wait that long, Aaron?"

"Johnathon, to this day I have asked myself that question."

When we got to the doctor's office an ultrasound was done and my son was gone. We only had a few weeks before Anthony would have been born. The doctor sent us to the hospital in Iowa City. That night I watched my son be born, knowing he was already in Heaven. I was so angry and hurt. The umbilical cord was wrapped around his neck three and a half times. I held him for hours in my arms before the funeral director came to pick him up. We had pictures taken and after years of looking at the photos, I finally realized my wife at that time was smiling as she held Anthony."

"Why was she smiling, Aaron? That seems like the saddest moment any couple could share."

"I don't know, Johnathon, and I never asked her. We buried Anthony on Thanksgiving Day of 1997. Every day I tell him I love and miss him. I wrote a poem about Anthony. Would you like to hear it?"

"Please, Aaron, I would like that."

"It's called:

Not Forgotten

Cresting, waiting for a time

that I do not want.

A lonely existence ends.

It cuts sharp but has no blade.

Twisted in the barbs of the dying vines,

I fall endlessly upon time –

screaming, crying, I hear whispers from within.

A heart shatters like a vase upon the wall.

A child lingers in my hands.

Scared, alone, he must feel in the dark.

To be broken, hurt,

to be one, broken together.

Black and blue unveils in my flesh

that was his flesh.

The cord unravels in my mind.

Darkness approaches with uncertainty.

Wandering alone, together,

we have no light around us here.

I want to live with rain and without rain,

in a sadness I can't explain.

Walking in the wind,

I stand alone in the harvested field.

In the night, together again,

I whisper good bye.

I don't want to let go.

Time fades in my eyes

only to be a memory.

Good bye, my creation,

Until I close my eyes."

"Aaron, that is a very powerful poem and it invokes so many emotions. How long after your son passed away did you and your first wife get divorced?"

"It was about a year and a half later. But before we divorced we had another son. His name is Isaac."

"Why didn't you mention him before, Aaron?"

"Because we do not talk and haven't for years."

"May I ask why?"

"Because the son I knew as a baby is gone. And, as I told you before, about Nicole, it's complicated. If you want, though, we can come back to the reason we don't talk."

"Fair enough, Aaron. I would still like to hear about what went on, if that is okay."

"That's fine Johnathon. After Isaac was born a few months had passed. My wife during that time changed. She was very distant from Isaac and would yell at him for one reason or another. The final straw of our marriage was on a Friday morning. I woke up around five a.m. to go to work. Isaac woke up and started crying. He was hungry and needed changed. I heard my wife start yelling at him. She said, 'why don't you shut up, you bastard child!' She would say things to him all the time like that. That morning we fought and then I went to work. By the time I got home that afternoon the whole house was cleaned out. She left with everything except Anthony's pictures, baby book and the ultrasound video. I didn't care about the household possessions. I wanted my son and was thankful she left Anthony's belongings.

She bounced from house to house until after the divorce was final and the child support started rolling in. Once I got the standard visitation rights, I took advantage of every moment I could. I paid my child support and believed in taking care of my obligations. I remember the last time I saw Isaac. He was standing in front of the screen door at her house, kicking and screaming crying for daddy."

"Why was that the last time you saw him Aaron?"

"After that she moved from state to state, tracking her down was almost impossible."

"Aaron, you and your wife Nicole both suffered loss and

hardships through the years."

"Loss is loss, and I won't argue that I've had my share of challenges, Johnathon. But Nicole's life was much harder than mine will ever be."

"How old was Isaac when he was yelling for you?"

"He was almost three years old. To this day I can see the images in my mind of that day I dropped him off."

"And you've seen him again since then?"

"Eventually, yes, but he had changed into someone unrecognizable. I remember back to when I would have him on the weekends. I lived in a small apartment, but I called it home. It had a bathroom, living room and a kitchen, with a door that led to the roof. I didn't have room for a bed, so I slept on the couch. When I had Isaac, I would put the love seat and couch together. That is where Isaac and I slept. Johnathon, some memories can make everything okay."

Chapter Ten

Isolated in Life

"Not to change the subject, Aaron, but can I hear more about Dick and Nicole?"

"Right. That's fine, Johnathon. When Nicole left Jacob, that night Dick got exactly what he wanted."

"What was that, Aaron?"

"Someone to control, manipulate and abuse. Nicole told me on the night she left Jacob that Dick had beaten her."

"Yes, I remember you saying that. What else happened to her that night?"

"Dick had Nicole sleep with three other men. They forced her to have sex with them as he sat back and watched. The reason they physically beat her was because she didn't want to have sex with them. She tried fighting them off and begged Dick to make the men stop, but he didn't lift a finger to help her. Over time, the drugs and abuse allowed him to have total control over Nicole and she became dependent on him. She had nowhere else to go and no one to turn to. You had asked me, Johnathon, why she lost contact with her sisters and her brother."

"Yes, Aaron, I remember."

"Well, Dick didn't want Nicole having any contact with them. He knew if she was talking with her family she would have an outlet to call for help if she needed it. So he forced her to get rid of her family's phone numbers and addresses. This led to fights between him and her, which ultimately ended up in him beating her until she agreed to his terms."

"What were his terms, Aaron?"

"To never talk to her sisters and brother again and do as he commanded. He really wanted to isolate and control Nicole. As time went on she found herself selling drugs and being forced to make money however she could. She sold cocaine, heroin, marijuana, and anything she could get her hands on. They would break into houses and steal possessions from the people who lived there. One time Dick stole a truck filled with automotive tools, which led him to ditching the truck and running from the police. Other times, he would steal motorcycles, cars and trucks to sell at chop shops."

"What kind of home did they have, Aaron?"

"They lived in a trailer in a rough neighborhood. Dick's mom rented the place and let them stay there. He had a sister that was married, and most nights his sister and her husband would stay with him and Nicole. Eventually, Nicole became pregnant with their first child, Sasha."

"Was Dick a religious man Aaron?"

"No, he didn't believe in God, nor did he want anybody else believing in Him. This reinforced Nicole's belief in the Devil. Many times, she would tell me she was the Devil's daughter."

"Did Nicole really believe that, Aaron?"

"To a degree she did, Johnathon. Through the years Nicole and Dick would find themselves in more situations with law enforcement. She would turn up with bruises from him physically beating on her to relieve his frustrations. Dick's brother-in-law would try and force Nicole to have sex with him when he was away. One time, she had to fight the brother-in-law off after he slammed her against the kitchen stove."

"Didn't Dick do anything about it, Aaron?"

"No, because he was always scared of him. Dick's sister wouldn't do anything, either. If she did, or tried, her husband would slap her around. But, as Nicole raised her daughter through the years, she became pregnant with her second child, Sabrina. They eventually started moving from one place to another and there was little stability – only Nicole's love for her children. Dick always did what he wanted to do, and he only used Nicole when it benefited him or his pocket. But how about we stretch our legs and walk to the river?"

"I am good with that, Aaron."

They begin walking toward the river that cascades down from the caps above. The rushing water sounds peaceful and the wildlife is amazing. The sun is on the downward slide as evening approaches. Closer to the river, they see a wooden bench sitting about five feet away from the bank. It's hand-crafted and appears to be made from oak. After wiping the leaves and pine needles off the top of the bench, they see an inscription:

Thoughts of the Shadows

Why are the unseen like the music that plays for no one to hear? Why do the shadows surround the living in the depth of darkness? Why are the souls of people dead to those who move upon the breast?

I say this to you! The music that plays in the bark of the trees that twist in the wind with no direction loses its sight of the cello whispering in the air we breathe. As we breathe, the silence of the cello marks the emptiness of the shell blind to the beauty of the ones standing in the darkness. A seed holds value to creation, but begins planted in the minced terrain below the surface. Even though the seed is stained by the hands of those who are dead, they still hold true, waiting for the life to arrive. As the dead that have no sight stand, wait, and look upon the breast of the depth of darkness within the earth, they become the infants born from the mud that once covered the flesh of the seed. Is no man nor woman like the seed hidden in the abyss? Are we driven by the night only to lose our senses upon the attention of falsehood? To understand what moves upon the breast, one must understand how the pendulum swings.

"I wonder who inscribed this, Johnathon."

"Does it mean anything to you, Aaron?"

"I don't know, should it? Should any of this?"

"I am not sure, but it's very complex and filled with many hidden meanings."

"Johnathon, let's head back to the cabin."

As the sun begins its descent into the horizon, they return to the cabin, remove their boots and throw a few logs into the fireplace. Johnathon lights the oil lamps and they find their seating in the sitting room.

"Aaron, do you think Nicole loved Dick?"

"If she did, it was a forced love. With all she had faced in her life up to that point, she learned to adapt to almost any circumstance. Nicole was still blacking out and losing time. Her drug and alcohol use continued, and she was just trying to survive. Dick controlled things to the point where she couldn't leave. After they had their third child, life got even harder and eventually they left Arizona. He had multiple warrants out for his arrest, so they had to move. When they left, they put their stuff in storage and moved to Iowa, where they found a house and started over. The unfortunate part is that Dick's mother, sister and her husband, along with their two children came with them. The home they lived in was on an old highway in the country. This left nine people living in a three-bedroom house. I remember once Nicole told me about the time Dick kicked her out of the house because she wouldn't do as she was told. It was in the middle of winter and Nicole had to sleep in the back yard in a shed. Years later, she showed me the home and where she slept.

"I cannot believe what she continued to go through with him, Aaron."

"She was a survivor, and I always told her I was proud of her when we were together. After a few years had passed in Iowa, Dick finally left Nicole and kicked her out on the street. She met another man and moved in with him until she could afford a place of her own. This guy was into drugs, but he did not beat on her like the rest of them did."

"How long were Dick and Nicole together, Aaron?"

"They got together when Nicole was seventeen and they separated when she was thirty years old. After about a year, she was able to get a place of her own. It was an apartment on the south side of town, with two bedrooms, a bathroom, a modest kitchen, living room, outside porch and a basement. She started working in retail, despite all her psychological issues, and all she wanted was for her kids to come back home."

"Aaron, if I may ask, how did Nicole come across the apartment?"

"Johnathon, there was this man named Cameron, who was her Income Maintenance Worker for CPS. Cameron always showed Nicole respect and helped her as much as he could. He told Nicole about this place which led her to renting the apartment. Nicole always talked about Cameron and how he was compassionate, understanding and, how much she respected him. Nicole always smiled when she talked about him. When Nicole and I were together she always thought CPS workers didn't care about people. But Cameron impacted her life in a positive way and Nicole said she was thankful for Cameron, and what he did for her."

"Aaron, he sounds like a good man."

"He is, Johnathon."

"Did Dick let her see the children Aaron?"

"He did, but always on his terms. He knew Nicole had very little money and food was scarce. When he brought the children over he would also bring fast food so he and the children could eat in front of her, I suppose to make her jealous or torment her in some way. He would also bring his new girlfriend over with the children to see Nicole."

"Aaron, I have no words, and what words I am thinking I will keep to myself."

"Nicole made journal entries about her life when she was alone. She wrote about her hatred toward Dick and how she would have to beg to see her kids. But there were also times when she wrote about Jacob. There was a lot of sadness coming from her in her writings. She would write a lot about how she didn't understand why she had to suffer through life. When I look closely at the pages of her journal, I can see what appears to be stains from tear drops."

"Aaron, if I may say, it sounds like the Devil wrapped his arms around Nicole and made her life a living Hell through her whole existence here on Earth."

"He did, Johnathon, and that is why I despise that son-of-a-bitch, and he knows I do. The Devil also knows I am a patient man, and the day will come when I will find him."

"What will you do, Aaron, on that day?"

"When I die, I hope my Father in Heaven sends me straight to Hell. I have some unfinished business there..."

Chapter Eleven
A Solution

"*I* will find the Devil. I may not kill him, but I am damn sure going to take a piece out of his ass for what he did to Nicole. When I am done, and I ascend back to Heaven, my Father will not ask me if I won the war. He will just ask me how hard I fought."

"Aaron, your anger for the Devil runs deep."

"Yes, it does, Johnathon, and believe me it's warranted. Ever since Nicole was young he plagued her with every kind of torment he could."

"But, Aaron, what I am trying to say is vengeance is not for you to carry out on the Devil. God will take care of Lucifer."

"Maybe so, but I still want my turn at the Devil, at any cost. You will understand, in the end, why my hatred grows deep within. I have even written about it if you would like to hear what I wrote. It's titled:

Hunting the Devil

I stand at the edge of the forest, gazing up. The

night is black with no moon and stars to shed light.

Stepping inward to the wilderness I am careful

not to make noise. My adversary is wise,

deceptive and cunning. His soul burns with fire.

His horns are pointed, his power is great,

and his senses are many. He knows I am hunting him.

He knows the time is near when I settle the score.

My sword is as sharp as a razor. My armor is my faith

in our Father. I am aware

of my surroundings. I see without sight,

smell without smelling, hear without hearing,

touch without touching, and taste without tasting. Deep

in the woods I feel his presence. He hides

in the shadows like the coward he is.

Without fear I break the silence,

call out the Devil, and draw my blade."

"You certainly aren't afraid to stand your ground against the Devil, Aaron."

"No, I am not, nor have I ever been during the times we've met."

"Just remember, Aaron, God will prevail over the Devil and, on that day, Lucifer will be destroyed. But, until then, we must have faith in God and carry that faith with us every minute of the day. God is not blind to what the Devil is doing to people, nor was God blind to what Satan was doing to Nicole. God loves you, Aaron, and he has always loved Nicole. We are all his children and it was Our Father that said the Kingdom of Heaven is within us.

"This cross I wear shows I believe you, Johnathon. I also know God has shown his power and His anger towards the Devil's demon's on earth."

"What do you mean Aaron?"

"Well, Johnathon, some years later, Nicole's adoptive father Samael died a horrible death as he deserved, in my opinion."

"Aaron, what happened?"

"Samael worked for an armored car company after his discharge from the Navy and was headed up interstate seventeen towards Flagstaff. As he was driving up the mountain, an eighteen-wheeler, fully loaded was coming down the mountainside when the driver of the semi lost control. The semi hopped the median and hit the vehicle Samael was driving at seventy miles per hour. The driver of the eighteen-wheeler survived, but Samael did not. The vehicle was blown apart and he was ejected onto the pavement where he suffered, pain and anguish before he died."

"Aaron, if I may say, God carried out vengeance and justice as He saw fit, and what He felt Samael deserved. It sounds like God had enough of the evil he projected on Nicole, and the others he may have tortured in life." What happened to Jezebeth?"

"Johnathon, I feel the same way, and Jezebeth died years later alone. I am not sure of the cause, but I do know she had no-one to be with her in the end."

"Aaron, I have to say it, God is God, and He is very loving, but He also strikes down those who cross over to the darkness to work for the Devil."

Filled with many emotions Johnathon asked, "What finally happened between Dick and Nicole?"

"Dick had kept the kids from her until the middle and youngest daughter wanted to live with their mom. With him, it was always an uphill battle because he didn't want to pay child support. After a while he had no choice but to let the girls stay with her. The two daughters were causing trouble for Dick because they wanted to live with their mother. He couldn't take it any longer and let the two girls go. Nicole was excited to have her children living with her. Once she obtained custody of the children she was eligible for state assistance, which helped her a lot with rent and groceries. All she wanted was to be the best mom she could to her children, so she again began working retail. She struggled, but kept going for herself and her girls. Since she never had a driver's license, or even owned a car, she would ride her bike everywhere. Eventually, though, Nicole's boyfriend began stealing her money. That left her struggling even more, and the stress of losing all her money mounted on her. She had worked hard to overcome her challenges and now she had a setback and no one to turn to."

"Aaron, my heart goes out to Nicole. I think I am going to turn in for the night if that's okay?"

"Sure, we can call it a night. Are you okay, Johnathon?"

"Yes, I just need to lay down."

Aaron could see Johnathon was troubled, and who wouldn't be after listening to what happened to Nicole. Johnathon made his bed and crawled under the covers. His eyes close as Aaron finishes taking care of the fire and the lamps. Walking through the cabin, he thinks about Nicole and wonders what Johnathon is thinking. He makes his way to the couch to get some sleep. Aaron looks over at Johnathon to make sure he is okay.

"Johnathon?"

"Yes, Aaron."

"Sorry if I woke you. I just wanted to tell you thank you for being my friend."

"It's okay, Aaron, and you're welcome."

Johnathon and Aaron close their eyes and sleep peacefully through the night. Morning arrives, and Aaron starts the wood stove in the kitchen to brew a fresh pot of coffee. Looking out the window, he can see the sunlight sparkling on Mother Earth. A smile appears on his face.

Softly, Aaron utters, "I wish I could bottle up the beauty that resides in this place that has no name and take it everywhere with me."

"What was that, Aaron?"

"Oh, Johnathon, I didn't realize you were awake."

"I smelled the coffee brewing and I couldn't help but get out of bed."

"Aaron, if I may ask, what was that you said?"

"I was looking out the window and wished that the beauty of this place could be something that I always carry with me."

"Well, you can, Aaron. If you just relax and capture the moment of all you see, your mind will create a picture for you to hold as a memory."

"Johnathon, would you like to go outside and sit on the porch?"

"Yes, let's get a closer look at all that splendor."

"Johnathon, this is gorgeous, like a flawless painting brushed by His divine hand."

"Aaron, God can do anything. Creating beautiful things is just one of his many talents."

Johnathon and Aaron find their seats on the front deck and begin enjoying the fresh mountain air. Aaron looks up at the sky and follows the flow of the morning sun back down to Johnathon. Suddenly, a thought flashes through his mind.

"Johnathon, have you noticed there are no eagles soaring in the heavens?"

"I haven't, Aaron."

"Come to think about it, the last time I saw an eagle was right before you showed up at the cabin. Don't you think that is a little odd?"

"Not really, Aaron, given all of the unknowns in Mother Nature's kingdom."

"I find it curious…"

"Aaron, since you have been at the cabin, have you seen the bright light anymore?"

"No, I haven't, and that's another mystery, Johnathon."

"So, how long was it before you entered the picture with Nicole, Aaron?"

"When she finally broke it off with her boyfriend, some time had passed, Nicole was still struggling but doing the best she could."

"If I remember correctly Aaron, you and Nicole had been dating for a few weeks and there was a meeting going to take place with CPS."

"That is correct, Johnathon. But before I discuss the meeting with CPS, I should tell you about Nicole and I and our dates prior. It was an exciting time for us both. We met on a Saturday night at about seven o'clock. I picked her up in my maroon Escort. The night air was calm, the stars were out, and the moon shimmered. We drove to the bar downtown. Upon entering the bar, I asked Nicole what she liked to drink. She told me her favorite drink was called Sex on the Beach, and I ordered her one when we got inside. She smiled as we walked to a table and her eyes glistened in the light as she asked me if she could have a cigarette. I told her I would do her one better. I walked to the bar and bought her a pack of Marlboro red one-hundreds. Nicole was surprised, but very thankful. As the night moved on she danced, sang and had a good time. She would smile at me and I would smile back. It was like she could relax around me. She was absolutely gorgeous that night, Johnathon, with her long, black hair and perfect makeup. After I had been seeing her for a week, she called me on a Thursday and asked if I would come over to her apartment in the afternoon. I came over and, after being there for a few hours, guess who showed up?"

"I could guess, Aaron, but I will let you tell me."

"Nicole asked me if I would answer the door and I obliged. It was Dick. He showed up wanting to harass Nicole, as he did sometimes, putting her down and calling her names. As the door opened, Dick stopped in his tracks and just stared. Looking at me, he asked, 'who are you?' and I replied, 'I am Aaron, Nicole's fiancé.' Dick was very standoffish, but I think he was more intimidated because I'm six feet, four inches tall and weighed two-hundred and fifty-five pounds."

"Aaron, how tall was Dick?"

"He stood about five feet nine inches and weighed about one-hundred and fifty pounds."

"I could see why he would be intimidated by you, Aaron."

"He wasn't very big, but still big enough to beat on Nicole all those years and force her to do things against her will. I guess seeing her with me was a slap in the face for him. It's like he knew he couldn't hurt her any more with me standing by her side. I didn't like him, and he knew it. I told him, from now on, he would respect her as long as I was around. Dick had a few choice words for me. I laughed and told him he needed to back off and leave if he wasn't going to be respectful, which he finally did. I worked hard to keep my anger at a minimum when dealing with Dick, out of respect for Nicole and her children."

"I am sure that was a very difficult thing to do, Aaron."

"My self-control improved greatly during those times. Back to the meeting between CPS and Nicole. Remember Johnathon, I had told you that Dick let the two girls live with her and that she had been struggling with keeping food in the house, paying the bills, drug and alcohol issues, and psychiatric problems."

"Yes, I remember, Aaron."

"Well, CPS wanted to take the children, and I spoke up during the meeting and offered a solution. I looked at the CPS worker and said, with confidence, 'What if I put new furniture in Nicole's apartment, fill her cabinets with food, get her bills all caught up and pay her rent? While I take care of everything at her apartment, Nicole will go into drug and alcohol rehabilitation and get clean. During that time, the girls could live in a foster home.'"

"Why did the two girls have to go into foster care, Aaron?"

"Because their biological father said if his daughters wanted to live with their mother, they had to be accountable for their decision. He was punishing the two girls because they loved their mother, and he stuck to his guns and refused to let the children stay with him."

"So, what did the CPS worker say to your proposal, Aaron?"

"They agreed, and Nicole started crying. When I asked her what was wrong, she said she was scared. I put my arms around her and told her it would be okay. I told her I would visit her every day and make sure she had a place to come home to. The next day I took Nicole to the drug and alcohol rehab building and admitted her. The children went into foster care and I began to take care of the food, bills, rent and furniture."

"Aaron, what kind of work were you doing to be able to do all that for Nicole?"

"I worked as a truck driver, making twenty-eight hundred dollars a month, with full benefits and quarterly bonuses. I still had to pay child support and take care of my own bills, Johnathon, but I managed. After I got all the utilities back on and the rent paid, I went to Nicole's apartment and started cleaning. It was several days before I got the place clean and all the laundry done. I went grocery shopping and filled the cabinets, refrigerator and freezer full of food. Then I bought new beds for Nicole and her daughters, and brought in a new couch and love seat, with a coffee table and end tables, for the living room."

"How often did you visit Nicole?"

"Every day, Johnathon, at five o'clock in the evenings. Before smoking bans were initiated, the patients could smoke in designated areas inside the rehabilitation center. I always made sure she had cigarettes and a warm smile from me. She would always smile back and thank me. During each visit I would remind her to look out her window around nine o'clock at night. When she did, I would blow her kisses and she would give kisses back."

Chapter Twelve
Finding Life

"Nicole would tell me she wished I could be with her while she stayed in rehab. I asked her why and she said she would get scared at night and sometimes during the day. I told her I would sneak myself in there and always be with her."

"How were you going to do that, Aaron?"

"At the rehab center they could watch movies, so one day I asked the supervisor if I could bring a movie to Nicole and have everyone watch it. Inside of the VHS case I slipped a picture of myself with a note that said 'I love you' and 'I told you I would sneak in to be with you.' I went to visit her that night and she started crying. I asked her what was wrong and she replied, 'I am not alone any more, am I?' I told her that I was there for her, and after her tears stopped, I took my hand and softly wiped her cheeks."

"Was she finally able to begin to heal, Aaron?"

"Let's go back inside and I can tell you more."

The sun had already begun its frame-by-frame descent to the edge of the horizon. Stepping back into the cabin, Jonathon couldn't help but to feel heavy-hearted for Nicole. He thought about what it must have taken for her to deal with the deeply buried emotions she had been masking with drugs and alcohol for all those years.

Aaron and Johnathon fill their cups with fresh coffee and make their way to the sitting room. The moonlight through the cabin windows adds warmth to the heat from the fire. Aaron's thoughts move forward and backward through time and space before resurfacing in the present.

"Thank you, Johnathon, for being my friend."

"You're welcome, Aaron, and thank you, too, for everything you have done for me."

"It sure is peaceful in this place that has no name. I love it here, but something in my gut tells me I will have to leave this place, or this place will leave me. Before that time comes, I hope I will understand why I am here and what all of this means. Johnathon, would you like to hear a song on the piano that Nicole said would always be our song? It's called 'From this Moment.'"

"It sounds like a beautiful song, Aaron."

I sit at the piano and prepare to play as the fire dances in the fireplace.

"Johnathon? Did you hear that?"

"Hear what, Aaron?"

"That noise on the front porch."

"I didn't hear anything."

Getting up from the bench, I walk to the front door, but before I can open it someone begins knocking. I open the door and standing before me is a lady with long, flowing brown hair and violet blue eyes. She appears to be about six feet tall and weighs about one-hundred and thirty pounds and is wearing a long-sleeved shirt, blue jeans and black cowboy boots. I stand for a moment and look at her before I remember my manners.

"Hello, can I help you?"

She replies, with a smile, "I hope so."

"What can I do for you?"

"May I come in?"

"Yes, you may. Johnathon, we have company. What is your name, young lady?"

"I am Bridgett."

"Nice to meet you, Bridgett. I'm Aaron and this is Johnathon. Would you like to sit with us and warm up with a cup of coffee?"

"I would like that, Aaron, thank you."

As Johnathon and Bridgett talk, I move into the kitchen to pour a cup of coffee and think to myself, how is it possible that I now have two visitors in this place that has no name.

"Here is your cup of coffee, Bridgett. May I ask where you came from and how you found us?"

"Aaron, I heard from others far away that there was a man traveling and staying in a cabin and I wanted to meet you."

"But why did you need to meet me, and who are the others?"

"It's not important right now, Aaron. What's important is that I am here."

"How did the others hear about me?"

"Sometimes the wind blows and the trees talk. Trust me – it's okay."

"That's what Johnathon says all the time, Bridgett. You two think alike. Smiling, I ask, are you two related?"

"We are all God's children, Aaron, and in His image we were created."

"Fair enough Bridgett, I suppose. I was just getting ready to play the piano when you showed up. Would you like to hear me play a song my wife loved and coined as 'our song'?"

"I would love to hear the piano, gentlemen. Are you any good at playing, Aaron?"

"When he plays the music echoes in the cabin like a symphony hall would," Johnathon answered.

"Thank you for the compliment, Johnathon. Bridgett, this is

'From This Moment by Shania Twain.'"

With the oil lamps going and the fire crackling, I find the bench and begin to play. Johnathon and Bridgett sit and listen to the music and, as I look over from playing, I see tears falling from Bridgett's eyes. She must be feeling the emotions coming from the song. Johnathon wears a smile on his face, as if he knows what this song means to Nicole and me. I can softly hear him tell her, "it's okay."

As the last ivory key is played, I stand and close the fallboard.

"That was beautiful, Aaron."

"Thank you, Bridgett. If you two don't mind, I am going to step outside and smoke a cigarette."

I close the cabin door and am struck by the moon's immense glow – the kind that makes night look like daytime. I think to myself that no child would be afraid of what hides in the darkness on a night like this. Looking back in at my new friends talking, I wonder who these guests are who have appeared out of nowhere, and if I am behind the glass or in Heaven. I ask myself why Bridgett needed to meet me, but get the feeling that neither Bridgett nor Johnathon would tell me no matter how many times I asked. It still might be worth another try, I consider, and re-join my group inside the cabin.

"Aaron, I hope you don't mind, I was just telling Bridgett about you and your wife, Nicole, and how you helped her so she didn't feel alone anymore."

"It's okay, Johnathon. There must be a reason why we're all here."

"Do you mind if I stay and listen?" Bridgett asked, as if she already knew the answer.

"Not at all, Bridgett. After I comforted Nicole at the rehabilitation center, I had to leave for work. But before I did, I told her that if she gets scared at night, or during the day, to just take my picture and hold it tight and everything would be all right. She smiled and said 'okay, Aaron.' Before my day of truck driving began, I went to Nicole's place to check on everything. I had placed the new furniture where I knew she would like everything. The new couch was on the south wall. The love seat was on the east wall. I also put a television and DVD player in her apartment, and had cable installed so she could watch her favorite shows. I wanted everything to be perfect for her and I felt it was."

Interjecting, Bridgett asked, "Johnathon said you did a lot for mom through the years."

"What did you say, Bridgett?"

"I said it sounds like you did a lot for Nicole through the years."

"That is not what you said. You said 'mom.' Or at least that's what I thought I heard."

"You must have misheard me, Aaron."

"Okay, I must be getting tired. I'm sorry, Bridgett."

Johnathon, as if to move past the matter, offers in agreement, "Yes, it has been a long day."

"Aaron, why don't we get some sleep and talk tomorrow?"

"Johnathon, I am good with that if Bridgett doesn't mind."

"I don't mind Aaron."

"Bridgett?"

"Yes Aaron, do you feel comfortable staying here tonight? You could take the couch and Johnathon and I will sleep on the floor."

"Yes, but I don't want to put you out, Aaron. That is very nice of you."

"Bridgett it's no problem at all, I'll see if there are more pillows and blankets."

Jonathon puts another log on the fire and puts out the oil lamps. Aaron returns with more blankets and pillows. Bridgett gets comfortable under the blankets on the couch. Johnathon and I lay down in our beds on the floor and close our eyes, but I am restless, still wondering why I can't get a straight answer from anyone and why I thought I heard Bridgett say 'mom' when I was telling them about Nicole. Time slips into the night and the others are sound asleep. I finally resolve, as Johnathon says, that sometimes we don't need to know why things happen. My mind clears and I fall deep within as my eyes close...

* * * * *

I awaken before sunrise, brew the coffee, and qu
onto the porch. The moon's night shift has ended, but its
brightness allows me to see a family of deer looking at n
water fountain. Sitting in the rocking chair, I look out upon Mother
Nature and watch her come to life. I wonder if my wife is looking
down on me from Heaven. I hope she is, even though I failed her in so
many ways. I hear the door crack and it's Bridgett.

"Good morning, Aaron. How are you?"

"It's another beautiful morning Bridgett, and I am doing okay.
How did you sleep?"

"Very peacefully, thank you. I hope you don't mind, I poured
myself a cup of your coffee.

Aaron replies with a smile, "Bridgett, you can have coffee any
time."

"Thank you, Aaron. Do you mind if I sit with you, Aaron?"

"Not at all, Bridgett."

As the deer slowly and silently disappear, a gentle breeze flows
against my face.

"What are you thinking about?"

"Just how beautiful this place is and how I miss Nicole."

"You loved her a lot, didn't you Aaron?"

"Yes, Bridgett, I did, and I always will."

"I'm sure she misses you, too, Aaron."

Johnathon emerges from the cabin and takes a seat next to
Bridgett.

"Good morning to you both."

"Good morning, Johnathon. Bridgett and I were just talking.
Well, actually, we just started talking about Nicole."

"Aaron, you were telling us about the apartment and Nicole
being in rehab."

"That is right Johnathon. The apartment was clean and fully stocked. So, at that point, I called the CPS worker and scheduled a time for her to come over and inspect. I was surprised to learn that the CPS worker could see me that day, around two-thirty in the afternoon. The social worker showed up and we did a walk-through of the apartment. She made sure to check the cabinets and refrigerator to see if there was enough food in the apartment. The electricity, water and gas were all turned on, and she also checked with the landlord to make sure the rent had been paid. I told the social worker I would maintain everything for Nicole. She was actually very nice and said I was doing a good job. I told her thank you, but I wasn't doing all this for a pat on the back, or to be a saint. I did it because I loved Nicole and it was the right thing to do. Satisfied, she left, and I went to visit Nicole. When I got there, I could see she was having some withdrawal issues. I just held her tight, whispering in her ear that it would be okay."

Chapter Thirteen
When You Love

"*N*icole asked me why I cared so much for her and why I was doing all this when we had only been together for a short time. I smiled and told her I wrote something special, just for her, and I read it to her."

"Could we hear it, Aaron?"

"Okay, Bridgett, I will share it with you:

Strings of the Heart

For years, the traveler walked day and night through wind, rain, sunshine and storms. Sometimes he would rest during the night, perched against a lonely old tree with the cool breeze grazing his flesh. Other times, the traveler would walk without sleep. During the day, as he moved down the lane, he would absorb all the beauty that God had to offer. He would smile and take pause, and listen to the birds, the trees, and the other wildlife that flourished upon the lands.

He would be weathered from the journey, with dust, dirt and

tattered clothing. He stood six feet, four inches tall and wore old boots that oftentimes tried to fall apart. But on his back, he carried the one thing that soothed his soul – his violin. When he played his violin, the world heard it, even though no one was around to hear. The traveler played the strings of his life and he was happy, but lonely, too.

Then, one day, the traveler was softly playing the strings as he sat on the old grey stones next to a flowing, beautiful waterfall, enjoying every moment of the sweet, soft music he was producing from the gift he held close. Then he stopped, looked out of the corner of his eye, and noticed the silhouette of a lady approaching. She smiled at him, and he at her, and after exchanging hellos she gazed upon him longingly. Finally, he asked her, 'Why are you looking at me, smiling?' and she replied, 'Because there's something about you. I don't know what it is, but I feel something.' He replied, 'It's okay not knowing. I didn't know, either. But, if I may say, in all these years of wandering, I always thought I was alone. But now, seeing you, I know I was never truly alone because you were always in my thoughts and my soul. I just never knew who you were till now.' She smiled and asked, 'Who am I? to which he replied, 'You, my lady, are my home, my life, what I have walked so long for.'

They gazed into each other's eyes, embraced, and talked all night long. The traveler whispered in her ear as the sun dawned over the misty waters from the fall, 'We have both wandered for so long, not knowing the right path to reach our destination. But our destination, our paths, were always connected.' She kissed his lips, smiled and spoke these words, 'I followed the music and the melody led me to you, my life.'" The traveler smiled, and a tear trailed along his cheek and he softly said, 'Come into my heart, Nicole, and I shall forever hold you dear.'"

"I told her that short story was about us and I loved her."

"Aaron, that was so beautiful."

"Thank you, Bridgett. I'm glad you enjoyed it."

"Where do you find the words you write, Aaron?" Johnathon asked.

"I don't really know. They just appear when my emotions are running strong."

"I think you could call your writing a gift, Aaron."

"Thank you both for the compliments. After I read her 'Strings of the Heart,' Nicole and I talked to each other and I held her tight. She loved the piece I wrote and kissed me. That's when she asked me if I would move in with her and I said yes. I told her one day she would be clean from drugs and alcohol. I did notice that, as she became less dependent on drugs and alcohol, she would have mood swings and fits of anger sometimes."

"I think that would be expected, Aaron, don't you?"

"Absolutely, Johnathon, but this was a different kind of mood swing."

"What do you mean, Aaron?"

"It's hard to describe, Bridgett. Sometimes her moods were just different. I couldn't figure it out in the beginning, but I loved her, nevertheless. In fact, every day I loved her more and more. After three months of drug and alcohol rehab, Nicole was finally clean and released. It was a Friday when I picked her up and took her home from the rehab center. As she and I entered the apartment, the first thing she noticed was the Bibles. She looked at me and said, 'What the hell are *those* books doing in here?!' I told her, 'If the Bibles go, then so do I.'"

"What did she say to that, Aaron?" Bridgett asked with a coy smile.

"She said the Bibles could stay, but not to expect her to read them. I acquiesced and told her that I wouldn't push religion on her if that is what she wanted. As we walked through the rest of the house, I could see by her face that she loved the new furniture. She was truly happy: she had food, utilities, clean clothes and a place where she could take a hot shower. I was grateful that she had made it through rehab and was back home. After a few days I talked with her about seeing a psychiatric doctor to help her deal with her past. She was scared to dig up even more old wounds than she did over the past few months getting clean, but reluctantly agreed, as long as I promised her I was going to be there for her as she dealt with everything. When we tried to schedule an appointment, they said we couldn't get into the doctor for a month, so we had to wait. Nicole's moods were changing drastically, and her anger was coming out more than it had before."

"Do you think it was because she didn't have the drugs and alcohol to mask her pain like before, Aaron?"

"Yes, that was probably part of it, Bridgett. I could see the hurt and anger living deep within her. She tried hard to keep it all in, but it was too much.

"Johnathon, do you remember when I said that you might not believe everything I tell you?"

"Yes, I remember, Aaron, and like I said, I like to keep an open mind. Why do you ask?"

"Because even I have a hard time believing what happened after Nicole left rehab and throughout the rest of the years that we were together."

Bridgett interjected, "Aaron, there are many things in life that may be hard to believe, but those things that happen to us in life are real and you must have faith."

"Now, we are ready to listen if you feel like sharing more with Johnathon and me."

"Okay, then. One calm night, with the moon full in the sky and a soft breeze blowing, Nicole and I were sitting in lawn chairs on the north side of the apartment, just talking. After an hour had passed, she and I decided to go inside and grab something to eat. Together, we walked into the apartment and moved into the kitchen. I remember we were sharing a fruit bowl filled with strawberries, cantaloupe, green and purple grapes, and honeydew melon. I set the fruit bowl down on the stand next to the microwave. As I leaned against the counter, I noticed that Nicole was by the window on the south wall. She began to look different and her voice seemed to change. She started telling me about some of the things she had gone through in her life. Then, suddenly, she said, 'so what's the matter with us, doc? Can you help us?' I knew something was off and I didn't know what it was, but I did know I was dealing with something I had never encountered before."

"Aaron, she used the word 'us,' in the plural sense?"

"Yes, Bridgett, and I didn't know what to make of it. I told Nicole, or who I thought was her, that I was stepping outside for a moment. I feared the unknown but, as I was walking toward the front door, I heard a voice inside my head telling me it would be okay. So I turned around and we sat on the couch. But Nicole was not Nicole. She introduced herself as April.

"Who was April, Aaron?"

"Evidently, Johnathon, and I didn't know this at the time, April was a personality that Nicole manifested from years of abuse. She was Nicole's first alternate identity to come out."

"The first? What was she like?" Bridgett asked with a frightened look on her face.

"She was blunt and straight to the point. April told me that night a storm was coming and it would last for years. I asked her who she was, and what storm was coming? April replied, 'Aaron, you will find out soon enough,' and then stated that she was the first, but not the last, and there would be many more to come. I asked her what that meant, but she was gone and Nicole was back. She couldn't remember how she went from the kitchen to the couch, or that I had said I was stepping outside. I told her it would be okay and she started crying, asking me to help her. I wiped her tears and held her. She didn't understand what was going on, nor did I begin to understand until later that night."

"What happened later, Aaron?"

"After a few hours had passed, Nicole and I moved from the couch to the front porch to enjoy the night air. That's when she started staring at me with this strange look on her face. I asked her what was wrong, and she didn't answer me. I asked her again and no reply. She just looked at me with this unexplainable facial expression I had never seen before. Five or ten minutes had passed and then Nicole asked me, 'do you know who I am?' and I said, 'You're Nicole?' She replied, 'No, I am not Nicole. I am John, and I would like to walk with you, Aaron.' I want you two to remember that this was at night when John came out to talk."

"Why does that matter, Aaron?"

"I will explain shortly, Johnathon. As John and I walked down the street, he asked me how much I knew about the Book of Revelations and demonic possession. I told him that I knew a little bit about it, explaining to him that I knew the Devil sends his demons out into the world to destroy lives by consuming their mortal bodies. I asked John why he wanted to know. He replied, 'Aaron, it's time.' I asked John, 'What must I do?' and he told me that I must fight for what I believe in. I asked him what is it that I believe in and who would I have to fight. He told me, in a very powerful voice, 'Aaron, you believe in Father in Heaven, and with all your faith you must fight those who live in the fire in order to help the one you love.'"

Johnathon, struck by the words from an earlier conversation, interrupted, "Aaron, you had told me your friend said there would be a time when you would have to fight."

"That is right Johnathon, he did tell me that years ago. At that point my mind was over-loading from everything that was happening. I was trying to comprehend what was going on as Nicole (John) and I were walking."

"Aaron, how does someone develop or manifest a personality?"

"I will answer the second part of the question first, if that's okay."

"Yes, please, Aaron."

"A person develops multiple personalities from constant abuse, or a severe traumatic event in his or her life. As the severe abuse continues, he or she will develop a defense mechanism that allows the mind to birth a new identity. Each identity endures a certain amount of abuse until the personality reaches his or her pain threshold. Once the pain threshold is met, another personality will manifest and come forward to endure the higher levels of pain. Multiple personalities, or what psychiatric doctors call Dissociative Identity Disorder (D.I.D.), is the defense mechanism that is designed to protect the original host. In this case, that was Nicole.

Chapter Fourteen
Believing

"Each personality may or may not be aware of another. He or she will hold their own memories that the original host is not aware of until the integration process. However, in some cases, the personality may join memories to the original host, who will then be aware that the other is present. This action allows both the original host and the personality to coexist together, which means more than one personality can be present without suppressing the original host, allowing them to interact with one another. Furthermore, each personality has its own identity, with distinguishing characteristics. For example, one personality may eat with his right hand and another may eat with her left hand. They may talk differently, or speak different languages, or have a different way of walking and moving. The original host can manifest males and females as their defense mechanisms, depending on the situation. Now, Johnathon, you asked me what I meant when I said Nicole was in a different state. She was suppressed within herself because John was a strong personality. As the original host manifests each personality, one is stronger than the other."

"So, what you're saying, Aaron, is that John suppressed her to make her unaware of his existence."

"That's right, Bridgett."

"But where does Nicole go when a personality does that to her?" Jonathon asked after a long, thoughtful silence.

"Jonathon, one could say that Nicole goes 'dormant,' if you will, or to a safe place that she calls her domain that resides within herself. Now, there is another explanation for these types of occurrences other than Dissociative Identity Disorder, which is that the individual has a spiritual affliction or an unclean soul. Before the new psychology was started in the early 1900s, psychiatric disorders were viewed as religious or spiritual afflictions. Even the American Psychiatric Association still defines the Lucifer effect in their dictionary as an action that resembles demonic possession. When someone is possessed by a demon, he or she loses the ability to control his or her body and may lose track of time or certain memories."

"Aaron, you said demons can possess a person, but isn't it also possible to have a heavenly host occupying Nicole or any other person?"

"I like that question, Johnathon. As you stated before, in the seventeenth chapter of St. Luke it was Christ who delivered the Sermon on the Mount and said that the Kingdom of Heaven is within man and woman. Therefore, it is possible with faith, believing in what Christ said during his sermon and knowing all things are possible in Christ's name. The Father, Son, and Holy Ghost are, and have been, within us, along with Father's angels, from the beginning of time. Do you remember when I spoke about the different planes of existence?"

"Yes, I do, Aaron."

"Well, for me, it's looking inward and hearing without hearing, feeling without feeling, touching without touching, smelling without smelling, and tasting without tasting. It is also the ability to move freely within the different realms of Heaven, Hell and Purgatory while being on Earth. Our Lord in Heaven gave everyone this gift because the Kingdom of God is within us. It is the gift bestowed upon every man, woman and child."

"Are you talking about walking by faith and not by sight?"

"I am, Bridgett, and I am also talking about looking deep within myself and listening to the words spoken. Christ is our Lord and speaks to us all the time, in all ways and in all manners. It's looking at the smallest signs that Father in Heaven has given me along the way. It's being self-aware and understanding that Heaven and Hell are real and not some fairy tale that mankind made up along the way. Demons do exist and walk this earth to create chaos, pain and suffering. As psychology has progressed, our society has waned away from the unclean soul afflictions and has allowed the Devil to hide in the shadows to torment people like Nicole over the course of her entire life. The Devil mocks God any way he can, by destroying people's lives. It was Lucifer in the beginning when God created man and woman in his image. That said, he would not kneel to God's beautiful creation when God instructed all of his angels to kneel before man and woman. That led to the war in Heaven between Lucifer and God. The angels took sides and, in the end, Lucifer was cast out of Heaven and bound in chains."

"I remember hearing about the war in Heaven, Aaron. It was a battle of battles between the angels that followed God and the angels that followed Lucifer."

"Yes, it was, Johnathon."

"What else did John say, Aaron?" Bridgett asked, as if trying to place a memory or recollection.

"John told me about the time the Devil met with God. The story went something like this:

God and the Devil

"And the heavenly hosts saw an unclean spirit come forth upon the Holy Land in Heaven, holding a scroll. They moved forth upon the unclean spirit to protect the Kingdom of Heaven, and when they did so they parted like the ocean in the time of Moses. The unclean spirit stopped. An angel appeared bathed in Gold and Jewels from behind God's most heavenly hosts and approached the unclean spirit with his sword in hand. The angel bathed in Jewels and Gold stood before the unclean spirit and took the scroll. The unclean spirit told the angel bathed in Gold and Jewels that his master, his God in Hell, wanted to speak to God in Heaven. The angel bathed in Gold and Jewels destroyed the unclean spirit and went forth to God the Father with the scroll.

The angel bathed in Gold and Jewels read the scroll to God the Father, who went to the mountain with his most heavenly hosts. Our Lord in Heaven met with the Devil on the day of rest and the Devil approached with darkness about him. And our Lord God brought forth the light with his almighty power and destroyed the darkness that surged about the Devil. God spoke in a thunderous voice that made the heavens tremble. As the heavens trembled, our Lord's most heavenly hosts were ready to follow any commandment set forth by God. And God said to Lucifer, 'speak on the matter of which you want.'"

"I want unchained by your hands."

"God and his heavenly hosts stepped forth to the Devil, and the Devil spoke…"

"I will choose a man or woman on earth to corrupt with drugs, alcohol, abuse, fill with hate, and possess. He or she will worship me and despise you. And I want you, God, to choose a man or woman on earth that can be filled with faith, love, and understanding. I want whomever you choose to love everything about you and Heaven. And, in a loud thunderous voice as lightning flashed in the heavens, God spoke to Lucifer…"

"Move forth, Satan, with your serpent's tongue."

"The chosen ones will meet on Earth when the time is right. Your child, chosen, will have the armor of faith. And my chosen child will despise your works and have the armor of hatred. As the war between the chosen ones begins, your heavenly hosts can watch and guide, and my unclean spirits will fight to keep the hurt and hatred alive through the years. Just as my demons will possess his or her body, your heavenly hosts can be present, too. If my chosen one can convert your chosen one into embracing the depths of Hell and be made to worship me, the Devil, then I will have freedom beyond the boundaries of constraint. If your chosen one converts the one I destroyed, the one I made to love me, the Devil, and will worship everything about you, God, with love, faith and honor, then the seals remain, and I will stay chained by your hands."

God then spoke to the Devil, "What if the fight to convert our chosen ones boils over into our worlds?"

Lucifer, smiling gruesomely, replies, "That depends on the manner of my unclean spirits and your most heavenly hosts."

And in a loud, thunderous voice, God tells Lucifer, "The mark will be made, but if you, Lucifer, cross the line, I will revisit you on this matter."

Then God raised his hand and showed Lucifer his almighty power by casting him back into Hell.

"At the end of the conversation between John and me, he said, 'I want to show you, Aaron, who I am.' He asked me to raise my head and look to the Heavens above. I looked up into the night sky and, in an instant, I could see the sky being filled with different colors. I was amazed. Everything was calm, and the night was beautiful. John's final words to me were, 'I have faith in you, Aaron, and I must go.'"

"Aaron, what was that like hearing about God and the Devil, and seeing the lights in the night sky?"

"Johnathon, it was amazing to watch the night sky be dark with the stars shining and then the next minute be filled with different colors."

"Aaron, God's angels can do many things."

"Yes, they can Bridgett, and I have seen many things happen since that time." But it was also confusing. With all my faith in Father in Heaven, I believe with all my heart that it was John."

"Do you mean John from the book of John?"

"Yes, Bridgett, I believe it was, but the confusing part was why me and why Nicole? Sometimes, I would just simply like to know why things happen."

Johnathon replies. "Many people, Aaron, throughout the world, ask why things happen. And yet, God will reveal it to them when the time is right, just as John showed you the vast array of colors in the night sky."

"Aaron, did Nicole come back after John left?"

"She did, Bridgett, and right away she asked me where we were. I told her that we went for a walk. Nicole was very confused and, since her new personality had just emerged that night, so was I. When we got back to the apartment, we decided to lay down and try and get some rest. Nicole was on edge and asked me if I would stay up to watch her until she went to sleep. I told her I would, and I gently ran my fingers through her hair and told her it would be okay as she was drifting off to sleep. About a half hour after she went to sleep, I walked outside to get some fresh air. I looked up at the night sky and prayed to Father in Heaven."

"If I may ask, Aaron, what did you pray about?"

"Bridgett, I would like some coffee, the fire needs another log and I need a cigarette."

"If you want to smoke, Aaron, I will get the coffee," Johnathon offered.

"And I will throw another log on the fire," said Bridgett, already halfway across the room toward her task."

"Thank you both very much."

I make my way to the front porch and, opening the door, feel a cool breeze brush against my skin. I breathe in deeply and absorb the gifts that blow in on the wind from these pristine mountain landscapes. I sit in the rocking chair and get the sensation that I am not alone. Directly across from me, perched on the railing, I'm struck by the sight of a sleek, white owl looking at me. I admire its soundless approach and sheer beauty, but I am afraid to move because I don't want to scare it off. I smile at the white-feathered messenger as it takes off into the night. My mind had wondered where the eagles went and now I wonder where the owl has gone. The porch door opens and Bridgett hands me a cup of coffee.

"Thank you, Bridgett."

"Are you coming back in, Aaron?"

"Yes, I am just finishing up. I will be in soon." My heart feels heavy tonight as I think about Nicole. I put out the cigarette and re-enter the cabin, finding my chair in the sitting room with a fresh cup of coffee and my two unexplained friends."

"While you were away, Aaron, I was thinking how Nicole's life sounds a lot like what Job went through in the Bible. Pain, suffering, hurt, and anguish was at the forefront of her entire life."

"Yes," Bridgett added, "and even as Job was going through his torment, God the Father was in Job's heart, just as God was in Nicole's heart. Aaron, you must believe in Him and His will. There is always a reason why something happens."

"I know, Bridgett, and it has taken me years to fully understand some things, and other things are still without answers. Don't get me wrong. I have been upset with Father in Heaven many times because I have not agreed with him. But I love my Father nonetheless."

"Aaron, it sounds like Nicole's heart ached many times throughout her life."

"That's an understatement, Bridgett. I tried to help both of us with the healing process by writing. There are two pieces that come to mind that I would like to share:

Thoughts of the Multitude

How many times does one fall in the book called life?

How many times does a heart ache?

How many times does one look to the heavens and ask Father to be our guide?

How many times do we walk upon the waters

Only to drown in the world below the sea?

The Voice Echoes

Behold, my life is forever

as the kingdom of Heaven is

without pain and suffering.

I say this to you: to know

who we are, in the beginning and the end,

one must fall against the rain to understand one's life.

A heart aches like the ocean tides,

flowing against the breast of Mother Earth.

If one can count the stones against her bosom,

then one knows how many times he or she looks

to our Father in Heaven to be our guide.

Falsehood is in the bark of the tree

that forms the vessels of illusory perceptions

between shadow and light. Drowning in the world

below the sea is to live within the soiled land above.

Chapter Fifteen
The Most Beautiful Lady

"Johnathon and Bridgett, I'm tired and I'd like to go to bed."

"Are you okay, Aaron?"

"I am fine, Johnathon. I just need to get some sleep."

"I understand, Aaron."

Johnathon and Bridgett make their beds while I move through the cabin and put out the oil lamps. Looking at the fireplace, I notice the flame is burning down so I put one last log on the fire for the night. I find my bedding on the floor next to the china hutch. As I begin making my bed, I look over and see that Bridgett and Johnathon are already sound asleep. I can hear the crackling of the fireplace and my mind will not slow down. I quietly get up and return to the sitting room.

I re-light the oil lamp that sits on the table in between the chairs and watch as the flame dances. I see my cup of coffee still sitting on the table and reach for it and take a sip. The coffee is a little cool, but still very good. I try to not make any noise so I can relax in the night. I gaze at the piano and think about the time when God the Father came to me when my wife laid in the hospital bed. In my mind I can hear myself telling my wife about the conversation God and I had, as if she was here at the cabin with me. Softly, I whisper. Nicole, I was:

Talking with God

Nicole, last night God the Father came to me

and asked me: Aaron, how are you doing? I replied to my Father,

Oh, I am hanging in there. How are you Father?

God the Father replied

I am the same today, tomorrow, and forever. Aaron

what is the most beautiful thing

in the world I created?

Well, Father, some could say

it is the meadowed field with the lilies

softly dancing in the wind. Some could say

it is the snow-capped mountains that glisten

as the sun peaks through the clouds. Or

some could say it is the sunrise or sunsets over the oceans.

And when the light hits the waters

it's like diamonds dancing on a ballroom stage.

God replied. Aaron, those are all wonderful sights to see,

but the most beautiful thing I created

was your wife, Nicole.

My eyes begin to mist as I remember how she would smile even though she was in all that pain. Tears fall from my eyes like the streams that flow from the caps above. I wipe the tears, but the waters continue to run. I lay my head in my hands, feeling the sadness of tonight. Suddenly, I feel a hand rest on my shoulder. I raise my head and see Bridgett standing there.

"What's wrong, Aaron?"

"I am sad tonight, Bridgett. I miss my wife, I miss my son Anthony and tonight my heart is heavy."

"May I give you a hug, Aaron?"

"Yes, I could use one, Bridgett."

"It's okay to cry, Aaron. It cleanses the soul."

"I used to tell Nicole that all the time."

"Would you like to talk about her?"

"Not right now, Bridgett. I just want to go back to bed. Thank you for the hug."

"You're welcome, Aaron."

Bridgett and I head quietly back to the living room and we both lay down. The night moves slowly as we all sleep. The morning sun wakes Johnathon and he slowly rises out of bed. As he looks around, he notices Aaron is not in his bed. He looks in the kitchen, throughout the cabin, and outside on the porch, but no sign of Aaron. He goes back inside and wakes Bridgett.

"Bridgett, get up!"

"I am up, Johnathon. What's the matter?"

"Aaron is gone."

"What? Are you joking, Johnathon?"

"No, I'm not. I've looked everywhere for him."

"Oh, dear heavens."

"Did he say anything to you last night, Bridgett?"

"Well, I woke up and found him in the sitting room, crying. He was sad and said he was missing his wife and son. I gave him a hug and asked him if he wanted to talk. He said no and that he just wanted to go to bed, so we did."

"That's all, Bridgett?"

"Yes, Johnathon, I thought he would be okay."

"We must find him," Johnathon said with an uneasiness in his voice.

Just as Bridgett and Johnathon step outside, they see a man standing by the marble angel fountain.

"Oh, my dear heavens, Johnathon," Bridgett utters as if she saw a ghost. They are both frozen by the image, who begins to speak…

"What's wrong?" the man questions in a strange, far-away voice.

"Aaron is gone from the cabin."

"Why is he gone, Johnathon?"

"I don't know. I awoke and he was nowhere to be found."

"You need to find him."

Bridgett and Johnathon both reply to the man. "We will find Aaron. We promise."

"I know you will, and I have faith in you both." With that, the man turned and walked down the path, disappearing into the canyon.

"Bridgett? Was he here last night watching?"

"I don't know, Johnathon. I didn't see him when I spoke with Aaron, but he could have been. We should have told Aaron who we are."

"No, Bridgett, it's not time yet."

"I still think we should have told him Johnathon."

"Come on, Bridgett."

"Which way do you think he would have gone?"

"Bridgett, I think we should walk down by the river towards the woods."

Bridgett and Johnathon make their way to the flowing river behind the cabin. They near the river and both begin calling out for Aaron. Johnathon turns his head towards the bench he and Aaron sat on the other day but he isn't there, either. They decide to cross the river and walk into the woods. Not too far from the table, they spot an old wooden bridge with rope railings. Crossing the well-worn bridge, Bridgett reaches an almost panic-like state.

"Johnathon!? I am very worried about Aaron. His heart was feeling a lot of sadness last night and..."

"Bridgett, he will be fine. I promise you."

With each step Johnathon and Bridgett take in the woods, their footsteps can be heard from the crackling of the fallen branches, leaves and pine needles. Bridgett looks to the heavens and sees a white-feathered owl in the sky. Slowly it descends to perch on the branch of an old oak tree."

"Johnathon? Look at that old oak tree and tell me what you see."

"I think we have another set of eyes helping us look for Aaron."

"I bet he was at the cabin last night and sensed something was wrong, and now he is helping us by being the messenger."

"I think you are right, Bridgett. Let's see if he gives us a sign."

Deeper into the woods, Bridgett and Johnathon stop for a moment and rest under an old pine tree. The sun is at its highest point in the sky, and Bridgett and Johnathon are far from the cabin. The owl had not followed them any further and Aaron's whereabouts were still a mystery.

"Bridgett, we should head back to the cabin before nightfall arrives."

"I agree, but I just don't know where Aaron could have gone."

Turning back, they begin the long journey through the woods. Nightfall is upon them and they still have the bridge to cross to get to the cabin.

They reach the bridge and carefully cross, holding onto the weathered rope railings. Safely across, they stop at the bench by the river and sit to catch their breath.

"Johnathon, let's start fresh in the morning looking for Aaron."

"That is all we can do for now, Bridgett."

As Bridgett and Johnathon return to the cabin, their minds are filled with worry and they wonder if Aaron is okay. They open the front door of the cabin and take off their boots. Walking toward the sitting room, they hear a voice.

"Hello, Bridgett and Johnathon. Where have you two been?"

They both stop where they stand, shocked to see Aaron before them.

"Oh, thank goodness! What are you doing here? We have looked all over God's creation for you!"

"Well, I was relaxing. Is that okay, Bridgett?" Aaron asked with a wry smile.

"Yes, but where have you been?"

"This morning, I got up and went for a walk to clear my head and when I came back, you and Johnathon were gone. So, I just stayed here and had some coffee."

Bridgett turns and looks at Johnathon and slaps his arm and softly whispers, "Good job, Johnathon."

Smiling Aaron asked. "Did I miss something?"

"No, Aaron, you did not. Johnathon just needed a reminder."

"What reminder is that, Bridgett?"

"Never mind Aaron; it's nothing."

"Would you two like some coffee? I will get you both a cup and bring them into the sitting room."

Both Bridgett and Johnathon reply. "We would Love some coffee."

As Aaron walks into the kitchen, Bridgett and Johnathon talk softly so he cannot hear.

"Johnathon, you had me worried."

"I'm sorry, Bridgett. It scared me when I didn't see Aaron laying in his bed and, when I couldn't find him, I was worried even more. You know how much he means to us both."

"I know, Johnathon, and I understand, but next time don't scare me like that."

"I will be more rational next time."

Aaron pours two cups of the fresh coffee for Johnathon and Bridgett and enters the sitting room where the low talking has stopped.

"So, where did you two run off too today?"

"Bridgett and I went for a walk, just as you did."

"Was your walk relaxing?"

"Yes, it was, Aaron," Johnathon softly said under his breath.

"If that's a relaxing walk we had, then I am the sun that shines down."

"What was that, Bridgett?"

"Nothing, Aaron."

"Well, before we catch up, I am going to step out on the porch and smoke."

"Go ahead, Aaron."

"I promise I won't go too far, as I wouldn't want you two to worry about me," I said with a chuckle.

"We will wait in here for you," a sheepish Bridgett offered.

Outside, I feel that familiar, gentle wind blowing against me. The angel fountain shimmers in the moonlight and the magnificent sounds of the wildlife give me peace. As I am finishing the cigarette, I notice the white-feathered owl has returned to the railing. But as quickly and silently as it arrived, it again disappears into the night. Inside, I share my witnessing of the majestic visitor...

"While I was outside, I saw the most beautiful white-feathered owl on the railing. That makes twice I've seen it in the same spot. Both times, as soon as I make eye contact with it and smile, it soundlessly disappears into the darkness."

Johnathon and Bridgett both look at each other and without saying a word they both know now the owl was watching.

"While you were outside, Aaron, Bridgett and I lit the oil lamps and threw another log on the fire."

"Thank you both. Now that we are comfortable, would you like to hear more about Nicole?"

"Yes, please," Bridgett answered for them both. "Aaron, we left off with you on the front porch praying to Father in Heaven after Nicole went to sleep."

"Right, I remember now. I asked Father in Heaven to help me understand what was going on with Nicole, John, and April. It was at that moment when I heard the voice inside of my head tell me, 'With faith, Aaron, no explanation is necessary. Believe in the seen, the unseen, listen to your heart beating within, and blessings will be upon you.' There was a gust of wind at that moment and the trees seem to whisper a calming sensation all around my body. I was relaxed and went back inside to lay down with Nicole. I crawled into bed and covered up and went to sleep. We woke up early in the morning and the day was quiet. We spent the day watching movies together and we visited her two children in foster care. Nicole was happy and so were the children.

She and I were able to take the two girls a gift. Their eyes lit up and they had this look on their face of peace and contentment, even though the situation was what it was. We said good bye to the girls and told them we would be back to visit them. Nicole gave her girls a kiss and a hug. After we left the foster home, we went back to the apartment and played a game of dice called 'ten-thousand.' We laughed and enjoyed every moment we could together. Night was approaching, and I cooked dinner.

"Do you remember what you made?" asked Bridgett.

"I made lasagna and garlic French bread."

"Aaron, throughout the course of the day, had anybody else come out or appeared?"

"No, the day was quiet, Bridgett, but that night was a different story. After dinner, Nicole and I laid down in bed. I remember I had drifted off to sleep and was awakened by this eerie feeling that someone was watching me."

Chapter Sixteen
Signs in Life

"The headboard of the bed was against the north wall of the apartment. Nicole was laying on the right side of the bed and I was on the left. She was on her side, staring at me with this absent look on her face."

"What do you mean by 'absent,' Aaron?"

"She had no facial expressions and her eyes seemed empty. I asked her if she was okay and she didn't respond. A few minutes later she spoke in a language I didn't understand. I told her that I didn't know what she was saying, and then her words turned back to English."

"What did she say, Aaron?"

"Well, Johnathon, it definitely wasn't Nicole. He called himself Jackal. The windows started shaking throughout the apartment. The room turned cold, and the lights seemed to dim, as Jackal was in Nicole. With the windows rattling, Jackal told me that others were coming, and the one named James would have words with me. Jackal spoke and said, 'Just as John showed you, Aaron, who he was, I show you, now, who we are, and our power, for we are many.' I was numb and admittedly a little scared. I knew I was dealing with something of a spiritual nature, but I also thought some of it may be psychological."

"Aaron, that does not seem psychological," Johnathon interjected.

"What happened next?" Bridgett followed with fearful anticipation.

"It was like something grabbed the apartment and made it shake as if an earthquake was happening. Then, after about ten minutes, Jackal was gone, and everything stopped shaking. When Nicole came back, though, she was different. She told me an image was in her head of a man with a disfigured face. His eyes were black and he carried a curved blade like a scythe or a sickle. She asked me what had happened, but I couldn't give her the truth, for it could have manifested in her again, so I just said she had a bad dream and that it would be all right."

"So you didn't want to scare her with what really happened?"

"Right, Bridgett, and I also didn't know for sure what was going on, as that was only the third episode of me experiencing an alternate identity in Nicole. So I thought it was best to wait. She was feeling extremely confused and didn't know what to say or how to act. And I was struggling to keep calm and was trying to understand what I had just witnessed. Having the walls to the apartment violently shake for ten minutes was completely new to me, too."

"I totally understand," Aaron." Bridgett said reassuringly.

"Johnathon and Bridgett, there was one other thing Nicole told me about the man. She said the image of the man in her mind was like black smoke. I didn't understand what that meant at the time, but I knew that if he appeared again, it would be just as volatile, if not worse."

"Aaron, it seems like everything started happening after you and Nicole got together as a couple."

"You are right about that Johnathon, and since I have had a lot of time to think since her passing, I am beginning to understand that it was all part of a larger purpose. I remember Nicole telling me that before she left Arizona she went to a palm reader, who told her there would be a man she would meet in Iowa. He would stand over six feet tall and have hazel eyes. And that man would stand even taller to guide and protect her. He would become her guardian and a Watcher. When she told me about what the palm reader had told her, I was shocked."

"Aaron, do you believe in soul mates?" asked Bridgett, philosophically.

"I do Bridgett, but I also believe in those who God sends to help others."

Interjecting, Johnathon asked. "Aaron, how about we get some more coffee, and could we hear more about what happened after Jackal emerged from Nicole?"

Aaron's mind goes back to the time when everything began and wonders how in the world, he and Nicole made it through all of it. With the steaming coffee in hand, Johnathon and Bridgett find their seats in the sitting room.

"Johnathon and Bridgett, after Jackal was gone and Nicole came back, we both decided to go into the living room and smoke a cigarette together and talk. I turned on the radio and we were trying to just relax, but that didn't happen. It was about one-thirty in the morning and we were still on the couch when Nicole left again and another came forward. This identity's name was Julie, and when she came out and spoke, her voice was very dominating and powerful."

"What did Julie say to you, Aaron?"

"Johnathon, she said, 'Few have come, but more are on their way. You, Aaron, have met good and evil and soon you will speak to the one named by the unclean spirit. A choice you must make. Just as God my Father gave all his creation free will to choose, you, Aaron, must choose now. Will you fight for God, protect Nicole, and make your mark?' I told Julie that my faith in my Father is strong and I only serve him. I asked her who she was, and she replied, 'I am with God the Father's most heavenly hosts.'"

"Sorry to interrupt, Aaron, but can you explain to me what the heavenly hosts were again?" Bridgett inquired.

"The heavenly hosts were God's angels ready to carry out his commands when given. They were extremely powerful and well-organized."

"Aaron were these heavenly hosts like archangels, then?"

"Exactly Bridgett, and Julie said she was a part of them. After I told her my decision, she said the angels would be watching when the one called James came to talk to me. Just as I told her that was fine, once again, like the others, Julie was gone in a flash and Nicole was back. I think I need to take a break, so how about we settle in for the night and get some rest?"

"I like that idea, Aaron" Johnathon proclaimed.

"You both don't know what to think, do you?"

"Of course we believe you, Aaron, but it's a lot to take in."

"It sure is, Johnathon."

"Not to change the subject, Aaron, but tomorrow can you tell us a little more about you?"

"I can, Bridgett. Let's pick up with that in the morning."

Good nights are exchanged, and the night moves slowly with what feels like peace and protection all around the cabin." Rising in the east the sun breaks and the light dawns another day. As Johnathon, Bridgett and Aaron rise from their beds, Bridgett starts the coffee in the kitchen. With freshly brewed coffee in their mugs, the three gather in the sitting room to hear how he came to be here…

"I was born in the month of September and I was an unexpected child. My mother gave birth naturally and I weighed eleven pounds, three ounces. I was twenty-six and a half inches long. My father and mother always said that, when I was born, the doctor came out of the delivery room and told my dad, 'If you give your son a minute to put on his clothes, he will be out to shake your hand.'"

"You were a big baby, Aaron, weren't you? How did your parents decide what name you should have?" asked Bridgett.

"My mother and father were friends with the priest of the church they attended. His name was Father Aaron."

"Your parents named you after a priest?"

"Yes, they did, Johnathon. Why do you ask?"

"I am just curious Aaron."

"You can tell me, Johnathon. It's hard to believe, isn't it?"

"Aaron, I was just thinking that you and Nicole have had so many signs along the way in your lives. And, as you said, if you have faith all things are possible."

"But Nicole's faith was dampened by the Evil that surrounded her life, Johnathon."

Bridgett chimed in, "Yes Aaron, but God was still present in her life. God was with Nicole, and if you have faith, then no explanation is needed. Aaron, the signs along the way led you to her. They were there through the years and, yet, you still have some doubt in you?"

"I do Bridgett."

"Why are you smiling, Aaron?"

"Bridgett, I was thinking about what my mother would say to me as I was growing up. She would call me a doubting Thomas, because some things I would not believe."

Bridgett replied. "I can see that, Aaron. You doubt like he did."

"Johnathon and Bridgett, after my mother passed away, I was looking through my baby book and I turned the page and found a sticker of a semi-truck glued in the book. My first thought was, 'how did my mother know that one day I would be driving a big rig?' It was odd to me that she would have been able to predict that. There is much more to tell about my life but, most importantly, it's interwoven with Nicole's seemingly unbelievable story, so I would like to tell you what happened after Julie came out and spoke to me and then Nicole returned."

With anticipation Bridgett responds. "Absolutely, Aaron, we are all ears."

"After Nicole and I smoked our cigarettes, we decided to go back to bed and rest. The morning sun peeked through the windows and I asked her if I could bring her breakfast in bed. She smiled and said she would like that. I made her bacon, hash browns, toast with strawberry jam, and eggs over easy, and poured her a glass of orange juice. As I entered the room with her breakfast, she had this look on her face of disbelief."

"What do you mean, Aaron?"

"Well, Bridgett, it was like she didn't think someone should be doing anything kind for her."

"I can understand how Nicole would feel like that after years of being mistreated, Aaron."

"I later realized that, as well, but when I looked into her eyes there was a mountain of pain and it made me sad, too. Ultimately, though, the gesture made her smile, and after breakfast we both got dressed and went to the park for a walk. The park had several ponds and there were always geese in the water, or the geese were flying high above in the heavens. There were baseball diamonds and it was peaceful. The trees stood tall and the warm air felt good as we walked and talked in the park. Nicole admitted to me, after the night I asked her out on a date, that she hesitated about meeting me that next Saturday. When I asked her why, she replied that she feared being hurt again."

"I can understand that, Aaron."

"I could, too, Johnathon, but there was more."

"What did she share with you, Aaron?"

"Bridgett, Nicole remembered what the palm reader had told her. She said she was still shocked at that time, or rather, I should say she was surprised that it came true."

"That would throw anyone off, Aaron."

"It somewhat did, Bridgett, but as we were walking by the baseball diamonds she stopped abruptly. I asked her what was wrong and, to my great surprise, she punched me in the face. After I was hit, she said, 'do I have your attention now?'"

"Why would Nicole hit you Aaron?"

"It wasn't Nicole that hit me, Johnathon. It was James."

"What did he say to you, Aaron?" Bridgett asked, visibly scared of the answer.

"James asked me if I was going to help Nicole. I told him that I was going to help her and there was nothing that he, nor anyone else, could do or say to change my mind. He then replied, 'If you do this, and you help Nicole, we will destroy you, Nicole, and everything you hold dear to your heart – just like we did with your first son.' I asked James how he destroyed my first son. He replied, 'your son died in the womb with the cord wrapped around his neck.' Angered, I told James that he was a fool. He said, 'A fool is a man who thinks he can save this woman. We are many, and you cannot fight the unseen.' I told him that I will fight, and Christ, my Father, will be at my side. James, unshaken, stated, 'Your God is a weak God, and Aaron, make your mark. But, if you do this, and fight against the Devil, lives will be destroyed.' It was at that point that James spoke in a different language. And then James was gone, and Nicole came back."

"How incredibly frightening, Aaron! If I may ask, did Nicole know what happened to your son, Anthony?"

"Not at that point, Bridgett. There were a lot of things that happened that I cannot explain. When Nicole came back that time, she asked me why my lip was bleeding. I told her it was nothing. She didn't believe me, but it was okay. As she wiped my lip, she said, 'Aaron, there is a storm coming, isn't there?' I told her that I believed so, but to stay by my side and I will watch over you. She said she was scared and I didn't blame her, but I knew I had enough faith in me, for both of us, to hold onto. We left the park and went to my father's house. I told Nicole I was just running in for a minute and would be right back. I walked up the front porch and knocked as I always do when seeing my father and mother. As I entered, I asked my father if he had any Holy water. Dad asked me why, and I told him that I couldn't tell him; I just needed it. My father replied, 'Aaron, do not, mess with things you know nothing about.' I told him that it would be okay and that I now know what I must do."

"Did your dad give you the Holy water, Aaron?"

"Yes, Bridgett, he did, and he also gave me his Bible and said, 'Whatever you are into, this will help guide you.'"

"Aaron, you started preparing, didn't you?"

"I did, Johnathon and Bridgett, and after I left mom and dad's house, I got in the car and opened the vase containing the Holy water and asked Nicole if I could put the sign of the cross on her forehead. She asked me why, and I told her that I wasn't trying to push religion off onto her and she would have to trust me. Nicole agreed and when I put the Holy water on her forehead, she became irate and grabbed the tweezers off the dash. Whatever was in Nicole stabbed me in my right arm with the tweezers. Her voice changed and whoever she had become started saying things against Christ, God, and Heaven with some very choice words.

"Aaron, and Johnathon?"

"Yes, Bridgett." Johnathon responds.

"Would it be okay if we settled in for the night?"

"Smiling, Both, Johnathon and Aaron respond. "We don't mind at all Bridgett."

Chapter Seventeen

Learning Faith

*J*ohnathon and Bridgett make their way through the cabin, collecting the bedding. Aaron turns the oil lamps out and puts another log on the fire to keep the cabin warm through the night, but his thoughts are with Nicole. He wishes he could hold her one more time, but in his mind and heart he knows that day will never come. A tear falls against his flesh and his heart hurts.

"What are you doing?" Bridgett asked.

Aaron swiftly pulls his hand away from the fire, not realizing the heat from the fireplace was causing the sleeve of his shirt to smolder.

"Please be careful," Bridgett said tenderly, like that of a caring mother.

"I usually am Bridgett. I guess I was deep in thought and didn't realize what was going on."

"Were you thinking about Nicole, Aaron?"

"I was, Johnathon. I miss her so much every day."

"I am sure you do Aaron." But let's all try to get some rest and talk in the morning.

"Thank you, Bridgett and Johnathon, for being my friends."

"You're most welcome, Aaron," they both replied, with a warm look in their eyes.

Johnathon, Bridgett and Aaron all lay down as the fire flickers in the night. The sounds of Mother Nature are present throughout the cabin, and the river flowing nearby brings a peaceful feeling to the room.

Bridgett, in a soft voice asked. "Aaron? Do you feel like you know Johnathon and I from somewhere?"

"You and Johnathon are my friends. Why do you ask, Bridgett?"

"I was just curious, "Good night everyone."

Both Johnathon and Aaron return Bridgett's bedtime sentiment. Slowly, the night moves along, and everyone sleeps as if they were nestled in a safe womb...

The morning light rises slowly into the cabin windows and shines down to make cross-like patterns through the windows. Aaron volunteers to get the percolator started for coffee while Johnathon and Bridgett pick up the bedding and wait patiently for his return from the kitchen. The bedding is folded nice and neat in the closet, and Bridgett and Johnathon find their seats in the sitting room. With the fire going and a good conversation under way, Aaron's footsteps announce fresh coffee.

"Here you both go."

"Thank you, Aaron."

"So, Aaron," Bridgett recalled from the previous night, "we left off with you putting the holy water on Nicole's forehead and you getting stabbed in the arm with a pair of tweezers."

"Right...when that happened, Bridgett, I knew it wasn't Nicole."

"Aaron, did you take her to the psychiatrist after that happened?"

"Johnathon, after James had appeared and the Holy water incident happened, I got Nicole into the doctor's office the next day, at two o'clock, because someone called in and canceled their appointment. We went to the local psychiatrist in town, and when we entered the room with the psychiatrist, the doctor shook our hands and seemed very kind and pleasant. After the doctor had listened to Nicole, he felt she needed several medications to help with her depression, anxiety, schizophrenia, bi-polar and anger disorders. He wrote out the prescriptions and told us he wanted to see her back in a month. We agreed to come back to see the psychiatrist but, before we left the office, he asked Nicole if she wanted me to be in the room with her as they discussed her past. She told the doctor if I could not come in with her, she would not come back to see him. The psychiatrist said that was fine and scheduled Nicole's next appointment. When she and I left the doctor's office, we headed to the pharmacy and filled the prescriptions. The day had been quiet, other than Nicole being confused.

"Did the medications work, Aaron?" asked Bridgett.

Just like with any prescription drugs, Bridgett, it takes a while for the medications to run through a person's body and take effect.

"Aaron, did you tell the psychiatrist about John, April, Julie, Jackal and James?"

"Not at that point, Johnathon. I wanted to see if the medications would reduce the personalities coming out, or if they would have no effect on the new identities emerging from her."

"So you were waiting to see if it was something psychological or something spiritual."

"Exactly, Bridgett."

"If I may say, Aaron, your mother was right to call you a doubting Thomas."

"Yes, mom called me that many times, and looking back I would agree with her. After Nicole and I filled the prescriptions, we went to visit her daughters as we did every day. She and her children were happy to see each other and we all talked. After visitation was over, we notified the CPS worker that Nicole had started seeing a psychiatrist. The CPS worker asked her if she was starting any medications and Nicole told the worker what she would be taking."

"Aaron, if I can interrupt, when you met Nicole, you were dealing with her ex-husband, something spiritual, her psychological issues, her drug and alcohol problem, child protective services, foster parents, her medications, and work at the same time."

"Well, Bridgett, when you break it down like that, I guess I was. And it was all by choice. I loved Nicole, and she loved me with all her heart. I had been in love before, but this was different. I felt this feeling deep inside of me that I had never felt before. And, despite what was going on with Nicole, I also had faith."

"Did you believe that Nicole had a spiritual war going on inside of her?"

"I would say, Johnathon, that ninety percent of my heart knew she was afflicted by the Devil and ten percent was attributed to psychological issues."

"And you still stayed with Nicole knowing you would be dealing with multiple storms?"

"I did, Johnathon. Nicole and I fell in love and I knew, for whatever reason, that we would have to fight what we later learned was the Devil in order to help her."

"I don't know what to say, Aaron, but thank you."

"Thank you for what, Bridgett and Johnathon?"

"We just appreciate you trying to help Nicole and standing up for her no matter the consequences."

"Well, you're both welcome, I guess. It certainly didn't come easy, but I would do it again a million times over. So, weeks had passed since Nicole graduated from the drug and alcohol program, and she and I were battling the different evil entities coming out of her. The angels came many times to help us fight the demons. During the nights I would have to stay up and watch over Nicole. If I didn't, the unclean spirits would hurt her."

Bridgett asked. "What would they do to her, Aaron?"

"I remember there was a man that called himself Ramon. He was from the darkness where evil resides, and it was a Sunday morning. After being up most of the night, I dozed off on the floor by the couch where Nicole was sleeping. I was startled by the sounds coming from her and I woke up with this look on my face of disbelief. Her stomach was cut up in many places. The man named Ramon was laughing as Nicole laid there bleeding. Ramon told me I would lose the battle and then he was gone. Her stomach had the pentagram cut into her, my name was carved backwards on her stomach, the crucifix was upside down near her breast line and there were other symbols on her flesh, as well. I went and gathered up medical supplies, and cleaned and dressed all her wounds. She asked me to help her and I told her to have faith in Father, the angels and me. Nicole said she didn't know how to have faith. After I cleaned and dressed all of her wounds, I asked her if I could read one of my favorite passages from the Bible.

Nicole agreed, and I read her Samuel two, verse twenty-two, the "Song of David." As I read her the Bible she asked me, 'how do you read the book?' I explained to her that it doesn't matter where you open the Bible – whether it's in the beginning, middle or the end, or whether you read one word, one sentence, one paragraph, one page or one chapter. What matters is that you took the time to pick up the Bible. For it's at that moment that faith found you and you found faith in Father in Heaven. She asked me if she could hold the Bible, and I handed it to her and she held it in her arms. That was the first time I heard Nicole utter the words, 'help me, Father.' She laid there holding the Bible and, then, from the lips of her mouth I heard a voice say, 'I am with you, my child.'"

"Who was it, Aaron?" An intrigued Bridgett asked.

"Johnathon and Bridgett, this was different."

"What do you mean, Aaron, by *different*?"

"Johnathon, she was still present, and not suppressed by the personality, or what she and I believed to be another heavenly spirit. It was the first time I had seen both Nicole and another entity be present at the same time. She said she could see this man standing in a white robe surrounded by light. The man spoke through her and said, 'you, my child, are my daughter and I love you just as my Father loves me.' Everything was calm in the room and it was like evil couldn't break through the barrier of peace the man in the white robe brought with him. Nicole held onto the Bible and I watched over her as she cried. From that moment on, she began learning the word of God the Father.

Before the man in the robe left, he took Nicole's hand and raised it up and placed the sign of the cross on my forehead. And, then, the man in the white robe did the same to Nicole. I remember Nicole's voice was different as she said, 'blessings and protection will always be with you both.'"

"Did Nicole ever say who the man was that came to her that day?"

"She did, Johnathon. She said the man was Jesus."

"Oh, my dear heavens, Aaron!"

"Are you okay, Bridgett?"

"That must have been amazing to see Nicole hold the Bible and then have the vision of Father in Heaven right before her eyes."

It was awe-inspiring to see the light of God the Father enter her life, Bridgett. But, as I have said before, it was also hard to imagine us in this spiritual war."

"If I may say, as you told us not too long ago, in the seventeenth chapter of St. Luke, Christ said, on the Sermon on the Mount, that the Kingdom of Heaven is within us always."

"That it is, Bridgett, and I believe in what Nicole had seen. For the first time Nicole didn't black out while someone else was speaking through her. And then, seeing her face as Father stood before her: it was peaceful, and she had this look I cannot explain."

"We all have said it, Aaron. With faith, no explanation is necessary." Johnathon added.

"Please continue Aaron."

"Alright Bridgett, as the day moved on, we stayed home and rested until it was time to see her children. Later that night we talked about her vision of Father in Heaven. Nicole asked me if she was losing her mind. I told her, as I held her tight, that because I cannot see what you see does not mean it isn't real. It just means I must learn to see beyond the picture, beyond the glass that is in front of my eyes. It also means I must learn to go within your mind to see what you see, and experience what you experience. She smiled and said she loved me, and I whispered in her ear, 'I love you, too, Nicole.' That day Nicole saw God the Father, and it was like I could feel this presence of peace, love, and warmth. Although I couldn't see what she was seeing at that point and time in my life, I knew something happened spiritually to her. I had nursed her day and night. I cooked dinner for her and served her food in bed, so she didn't have to move, but as I was bringing in her dinner, I heard her talking in the bedroom. I asked her who she was talking to, and a deep voice came from her, 'Are you Aaron?' Then Nicole spoke up and said, 'This man wants to speak with you, Aaron.' I asked, 'Who are you?' and he replied, 'I am Luke. I am here to help you and Nicole.' At this point, she didn't seem to fear Luke, as I watched her body language, and Luke did not seem to be malicious towards her or me. I asked Luke how he was going to help us, and he told me that our Father had sent him down to watch over Nicole and he was to teach me to develop my senses to a heightened level. I smiled a little and I asked Luke if he could really teach me to sense beyond sensing."

Bridgett asked, "What did Luke say, Aaron?"

"The first thing Luke said after he had seen me smiling was, 'Aaron, take heed to what I say and know that the lessons I teach are serious.' The second thing he said to me was, 'I know you believe in Christ the Father, Aaron, and faith you should have in me as one of his heavenly hosts. Then he stated, very emphatically, 'I can teach you, but you, Aaron, must look deep within yourself.' I questioned Luke about his faith and where he came from, to which he replied, 'I am from Heaven and you have met John, Julie, April, and Father in Heaven. I also stand ready to carry out Father's commandments. Aaron, you have watched what evil can do, and you must be able to sense the unseen in order to defeat the Devil. As you have seen, Aaron, through the weeks the unclean spirits have tormented Nicole and you every day.' I simply replied, 'I am aware of this, Luke." He concluded our first meeting by saying, 'And, Aaron, as you also know, Father's angels have been watching.'"

Chapter Eighteen
Parables of Life

After listening carefully, Johnathon observed, "Aaron, you have mentioned using what some people call the sixth sense multiple times, and we have talked about what you meant by walking by faith, and life not being one-dimensional and seeing 'behind the glass.'"

"Yes, I remember. What's your question?"

"Was it Luke that taught you that, Aaron?"

"Actually, Johnathon, it was a combination of Nicole, Luke and many other angels who followed. To this day I sense many things – some I am aware of as evil, in many forms, and some I recognize as goodness given from God. It reminds me of the time I was visiting my son, Anthony, at the cemetery. I don't remember what day it was when I went to see him, but I do recall it was a cloudy day and very peaceful. The wind was gracefully blowing from the northeast and the birds were singing a beautiful tune that echoed across the headstone-laden grounds. I was standing by my son's resting place when I turned toward the west. There was a man in overalls, much like the ones you wear, Johnathon.

He was a much larger man, and he wore work boots and an old cap that looked like a train conductor's hat. His car was a little, red two-door automobile that he parked next to an old maple tree. The man looked at me, smiled, and started making his way over to where I was standing. I began walking toward the man in bib overalls and we met, shook hands and exchanged names. He asked me if I was visiting someone at the cemetery, and I told him I was visiting my son and asked him if he had family at the cemetery, as well. The man said he was visiting an old friend who served in the war. Then he paused for a minute and said, 'Aaron, for all we do for our Father, you would think God the Father would part the sky and show us a little piece of Heaven and what we can look forward to.' I replied to the man that it would be nice if God the Father would do that for us, and he responded by saying, 'Aaron, but if you think about it, maybe God the Father already has shown us a little piece of Heaven and we just weren't looking.'"

"That is very profound, Aaron" Bridgett said with a look of longing on her face.

"After that, the man smiled and said he had to leave. When I last shook his hand, he said, 'Aaron, believe in God with all your heart and it shall be filled.' With that, he walked back to his car and I went back to my son. By the time I got back to Anthony's resting place, which was only about one-hundred feet away, I turned around and the car and the man was gone. I didn't hear the car start, nor did I hear or see him drive away."

"I don't know what to say, other than you have met some interesting people. But how do you explain his disappearance?" Johnathon asked.

"Looking back, I believe the ones I have met were angels. And when I met that man in the cemetery, it was like I developed a rolodex in my head."

"What do you mean, Aaron, a rolodex?"

"To this day Bridgett, I can think of a specific point in my life and flip through the pictures in my head, remember where I was, what I was doing, who I was with, and the layout of my surroundings – even what words were said. And, perhaps as an innate survival tactic, I have also built catacombs within myself to compartmentalize my most sacred memories."

"Catacombs, Aaron?" asked Johnathon. "What's in there, if I

may ask, and what does it look like?"

"The catacombs are made from white marble stones, with an iron door that is sealed. Inside the catacombs are chambers where I hold the most sacred memories of my son, my mother, my wife, and others that are irreplaceable. But there is one chamber where I go where the ancient warriors stand guard from the old days. They are two statues that have come and gone through time. They are the ones that have never wavered in times of chaos. They are the most trusted.

"Aaron, your place sounds beautiful."

"It is, Bridgett, but I also have a guardian in the catacombs to watch over the place when I am not there."

"Who is it, Aaron?"

"It is not a man, Bridgett. His name is Ladon and he is my dragon."

"Oh, my dear heavens, Aaron, a dragon?!"

"That's right. If you want, I can read you something I wrote about Ladon."

"Please do, Aaron" Both Johnathon and Bridgett respond.

"It's called:

Clarity

For a thousand years the Iron Gate has been sealed.

Deep within the catacombs Ladon moves, waiting

for my return. The door stands covered in black,

yearning to be cracked. I join iron with iron and twist,

and the musty air of the ancient halls fills my lungs.

Cautiously, I move down the stairs.

In the distance, glowing red eyes appear

at once, the lanterns blaze from the nostrils afar.

The guardian kneels before his master

to show respect. I smile and begin walking,

further into the halls, passing the sword.

The shaft leads me to the tomb

where the ancient warriors stand, holding the keys

to the foundation of my existence.

Pushing one left, and one right, stone on stone,

the granite slides and the chamber opens.

I remove my sandals and enter, gazing upon

millions of illuminated urns. I disrobe,

extend my arms, lay my head back, close my eyes

and become purified of my wounds.

I fall, curled like a newborn,

delivered from a mother's womb.

Slowly I regain my strength and rise,

forged in the armor of wisdom. Breathing

once again, I turn back. Out of the shadows

the dragon steps, and now I kneel

at his feet, realizing I was never the master.

I was always the servant.

"Aaron, in that poem it sounds like a transformation occurred to the speaker. Can you tell me about how the person went from thinking he was the master to understanding that he was the servant?"

"I can explain, Johnathon, but preferably after I take a break, have a cigarette and clear my mind."

"That sounds good, Aaron. We will get some fresh coffee and meet you here after you are done."

I stand and reach for the latch to open the door and, immediately, as the door opens I can smell the fragrances of Mother Nature. There's a sweetness from the wild flowers at the edge of the forest, mixed with a pine scent from the rows of towering trees at this elevation, and even a trace of mint from some of the thorny bushes in the thicket near the river. The wind softly blows all of this wilderness to me. I light my cigarette and, leaning against the railing where the white-feathered owl visited, I decide to go look at the angel statue. Walking down the front stairs, I look around me and wonder when I will have to leave this place that I have come to love. Standing before the statue, I envision Nicole and how gorgeous she was. My right hand grazes the marble angel and I think to myself, this is what she looks like in heaven – beautiful and flawless. My eyes mist like the waterfall flowing down from the white caps above.

I wipe my tears and think about Nicole, wishing she was with me, here at the cabin. But I know she is not, and all I have are the memories of her and me together. I finish the last of my cigarette and, before walking back to the cabin, I kiss the angel's cheek and whisper – like the soft, subtle breeze blowing – "I love you, Nicole." Moments later, I find myself standing at the cabin door ready to make my way inside. I enter and find Bridgett and Johnathon smiling at me as Bridgett holds out a fresh cup of coffee for me.

"Thank you, Bridgett. Are you and Johnathon up for hearing more about Nicole?"

"Yes, we put another log on the fire and we have plenty of coffee made."

Johnathon, Bridgett and Aaron move to the sitting room and get comfortable in front of the fireplace. Bridgett had already prepared the space by putting a blanket down on the floor with some pillows.

"Johnathon and Bridgett, I wrote 'Clarity' as a remembrance, so I don't lose myself in the bark of the tree called life. My catacombs help me understand that as much as I believe we are the masters of our own lives, we are not. Yes, we make free will choices daily, but our lives are forged upon the stones written on the stone tablets by the unseen. I also built the catacombs to protect what Nicole and the ones I love so dearly gave me throughout the years."

"What did Nicole and the other ones give you, Aaron, that you have held onto?"

"Bridgett, she and the others I love gave me everything – from laughter, to love, to hugs. Nothing I would consider *things*, but important to me, nonetheless. Simple, essential parts of life. May I tell you both the story of a homeless man?"

Bridgett responds with a smile. "We would love to hear it, Aaron."

"There was a homeless man sitting outside of a grocery store on the sidewalk. He was wearing a torn t-shirt, ragged old blue jeans and shoes that looked completely worn out with holes in the soles. He was in his fifties and didn't have anyone to call family. As the homeless man was sitting on the sidewalk, watching everyone pass by him, he noticed a gentleman wearing a three-piece suit coming out of the store. The man in the suit, black in color, and with shoes that shined, stopped in front of the homeless man and reached for his wallet. He set his grocery bags down on the sidewalk and pulled out five one-hundred-dollar bills. He put the money in the homeless man's tin-can.

The homeless man watched the guy in the suit pick up his bags from the sidewalk and said, 'Thank you and God bless you.' The gentlemen in the suit smiled and went on his way. A little later, a lady came out of the grocery store in blue jeans, a t-shirt and flip flops. The lady saw the homeless man on the sidewalk and stopped in front of him. She put her bags down and reached into her pocket and pulled out all the change she had. Now, the change the lady had was in the amount of three dollars and forty cents. As the homeless man watched the lady pick up her grocery bags, he said, 'God bless and thank you.' The lady smiled and went on her way. Now, Johnathon and Bridgett, who gave more, the man who gave five-hundred dollars or the lady who gave three dollars and forty cents?"

Johnathon replied, "Aaron, I would say the man."

Bridgett then offered, "I would say the lady gave more, Aaron."

"Well, one could argue that the man who gave five-hundred dollars gave more than the lady. However, the lady gave all that she had. She wasn't rich like the man in the suit. The point I am trying to make is this: the amount of money never mattered in the first place. It was the fact that the lady and the man took the time to stop and recognize the homeless man; to see beyond his tattered clothing; to not judge the dirt and hardship of his life. It was recognizing someone who is rarely seen by people that meant the most to the homeless man, and that is why he smiled that day. I tell you this story, Johnathon and Bridgett, because I took all the little things Nicole gave to me when we were together and cherished them.

If you both remember, she believed she wasn't good enough for anyone. After all those years of abuse, and being told she was no good and she wouldn't amount to anything by the people that were supposed to take care of her, Nicole's own image of what she saw in the mirror was stained by the hands who held the seed. I always saw so much more than what she was seeing and that is why she didn't understand, on many occasions, why I loved her. But, as I look back through the years, the enticements of the Devil were many and there were times when I lost sight of my direction."

"How did you lose your direction, Aaron?"

"Johnathon, I would get frustrated from the sheer stress of everything Nicole and I were going through. It was hard to understand and many times I thought about leaving. In my mind I could see myself walking out on her and never having to deal with everything going on ever again. The enticements were in the form of having a normal life, without all the medications, without fighting the Devil, and just being free from all that sharing a life with her entailed. But the voice inside my head would tell me to breathe, have strength and remember the love she and I had for one another. When I would get frustrated, my thought process was derailed and I needed to regain clarity."

"Aaron? Would you be able to get the clarity you needed?"

"I would Johnathon. I would walk within myself and go to the chamber, deep into the catacombs and become cleansed. By going into the tombs, I would gain clarity and it would also give me balance in life. Nicole knew that I needed to have balance in my life, just as

I strove to help her achieve that in hers, as well. It's what I call the teeter-totter effect. Our lives needed to be balanced in the middle of all the chaos that was going on around us, and within us. By gaining clarity and balance, I knew I could stabilize most situations. I also knew that chaos makes for blindness in one's life, and I did not want to be blind, nor did I want Nicole worrying. Without balance, I knew our lives would get much worse."

"Aaron, you were trying to fight many different things that most people would have walked away from in the beginning."

"I would agree with that, Johnathon, but I would also say I had to have balance and clarity because Nicole needed me for everything. Her confusion, sadness, heartaches and pain dominated her within, and she looked upon me as her rock, her guardian, and the watcher. When Luke talked about teaching me those things, I did learn how to use the sixth sense from him and Nicole and many others. Nicole taught me to be more aware and to open my eyes to other planes that existed. Because she was seeing images of angels and demons before her, and within her, I had to place myself within her mind to understand what was going on and what she was seeing."

"I remember you talking about that Aaron.' How did you place yourself within Nicole's mind?"

"Johnathon, I would listen to her every word and remember everything she told me, which included what the good or bad looked like, how they talked, walked, ate, smoked, and if the angel or demon caused her body language to change in any positive or negative way. All observable behaviors became new cards in my rolodex."

Chapter Nineteen
Love Is the Reed

"Now, you both might be wondering why I said I needed to watch the physical and emotional characteristics of the good and evil identities. It's because, at any given moment, the evil would come through Nicole. Sometimes, while she was smoking, the evil would become present and act like her, but it wasn't her. The demon, or unclean spirit, would take her body over and smoke the cigarette. Take Salone, for example. He was a demon that would smoke with the opposite hand of Nicole. I had to remember that aspect of Salone. If I noticed a shift like that, my guard would go up because I knew Salone, or any other evil spirit, would use the cigarette to burn Nicole. I knew angels didn't smoke cigarettes, which gave me an indication that only an evil presence was in her. Granted, Nicole smoked cigarettes and it wasn't every time she smoked that I thought someone evil was in her, but many times it happened that she would be burned. That is why I had to remember everything I could and keep a rolodex in my head, so I could see who was who. And, because it was Nicole's body that the entities were coming through, there would be other instances where she would be eating and the evil identity would do things to get her to choke on her food. Therefore, I was always watching her very closely."

"Aaron, couldn't the angels and you sense when the evil was coming forward?"

"Yes, we could, Johnathon, but there were also those times when Nicole, the angels and I were all taken off guard. The Devil is well-practiced at the art of deception, and some of the demons that came through Nicole were more powerful than the ones before. Looking back in human history, there have been numerous cases of demonic possession, written and logged by people from many different religions. When Christ walked the Earth and performed miracles, it was Christ that cast the demons out of the possessed man into the swine. But, before Christ cleansed the soul of the possessed man, it was He that said, 'I want to know your name' and the demons replied, 'We are legion, for we are many.' That is why it was hard, at first, to remember everything because there were so many of the demons. But, then it got easier to remember those who had come and gone, due to the repetition of them coming out and showing their different characteristics. After some time and experience in handling these identities. Luke taught me to tell certain information to the good ones that came through Nicole. He also taught me to listen to the wind, feel what was in the air, and to feel my surroundings."

"Why would you do that, Aaron?"

"Well, Bridgett, because the Devil works with deception, and many of the evil ones would act like an angel, even though they were really demons waiting for the time to hurt Nicole. For this reason, I would ask the entity what I had told him or her. If they couldn't answer me, then I knew something was wrong. The other way I would distinguish good and evil was by using Holy water, the crucifix and certain passages of the Bible. Since Nicole started reading the Bible with me, the more she learned faith the more I would have to watch over her so the evil could not hurt her."

"How did you manage to do all this and work, Aaron?"

"Many choices had to be made, Bridgett, and there were those days I would have to call off from work. We had to trust God and the angels completely and know that if one door would happen to close on her and me, God the Father would open another door for us to walk through. As Nicole began to find God in Heaven, the evil identities were taunting her more and hurting her in any way they could. As time went on, the angels would watch over her while I was working. Sometimes, Luke, Mathew, Mark, Julie, April, or another angel would stay in her while I was working."

"Would Nicole be aware of their presence, Aaron?"

"Yes, Johnathon, she would be aware of them. It wasn't an exact system, as sometimes I would come home from work and she would be hurt, but for the most part the good ones protected her. It all depended on who the good and evil were, as there are different levels of angels and demons. There is a hierarchy in Heaven and in Hell, with all of the angels as well as the demons."

"Aaron, you must have had an unwavering faith in Father in Heaven."

"My faith in my Father was strong, my belief in Nicole was great, and I felt I had to do what was right. Nicole dealt with the Devil, his demons, and her heartache, but by believing in God the Father and knowing I was watching over her Nicole stayed strong. Staying by her side was what I needed to do for her, but I won't pretend that it didn't present its fair share of challenges. I will tell you both about a time that was very trying to me. There were many of the angels that Nicole and I became friends with, as they would come out of her to help guide us. Trust was important, and we put our trust in those we knew were from Heaven. There was this time when Joshua and Luke were watching over Nicole. I had come home from work in the middle of the afternoon and a storm had set in for the day. Thunder and lightning dominated the sky and the winds were howling. As I walked into the apartment, Joshua told me Nicole was gone and an evil one had taken her deep within. I explained to Joshua and Luke that we needed to find her. Joshua told me the angels were already looking for her. Over the course of three days that Nicole was gone I had the angels stay in her."

"Aaron, who did you have stay in Nicole while she was gone?"

"Johnathon, I had Beau, Joe and Al rotating in and out of her, and Joshua and Luke were checking in on the other angels. These men were archangels and very good at watching and sensing, and their knowledge of Heaven was remarkable. After the third day, one of the angels found Nicole and brought her forward."

"Who was the angel that found Nicole, Aaron, if it's all right to ask?"

"Bridgett, her name was Janette, and she was an archangel. She worked with another angel named Billy. When Janette brought Nicole forward, she instantly started crying. She told the angels and me how a demon named Jade had taken her and put her in a casket-like box, sealed it tight and left her in an unknown place. She was terrified, and she explained how much her body hurt from being in the box. Once again, I didn't leave her side and tended to her every need. You see, when Nicole was taken by an evil spirit, she would feel everything that was going on in her mind, body and soul. She lived every moment the evil put her through, much like she did through the years of abuse. It was hard on her and some days were worse on her than others. I hated to see Nicole hurting, so I decided to watch and observe everything going on in our lives even more than I had been doing.

When what free time I had, which was very little, I read psychology books, one after the other. I studied the black mass, the Devil's Bible, the Holy Bible and every religion I could. I needed to know what elements I might encounter with each interaction I had with the angels, demons and Nicole. She was what kept me going, though."

"What were some of the other facets that kept you going, Aaron?"

"Johnathon, faith, love, understanding and compassion. You see, every now and then Nicole would walk up to me with a tear running down her cheek. She would look at me and give me a hug and say 'thank you for taking care of us, Aaron.' It was for that brief moment the world was okay and nothing else existed. I wouldn't see that part of Nicole very often, but when I did I knew I was loved and I was making a difference in her life."

"Aaron, it sounds like you and Nicole had a lot of special times together. And if I may say, you remind me of someone I hold very dear to my heart."

"Well thank you, Bridgett. May I ask who that someone special is?"

"He was like a father to me, but I didn't know him very well. May I give you a hug, Aaron?"

"I would like that, Bridgett."

As Bridgett gives Aaron a hug, he thinks about how special this man must have been to her. He is struck by a familiar feeling that he hasn't experienced since his wife's passing.

"Johnathon and Bridgett, I am going to lay down and get some rest."

Bridgett replies, "Going to bed sounds good, Aaron. It has been a long day for us all. Thank you for continuing to share your wife's story with us, and there is so much more we would like to know."

"I will gladly pick up where we left off when the morning light brings us a new day."

Aaron, Johnathon and Bridgett make their beds, turn out the oil lamps and throw the logs on the fire. As Aaron gets ready for bed, he feels happiness as he looks to Johnathon and Bridgett as his new family. He thinks to himself that, even though we are no relation to one another, if I could have another family with Nicole, I would want Johnathon and Bridgett to be a part of it. The peaceful thought causes Aaron to drift off to sleep with a smile on his face. Through the night the cabin is peaceful and Johnathon, Bridgett and Aaron sleep soundly, as if Mother Nature wrapped a swaddling cloth around each of them. Outside, the pine trees dance and sing a song through the cords wrapped in bark that can be heard through the walls of the cabin. As the night transitions to morning, Aaron wakes up early and decides to walk into the sitting room. He lights the oil lamp and moves to the piano, opening the fall board and housing.

He sits on the bench and begins to play *Clare de Lune* by Schubert. With the sounds from all that wakes in the mountain landscape in the background, and with every stroke of the ivory keys, his heart feels the love he had for Nicole. The fire from the fireplace joins in, as it reflects off the gloss black finish on the piano. Aaron remembers a poem he wrote after he lost Nicole. He recites the poem in his head as he plays, and he feels like Nicole is listening to him. In his mind a soft sweet voice says "read the poem to me, Aaron." With the music playing, he begins reciting his poem out loud:

A Love Letter

Dear Nicole,

Our hearts became one when the mountains formed

From the heavens above. Shades of grey, green and white

Capture the eyes of many as they stand desiring, wanting

to embrace something, anything they can, to feel

what we felt in life. What people see glistening

on the snow-capped mountains the angels brought forth

and formed our love with warmth

from the orb above that wraps around you and me

and the memories of how beautiful you have always been.

My heart cries out and longs to lay in the meadow

of peacefulness that resides in your arms.

The slanted blades of green, resting on the hillside,

so soft and delicate, give peace to our life.

Just as Father in Heaven calmed the sea

and gave the fishermen peace so many years ago.

Flowing in the wind with the sapphires,

your heart, Nicole, is loved and is as beautiful as you are.

Even now, as you sleep, my love, my heart will always be

your heart and in the distance, my future will soon cross the valley

upon the winds of the Onyx and together,

forever, my Dear Love, we shall be one again.

The last ivory key is pressed on the piano and Aaron's thoughts of Nicole overtake him, especially those of how he failed her. He looks deeply into the fire and wonders when he will have his time with the Devil. Startled, he hears footsteps behind him. He stands and turns around to find a strange man standing before him.

"Who are you and how did you get in the cabin?"

"Aaron, I will ask that you talk softly so we don't wake Bridgett and Johnathon."

"One more time, who are you? I won't ask again!"

"My name is Samuel, or as your son Anthony would call me, Sam, Sam.

"How do you know that Anthony called you Sam, Sam?"

"Because I watch over him, Aaron, and I have through the years."

Aaron loses his footing and falls back on the bench in front of the piano.

"Aaron, it's okay. You did not fail Nicole. You saved her in so many ways. I don't think you realize what you did for her in life. You are loved by many in Heaven and on earth. Believe in me as you have in our Father, for your heart is good. Take my hand, Aaron, and I will lift you up."

"But, you can't be Samuel."

"I am Samuel and you know I am because we have talked many times throughout the years when you and Nicole were together. If you doubt me, Aaron, ask me anything you want."

"Okay, Samuel, when Nicole and I were together, where would we go when evil would torment her and me all night long during the war?"

Samuel smiles and says, "You and Nicole would spend the night sleeping in the cemetery. Many nights you would drive her to Calvary and park. When you and she would park in the valley of the cemetery, you would hold her and watch over her, for you knew the land was blessed by many pastors."

"Samuel, I am sorry I doubted you."

"It's okay, Aaron, and I love you as my son. Remember, you did not fail your Father in Heaven and you didn't fail Nicole."

"That I cannot believe, Samuel, and I am sorry, but I did fail her, and her death is my fault."

Samuel kisses Aaron on the forehead and whispers, "Aaron, the human heart was not built in a day. It takes a lifetime for the heart to grow and yearn for love, understanding and peace. The beating of the heart is the voice that is closest to God, and love is the reed that feeds the soul. I must say goodbye, Aaron, until we meet again."

Sitting on the bench, Aaron looks at Samuel as he disappears. With his head in his hands, he is in disbelief at what just happened.

"Aaron! Aaron! Wake up. Wake up Aaron."

Startled once again, he opens his eyes to see Bridgett and Johnathon standing over him.

"Are you okay, Aaron?"

"Where am I, Bridgett?"

"You are at the cabin with Johnathon and me. Were you having a bad dream?"

"No, not a bad dream. I need a minute, please."

"Okay, Aaron. I am going to make some coffee."

Chapter Twenty
Old Friends

Bridgett walks to the kitchen and Johnathon and Aaron, after getting out of bed, sit down on the couch. Bridgett returns with everyone's coffee.

"Take a sip, Aaron. It will help relax you. At least I know coffee relaxes me."

"Thank you, Bridgett. It somewhat relaxes me, too, and also doesn't, if that makes sense."

"Are you okay?"

"I am, Johnathon, but I just had this dream that felt so real."

"Do you want to tell us about it?"

"Bridgett, I woke up early in the morning and went into the sitting room, lit an oil lamp and began playing the piano. Then I heard someone walking behind me. I turned around and this man was standing there looking at me."

"What?!" Bridgett replied with a start. "Who was he?"

"His name was Samuel."

"*The* Samuel, Aaron?"

"Yes, Bridgett, from the book of Samuel."

"Oh, my dear heavens, Aaron!"

"I hadn't talked with him for years.

"Aaron, was he one of the angels that you and Nicole saw throughout her struggles?"

"He was, Johnathon, and in my dream he asked me to speak softly so we wouldn't wake you two from your sleep. Then Samuel told me a few other things and then he was gone; he just disappeared. If you two don't mind, I am going to step outside and smoke a cigarette."

"Take your time, Aaron. Bridgett and I will stay in here."

Aaron steps outside to smoke while Bridgett and Johnathon talk.

"Johnathon, what do you think?"

"Bridgett, we have seen many things in our lifetime and I believe Aaron."

"So do I, Johnathon."

"Bridgett? When do you think we should tell Aaron?"

"Well, as you said before, it's not time."

Aaron walks back into the cabin and, hearing Johnathon and Bridgett talking, asks "It's not time for what?"

"For…us to make another pot of coffee, Aaron."

"Is the pot almost out of coffee, Bridgett?"

"No, there is a little left."

"Aaron, could we go back to Ramon and what he did to Nicole? What happened after Ramon had cut Nicole's stomach?"

"As Nicole's stomach healed from what Ramon did to her, we continued to deal with the demons that came through. With the help of the angels, we both became stronger and smarter, and our faith grew together in God the Father. Nicole started reading the Bible more and I tried to answer all the questions she had."

"So, you were teaching Nicole about faith, Aaron?"

"Yes, I was, Bridgett, and the only way that was possible was because she wanted to learn about the Bible and about our Holy Father in Heaven. Without her desire to be born again through Christ, I would not have been able to help her learn. Her heart yearned for healing and all I did was help – nothing more and nothing less."

"Aaron, you did more than that."

"I don't think I did, Johnathon, but thank you."

"If I may ask, Aaron, what religion did you teach Nicole?"

"I was brought up in the Catholic church, but I didn't believe a person needed to be within four walls to worship God. And Nicole and I did use Holy Water and the Bible against the evil identities that emerged. It was an every day and night occurrence regarding protecting her. But, to more specifically answer your question, Bridgett, Nicole and I went to the Brethren church, a Christian church, and many others, but our favorite place to commune with God the Father was in the woods by the river. Our religion was based solely on our faith in God, not in the name of a particular denomination or its distinguishing beliefs or system. Christ dwells in the hearts and minds of everyone and, for Nicole and me, our Father's heart was *our* heart. We felt at peace in the woods as we read and learned together about Christ, the disciples and the angels. Sometimes we would sit by the river and enjoy each other's company while being in God's kingdom on Earth."

"What do you mean, Aaron, God's kingdom on Earth?"

"Bridgett, there is so much beauty on earth and it's all around us, all the time. By appreciating the natural surroundings, we would embrace what Father in Heaven has given to us."

"So, your church was outside in the wilderness, Aaron?"

"That is an accurate assessment, Johnathon."

"So, if I may ask, Aaron, how was it going with CPS?"

"At first, it was going fine, but it seemed like there was always at least one hoop to jump through. First, Nicole had to get clean, and then I needed to get everything in order with her bills and food. Also, CPS required us to inform them about the doctor she was seeing, her medications, and how often she was going to see the doctor. After that, it was home visits with her and me. It seemed like it was one thing after another with the CPS worker, but looking back I'm sure she was just doing her job."

Bridgett replied, as if she knew more about the topic than she led on, "Aaron, I have heard once CPS gets their hooks in a family, they don't want to let go."

"I have seen many families fight CPS, Bridgett."

"Please go on, Aaron. Bridgett and I are listening."

"The children were still in foster care and the worker kept finding new things for us to do or complete. Nicole and I were frustrated and, finally, after a year of the children being in foster care, we had a court date for the child in need of assistance hearing. When we showed up at the courthouse, I spoke to the worker with Nicole and told her, very sternly, that I was tired of pleasing her. I strongly added, 'When you go speak with the judge, I hope you make the right decision to drop this case and return the girls to Nicole. I am not jumping through your hoops any more. I am done, and so is Nicole, and if it means me hiring an attorney outside of the court-appointed attorney to sue you, I will, so make the right decision or you will find yourself with a harassment suit.' The CPS worker asked me if I was threatening her. I told her that it's not a threat; it's a promise. I let her know that I could just as easily make her life hell like she was making mine and Nicole's."

"What did she say to that, Aaron?"

"Well, her actions did the speaking for her. She turned around, walked up the stairs to the Judge's chambers, and when she came down, the case was dismissed. But, before she walked away, she told us she would like to get her hands on Nicole's daughters. I told her I didn't care what she wants, and that she needed to stay clear of Nicole and her girls."

"Aaron, it sounds like you and the CPS worker had issues with one another."

"We did, Bridgett, due to the fact that she was trying to exert her power too much and I wasn't going to tolerate it. Despite her demeanor being kind in the beginning, things changed, as they do with many people when they are given too much power. And that was not the last time Nicole and I saw her."

"I bet that Nicole was happy to have her girls coming home."

"She was elated, to say the least. After we received the documentation from the courts, the lady from CPS called to inform the foster parents of the dismissal of the case. Nicole and I picked up her two daughters and the children smiled like I had never seen anyone smile before."

"What was it like for you and Nicole after you brought her daughters home?"

"Bridgett, it was encouraging to have the kids be so excited to be home and see everything in the apartment. Nicole asked her girls if they wanted a home-cooked meal, or if they wanted to go out and eat. Naturally, they wanted to go out, so we took them to a nice restaurant. After dinner, we took the kids to a movie and they ate popcorn and candy, and the two girls had their own soda."

"Aaron, were the evil identities still coming out of Nicole when you had the girls?"

"They were, Johnathon, and they didn't stop, but the one thing we had in our favor was the decision to have the angels staying in Nicole to govern what the evil ones tried to do to her."

What do you mean, Aaron?"

"As time went on, the heavenly hosts were still coming down to watch over Nicole."

"Did the evil identities ever try to hurt the girls, Aaron?"

"No, Bridgett, they never did. They knew better than to do anything to the girls. It was like there was a boundary set and the evil could not cross that line. With me watching from the outside, and the archangels watching from within, and Nicole not blacking out as much, the unclean spirits never did hurt the girls. At that time, more than a year had passed and the fight was still going on, but Nicole's faith was a hundred times what it was from the time we first met. Being with her was great, most of the time, but there were those moments when the children were away at school when the evil identities would come out and physically beat on me. It made me realize what Jacob was talking about."

"What do you mean, Aaron?"

"Just as Jacob would get hit when he was with Nicole, I would also get punched in the face. One time when Jacob and I talked, he said that one minute Nicole was an angel and then the next minute it was like she was possessed by a demon. When the evil would come out of her and begin beating on me. I would get on my knees, wrap my arms around her waist and say, 'I will not fight you.' In a sense, I knew I had to take the beating that every man gave to Nicole through the years, in order for her to heal. The psychological part of her years of abuse was the anger and hurt that resided within her. It needed to be released and I was the one who absorbed it. The medications didn't stop the evil or good from coming out, even when the doctor would prescribe new medications.

I remember once, when we had an appointment with the doctor, we discussed how I was getting punched almost every day. The doctor smiled and said, 'Aaron, you're a big man, I think you can take a punch or two.' I smiled back and said, 'I think I can, too, doctor.' Nicole told him about everything that was going on and the psychiatrist gave her some new prescriptions."

"Aaron, what did the psychiatrist think was going on with Nicole?"

"He diagnosed her with schizophrenia, unspecified psychosis, dissociative identity disorder and post-traumatic stress disorder. She was already diagnosed with bi-polar disorder and severe anxiety. The doctor stated he had suspicions that Nicole's case would be complicated, and he wanted another opinion, so he asked another doctor to come and evaluate her. It was about a week later when the other psychiatrist got into town. The nurse called Nicole and I to inform us about the appointment and together we went to see both psychiatrists. After the doctor that was called in to offer a second opinion was finished evaluating Nicole, he came out and asked to speak with me."

"What did this doctor think, Aaron?"

"Johnathon, the psychiatrist asked me if I journaled what was going on with Nicole. I told him I was journaling, and he asked if he could have the journals. I told him that he could not."

"Why did the psychiatrist want your journals, Aaron?"

"Bridgett, the doctor told me that he believed Nicole did have dissociative identity disorder, but he was confused about other aspects of her issues."

Johnathon interjected, "What do you mean?"

"The doctor thought Nicole had other things going on with her and my journals might help him figure out what he could not explain. I asked the doctor what he meant by 'other things going on' with her and he said, 'Aaron, she can talk in multiple languages on the drop of a dime and, given that she only has an eighth-grade education, that is unheard of and is inexplicable.'"

"So, Aaron, let me guess: the doctor wouldn't come out and say there was a spiritual conflict going on with Nicole."

"That is correct, Bridgett. Don't get me wrong. He was very nice and compassionate, but he was very adamant about reading my journals. I told him again that he could not have them. The last thing the psychiatrist said to me was that Nicole had a lot of conflicts going on and I should be careful when dealing with the unknown aspects not related to psychiatry. I smiled at him and told him that I was being careful."

"Aaron, I just realized how his advice sounds like what your father told you when you were getting the Bible and Holy Water."

"It does, Johnathon, and despite hearing that advice from two men I respected, Nicole's well-being hinged upon me not heeding their cautionary words. Quite the opposite, actually, because a few days later, after another appointment, I proposed to her."

"Before you tell us about it, Aaron, I am going to get some coffee. Would you both like some?"

"We would, Bridgett, and thank you. I am going outside and smoke."

Bridgett replies, "Okay, Aaron. We will be here waiting for you."

As Aaron steps outside to smoke, he looks to the heavens. Evening approaches and the sun is a soft, orange color that blends with the darkening sky. He smiles as he sees the first star of the evening.

The clouds slowly move as if they were ships sailing calmly over the ocean. Aaron breathes in deeply and takes in what Mother Nature offers him. Then, after the last drag of his cigarette, he makes his way back into the cabin and finds his seat in the sitting room where Johnathon and Bridgett await his arrival.

"Thank you for the coffee, Bridgett and Johnathon."

Smiling, Bridgett replied. "You are most welcome, Aaron. We are excited to hear about your proposing to Nicole."

"Nicole and I gathered the kids and we drove the children over to my parent's house, so they could spend the night with their grandparents. After we dropped the children off, I took Nicole to Wildwood Park. It was beautiful that evening and we went to a place where people drove up to the top of a hill and would park for peace and quiet. It overlooked the surrounding area and there were trees everywhere. The grass was green and it was peaceful. After we parked at the top of the hill, we both got out of the car, threw a blanket down and laid there for hours. Night was approaching, and I just held Nicole. When the moon crested on the horizon, it was the brightest, largest moon I had ever seen. It was like I could reach up and grab the moon with my two hands."

"That sounds so romantic, Aaron."

"Bridgett, it was truly amazing. Nicole got up from the blanket and reached for my hand and pulled me up. We embraced and then I got on one knee, held her hand and asked her to marry me. She smiled, started crying and then said yes. I asked her what was wrong, and she replied, 'I never thought someone could love me as you, Aaron, have loved me since we met.' She asked me if I was sure I wanted to marry someone like her. I told her that she was perfect in every way and, when I looked into her eyes, I could see her soul and everything about it was beautiful. I then asked her if she could see what I see and she said, 'I do not, Aaron.' So I asked her if I could read her something I wrote. As we laid back down, I began to recite this:"

Heaven's Lost Angel

Into her eyes I gaze, and softly

the images of her heart project outwardly

and inwardly into my soul. Saddened,

she does not know. I fall, with tears flowing,

filling my chamber. An angel I see, lost

within herself. Beauty in its entirety, broken,

in life. We listen to the Redeemer

and I whisper in her ear, "can you See what I see?"

She replies, "I am only me. What do you see?"

I engage her; go deep within her eyes,

looking into her soul. Gazing at the snow-capped mountains,

glistening from the illuminated sphere above,

an Angel, beautiful, with long, flowing black hair.

She stands on the coverings, her wings spread,

her feathers swaying in the breeze.

Gold, silver, and jewels inlayed upon satin

surround her soft, elegant skin.

Her lips are as red as rose pedals.

Her voice gently flows like the wind.

My heart flutters like the butterfly

dancing in the openness of life.

She is an Angel.

I slowly return from within her soul,

her heart, and I am once again saddened.

This lady, graced from God,

does not see what I see.

Morning approaches and her glass begins to fill

with my response and, on a whisper,

she, Heaven's Angel, is lost again.

Chapter Twenty-One
Beneath the Moonlight

"Aaron, I love what you wrote for Nicole. What did she say after you read that to her?"

"Thank you, Bridgett. She just smiled and said that she wished she could believe it. I told her that she should remember what our Father in Heaven told her – that night, Father told you that you were his daughter and he loves you unconditionally. She replied, 'Yes, I know he said that, Aaron, but it's hard to believe.' It was at that moment when I recited what my mother told me through the years. 'Nicole, you are being a doubting Thomas.' She laughed and gave me a hug as we laid together on the blanket, under the moonlight."

"What's wrong, Bridgett? Why are you crying?"

"They are happy tears, Aaron. To know someone could have loved my mother so much."

"What, Bridgett?! What did you say?"

Johnathon quickly speaks up and says, "Bridgett didn't know her mother and she feels like Nicole could have been like her mom."

With Bridgett crying, Johnathon wraps his arm around her and holds her tight. Aaron wonders what is going on with the two of them, and he considers that Bridgett might be getting attached to Nicole, as he has heard of people getting close to those they have never met before. Just as the thought enters his mind, Bridgett gets up and wraps her arms around him.

"What is this for, Bridgett?"

"It's just a hug and thank you for being you, Aaron."

"Well, thank you, Bridgett.

After hugging Aaron, Bridgett sits back down in her chair, having composed herself once again.

"Aaron, can we hear more about your courtship with Nicole?"

"Sure, Johnathon. After such an exhilarating night, with the proposal to Nicole and her affirmative answer, our emotions were elevated. We made love under the stars and I wrote about that night so I could keep the feelings alive forever:

Softly

Her hands slowly caress every ounce

of my flesh. Her lips press against

my neck. I feel the love, she feels the pounding

of my heart. My hands, my arms pull her body closer.

She whispers, I whisper, "love me forever." Impressions

upon mother earth take hold as our souls become one

in the heated desire between two, that is now one. Her flesh, my flesh

performs effortlessly in the night. Her sensual, soft body releases

as my hold tightens around her body. She lays her head upon

my chest in the moonlight, whispering

"I love you." I whisper to her,

"my princess, my wife,

I love you, too."

"Oh, Aaron, that was gorgeous!"

"You and Nicole were soul mates. I just know it in my heart."

"I knew it from the first time I met her, Johnathon."

"If I may ask, did any evil identities come out during the course of that particular evening?"

"No, Johnathon, it was like the day when Nicole had her vision of Father in Heaven. All was calm and peaceful."

"Where did you and she get married, Aaron?"

"We found a local preacher and we were married by a Brethren minister. It was a simple wedding, with only Nicole's girls there, as well as the two witnesses, the minister and his wife."

"Aaron, why weren't your mother and father at the wedding?"

"Bridgett, my father believed that if you weren't getting married in a Catholic Church, then the marriage wasn't legitimate in the eyes of God."

"What about your mother, then? Did she come to the wedding?"

"She did not because she was not allowed."

"What do you mean by that?"

"Bridgett, I remember my mom was sitting on the couch and looked at me and said she wanted to go, but dad said she wasn't going and that was final. My mother looked so sad that day and said she was sorry to Nicole and me. I told her it wasn't her fault and that I loved her. But, to this day, I still feel the emptiness from not having mom there to see me marry Nicole."

Bridgett visibly stirred, interjected and said, "Aaron, when two people love each other, and they love God the Father and want to be together, God is always present. It shouldn't matter what religion a person is, or isn't."

"I know Bridgett, but that was how my dad was behind the scenes. Anyway, Nicole and I were finally married, and it was a special day for both of us."

"I think it sounds perfect, Aaron, what you and Nicole did

together for your wedding. Did you get her a ring?"

"I did, Johnathon. It was a three-quarter carat marquise diamond ring, with a one-carat cluster of diamonds surrounding the larger stone."

"Oh, my goodness, Aaron, that sounds absolutely gorgeous!"

"It was a beautiful ring Bridgett, but not as beautiful as Nicole."

"Nicole loved the ring and that was one of many to come for her throughout our marriage."

"What happened after you two got married?"

"Nicole and I took the kids to Hannibal, Missouri, for the weekend. We went through the caves, stayed in a nice motel, and we all loved every minute of the trip. It was great to get out as a family. After we got back home with the children from our vacation/honeymoon, life went back to the way it was, with everything going on as it had before."

"How was the fight going over Nicole?" Johnathon inquired.

"We were still dealing with the evil spirits coming out and tormenting her and me. There were times when they would come out and pick up a knife and threaten me, or I would find pictures of Jesus torn up into pieces. Sometimes our Bibles would have pages ripped up. It was a different experience every day. Weeks had passed, and the medications helped a little, and the archangels were helping every second they could. Then, one night, I had my own vision: I saw this man standing before me in a place I had never seen in my life. It was made from white marble stone, and the man took my hand and led me through a hall with torches made from gold lighting the way. As the man in the robe and I walked down the hall, I turned my head to the left and there were three thrones next to each other. Behind the thrones was a crucifix bathed in gold. It had jewels of every kind embedded within the cross, and there were satin curtains that were in front of the room where the thrones were placed. I had seen two angels standing before the thrones bathed in jewels. Their wings were gorgeous. When the man in the robe and I passed by the room with the thrones, we came upon another room that had inscriptions above the door."

"What were the inscriptions, Aaron?"

"The writing looked Hebrew, Bridgett. As the man in the robe and I walked through the door, I was amazed to find that the room was filled with swords. I looked at the man and asked him what we were doing in this room. The man replied, 'Aaron, you must choose a sword, for one day your hands will need the blade to cut through time. And you, Aaron, must follow the path your heart is laid upon.' As I walked through the room, there were many swords to choose from."

"Was it peaceful, or did you feel a sensation of fear in that room?" Jonathon wondered.

"It was peaceful, overall, and I did choose a sword. It had a four-foot blade with a golden handle and markings on the blade that I couldn't understand. I asked the man in the robe what the markings meant. He told me the markings on the blade were made by the finger of God and the words inscribed on the blade read, 'The spirit of God is within you, and your heart.' The man in the robe smiled and said, 'Aaron, we must be on our way.' Then we left the room and walked back down the hall. As the man and I stepped outside, I raised my head. My eyes were looking at the most beautiful palace in the world. It had a golden dome on top and the entire place was miraculous. On the outside, in front of the palace, there were statues of angels that towered over us. The doors entering the front of the palace had markings on them of the old times. Each door looked to be crafted by a wood cutter, with carvings of the last supper and the markings of the Holy trinity. It was truly unlike any other place on Earth.

The man in the robe told me about a place in Heaven where peace is not peaceful. I asked him what he meant and he said there is a layer in Heaven that is constantly under attack by Satan. Just as Satan walks the earth, trying to destroy lives for his own pleasure, he also tries to wreak havoc in Heaven. This layer in Heaven, where angels fight the demons, is the same place where angels die in battle. When an angel dies, he or she, the heavenly host, will go to a special place."

"Aaron, you are correct. Just as a demon can be killed in battle, an angel can die, too."

"Johnathon, you sound like you know what I am talking about."

"I was just agreeing with you."

"That might be true, Johnathon, but you had a lot of confidence in your voice."

"Please tell us more about this vision, you had."

"I asked the man in the robe where this place is in Heaven, where the Devil's demons are trying to destroy God's kingdom. He told me he must show me God's heavenly hosts that stand ready to follow God's every commandment in the name of faith. The man in the robe waved his hand and showed me the place in Heaven."

"Where was it, Aaron?"

"Bridgett, as I looked around, standing by the man in the robe, I saw tens of thousands of archangels in the seventh layer of Heaven, where the seven angels walk, with the seven trumpets."

"Aaron? In the first book of Genesis, God said 'In the beginning God created the heavens and the earth.'"

"You are right, Bridgett, but many of the Bibles have changed the word 'heavens' to 'heaven' in the first book of Genesis."

"Aaron, who were the seven angels?"

"Well, the Bible only names three of the angels: Michael, Gabriel and Raphael; however, the Catholic Church denies the existence of the other four angels because they are from the book of Enoch, which were Uriel, Raguel, Sariel and Jerimiel."

"Why is that, Aaron?" Bridgett asked with a look of confusion on her face.

"The Catholic Church says the writings in the Bible must be canonical books of the

Bible; therefore, proper names of angels must not be recognized by the church."

Bridgett and Johnathon reply, "I do not agree with that at all."

"Nor do I, but again, it is a matter of one's faith and interpretation of the Bible. In my vision, as I looked out upon the heavenly hosts, there was an angel who was bathed in jewels and fine garments. He stood out among the other angels and, as I looked at him, I felt this power and greatness about him. That's when the angel bathed in jewels began looking at me. He turned, and our eyes met. His eyes burned bright with the spirit of God. I turned my head away because I could see and feel the power of our Father in that angel. All angels have the spirit of God in them, but this angel was exalted."

"Who was the angel, Aaron?"

"Johnathon, it was St. Michael the archangel. Then the man in the robe showed me the thousands of archangels and then he waved his hand. He told me that many angels have come and gone in the name of Father in Heaven. At that moment it was like my eyes opened and I could see beyond the thousands of angels. The man in the robe showed me the war that was going on in that layer of Heaven. I could see the demons and angels fighting before me. I felt the ground shake and the stampede of the horses sounded like thunder in the sky. The man in the robe informed me, 'Aaron, just as you fight the unseen, we fight the seen, but when you see the unseen you will understand many things.'"

"Were the angels fighting in Heaven, Aaron?"

"Yes and no, Johnathon. This place seemed to be outside of Heaven, but it was actually in Heaven."

"So, it wasn't the Great War in Heaven that the man in the robe showed you?"

"No, not exactly Bridgett, but how would you know about that war?"

"I have heard about it."

"Well, I will try and explain what I witnessed. As I stood there, looking at the place where the fighting was going on, I felt like it was protected by Heaven, but also like it was in between two worlds."

"Aaron, aren't there supposed to be many peaceful places in Heaven?"

"Yes, there are, Bridgett, but the place I was looking at seemed to be in the hearts and minds of those wandering upon the lands. Then the man in the robe spoke and said, 'Aaron, many times a man or woman will not succeed in the light of the sun, and many will fall into the wind. But, when a man or woman falls into the wind, the light will break the ground that leads to the heart of the moon. As the reed glistens from the mists of the river of Jordan, a man or woman can dissolve the seed that taints the life of the water.' I told the man I didn't know what that means, and he replied, 'Aaron, one must know the air we breathe to understand the kingdom of Heaven.' It was at that moment when I woke up. Never in my life had I seen such beauty and felt so much peace. But, on the other hand, I must say that I also felt sadness, pain and death in the one layer of Heaven where the fighting is always going on."

"Aaron, did the man give you his name?"

"He did, Bridgett. His name was Isaiah. Nicole was still sleeping when I woke up. I stepped outside and smoked a cigarette. As I smoked, I heard a voice inside my head say, 'I am proud of you, my son.' The wind picked up and the voice was gone. When I finished my cigarette on the front porch of the apartment, I went back inside. Nicole was awake, but still lying in bed. I told her about the dream I had and she was very supportive. It was like she knew what I was talking about. We laid in bed and talked for a while and then I got up to cook everyone breakfast. When breakfast was done, Nicole and I and the girls went to the basketball court and played 'around the world.'"

"Just curious, Aaron, but how bad was it when the unclean spirits were coming out?"

"Bridgett, it was getting really bad. The demons inside Nicole were cutting on her a lot more, and one night she got arrested for driving without a license and failure to maintain a vehicle."

"How did that happen, Aaron?"

"An evil spirit had come out and Nicole was taken over by this entity, who decided to take my car. I ended up bailing her out of jail early in the morning. Some of the evil ones that came out of Nicole she knew and could feel, but the other unclean spirits were powerful and more subtle. After she had her court date, I paid her fines and we went on our way."

"Strange question, but did Dick ever come back around, Aaron?"

"Interesting that you should ask that, and yes, he did, Bridgett. Dick had heard that Nicole was arrested and came down to the apartment to check on the kids."

"Why would he do that after all this time, Aaron?"

"Dick thought he would run his mouth to Nicole and put her down. He stood on the front porch calling her a loser and other choice words. At that point, I asked Nicole to step aside. She moved behind me and told the girls to go inside. I asked Dick, 'do you remember what I told you about respecting Nicole?' He laughed and said a few more choice words to both me and Nicole. So I looked him straight in the eyes, and I knocked him out cold. After I knocked Dick out, I went and got a bucket of water and threw it on him. I helped him up and told him that he will apologize to Nicole, right now, and it's not an option."

"I bet Dick apologized, didn't he?"

"Yes, he did, Johnathon, and after that I told him we were going for a walk to talk. Dick and I walked several blocks as we talked. After that day, Dick was a different man to Nicole."

"Aaron, the stress of everything going on had to be getting to you, too?"

"Yes, it did, Bridgett, but I also had to let Dick know he was not going to belittle Nicole any more. I am proud of what I did because he knew from that moment on he would respect her. After Dick left, Nicole was shocked that I did that to him and she told me I would probably get arrested for assault. I told her I didn't care because right is right, and wrong is wrong, and if it means me going to jail, then by all means send me to jail. Nicole smiled, said she loved me and gave me a kiss. I smiled back and gave her a hug."

"Did Nicole's girls know what went on outside, Aaron?"

"They did, but they said their dad deserved it for what he had been doing to their mother. Dick stayed away for a long time before Nicole and I saw him again. Don't get me wrong, we tried getting him to come and see the girls, but he would find one excuse after another not to come."

"Aaron, I am sure he feared you after you knocked him out."

"That might have had something to do with it Johnathon. But the girls had fun when they were with Nicole and me. They really enjoyed going over and spending time with my parents. Mom would bake them cakes and they would go shopping all the time. Nicole loved the fact that her daughters could have the things they never had before, and mom and dad enjoyed spoiling their grandkids. Finally, after about six months, Dick showed up and wanted to be in his daughters' lives. When he first arrived, he apologized again to Nicole and me. We both were surprised and, from there on, everyone got along. Dick and I had a conversation about him being in his daughters' lives. I told him that Nicole and I wanted him to see his daughters as much as he could."

Chapter Twenty-Two
Open Highways

"What did Dick say to you and Nicole, Aaron?"

"He agreed that he needed to be in his daughters' lives and asked if he could take the girls out to eat. Both Nicole and I said that was fine. After the girls were dropped off at their dad's, we stayed home and relaxed as much as we could."

"Aaron, how did you and Nicole keep what was going on with the evil from the girls?"

"It wasn't easy, Bridgett, but when the evil ones came out we would tell the girls that their mother was not feeling well. At that point, we would go into our room, and this would allow us, along with the angels, to deal with whatever the evil spirits did or tried to do to Nicole or me. As time went on, the fight over Nicole kept going, Dick was staying in contact with the girls, I was still working, and Nicole was clinging to her faith even more."

"Aaron, what happened to her job in retail?"

"Oh, Nicole left her job, as she couldn't deal with work and everything that was going on in her life. Before she quit her job, she asked me if I could handle taking care of the bills and other expenses. I told her I could handle the bills, but things might get a little tight with finances. She smiled and said, 'all I need in this world is you and my girls.' I kissed her and she kissed me. We had faith in the belief that we would survive somehow."

"Aaron, I can understand why she left her job. Will you tell us more?"

"I remember one time Nicole asked me if she could have her own Bible instead of reading mine. I told her that we would get her one. She smiled and asked me if she could have my large Bible. I asked her why she wanted that one. She told me that she liked reading it because it has prayers in the front of the book. I told her that was my son's Bible, but if she would like it, she could have it. Nicole asked me what happened to my son and I finally told her."

"I remember you saying that James knew about how your son died, but Nicole didn't, Aaron?"

"That is correct, Johnathon, and this was the first time I told Nicole about what happened to Anthony. She knew I had buried my son, but she did not know why my son died until now. Some things are hard to open up about."

"We completely understand your decision to wait to tell Nicole, especially with everything that was happening to her. Did she understand why you wouldn't talk about what happened to Anthony?"

"She did, Johnathon, but because of her love for me, it also was hard on her. I remember she started crying and said my son is in Heaven with her two babies and they were all happy. I asked her how she knew that the children were happy in Heaven, and she told me she just knew it in her heart. I smiled and told her she was an amazing lady. Then she asked me for one more thing. I told her to ask away. Nicole asked for Anthony's baby book. I said yes, went into the room, opened the foot locker and pulled it out. As I walked back into the living room, she smiled and said she would treasure the books forever."

Bridgett suddenly spoke up, "I just love Nicole."

Smiling Aaron replies, "I do, too, Bridgett."

"Does anyone need some coffee?"

Johnathon and Aaron reply, "I do, Bridgett."

"Bridgett, let me get the coffee and you sit with dad," said Jonathon.

"Did you just call me dad?"

"I'm sorry, Aaron. My mind was just wandering."

Aaron's thoughts begin to run wild, wondering why Johnathon and Bridgett keep saying things like that. But before he can make any sense of it, Johnathon returns with the steaming coffee in his hands.

"Bridgett, here is your coffee, and for you, Aaron, a nice hot cup, too. So, where were we, Aaron?"

"Nicole said she would treasure the baby book that belonged to my son."

"Did that concern you at all, given the deceptive tactics of the evil spirits? After all, that was a very special book, Aaron."

"You're right, Bridgett. It is a very special book and I wasn't worried about the unclean spirits. I gave it to Nicole because she loved Anthony as I loved him. His biological mother never cared for him and I looked at Nicole as his mother. I will also say this, she loved Anthony and cherished him as her own son."

"What happened after that, Aaron?"

"Nicole and I hugged and made another loving memory together. As time went on, we had our usual routines of dealing with the evil spirits, my work, and making sure the girls stayed in contact with Dick. But, the evil kept coming and creating chaos, and Nicole and I were becoming exhausted. We hung in there the best we could, though, and Dick was spending more time with his daughters."

"It sounds like he was finally doing what a father should do, Aaron."

"He was, Bridgett, but I also watched him very closely to see if the snake would once again try and strike at Nicole or me."

"Did he, Aaron?" Johnathon asked.

"For the most part, he was decent. Nicole and I had dealt with so many demons that we were just tired most of the time. That is when we talked about a potential change. With everything going on with the anger, the demonic attacks and her hostility towards me getting worse, Nicole and I talked about letting the girls stay with their dad for a while so we could go over the road together. I told her that would have to be her decision and I could not make it for her, but I would support any decision she made. She smiled and said she loved me and I told her I loved her, too. We talked with her two girls about us going over the road and they said they loved us both and they understood. We reassured them that we would be back every weekend to visit them. Nicole's daughters smiled and gave us both hugs. When Dick came for his next visitation with his daughters, we talked with him about what we needed to do."

"Aaron, did Dick know everything that was going on with Nicole?"

"No, not everything, Bridgett. He just knew what we wanted him to know. Dick agreed and said he would take the girls home with him. I told him it wouldn't be until I found an over-the-road job and he told us that was fine. After Dick left, I began looking for a trucking job that had the ride-along program so Nicole could go with me in the truck."

"If I may ask, Aaron, what is 'over the road'?"

"Johnathon, over the road, or O.T.R., is driving cross country, hauling loads from one place to the other."

"What did Nicole say, Aaron?"

"She said she would love to travel, but if we did drive over the road she wanted to collect shot glasses. I smiled and told her she could collect anything she wanted. We thought by driving over the road we could deal with the evil spirits better, without worrying her daughters. By being together in the truck, Nicole wouldn't be home alone to deal with everything by herself, even though the angels were with her. Everyone was okay with what we had decided. We still had the apartment and I left my job to be with her and help her. I remember I was hired on with a trucking company that hauled from the Midwest to the west coast. When Nicole and I first looked at the rig I would be driving, she said the truck looked 'mean' and it was huge. I smiled and told her it would be okay. How did you learn to drive, Aaron? When I first learned how to drive a semi, I was taught by the best. On my first day of training, my boss asked me if I wanted to see the semi I would be driving.

I said sure and my boss at that time took me in the yard where all the tractor trailers were and said, 'Before you get in the truck, walk around it and tell me what you see, Aaron.' I walked around the truck the first time and told my boss, 'I see a semi.' My boss replied, 'You're wrong, and walk around it again.' I walked around the semi and told my boss, 'I see a tractor trailer.' Again, my boss said I was wrong. I walked around the truck a third time and told my boss, 'I don't know what you want me to say.' He smiled and said, 'Fully loaded, this tractor trailer is a bullet when going down the road. The minute you disrespect the semi, you will kill yourself or someone else.' I told him that time I understood."

"What did he say next, Aaron?"

"He told me that, before I went home that night, I would have to dock the truck twice and ride a painted line, in reverse, 500 feet with the back tandems of the trailer without the line leaving the middle of the duals. Oh, and he also said if I hit his coffee cup that he sat next to the line, I would be fired."

"Aaron, your old boss sounds very intelligent."

"He was, Bridgett, and I still respect him to this day."

"Aaron, let's get back to you and Nicole walking up to the semi."

"Okay Johnathon, as you both know, she thought the semi looked mean."

An excited Johnathon asked, "What kind was it, Aaron?"

"It was a T-600 Kenworth, white in color, with blue stripes down the middle on each side. Nicole loved the colors and the bed inside of the berthing area was big enough for both of us to sleep. The gentlemen who oversaw hiring asked me what I thought and if I would like to work for the company. Nicole and I looked at each other and I said yes. We went in to the office and filled out some paperwork and I was officially hired on with the trucking company. The gentlemen who hired me asked when I could start. I told him in three days I would be ready."

Confused, Bridgett asked, "Why three days, Aaron?"

"Nicole and I needed time to spend with the girls, go grocery shopping and pack our clothes."

"Why did you need to go grocery shopping when both of you were leaving?"

"The semi had compartments under the bed to store food. By going grocery shopping we wouldn't have to buy food from the truck stops. I knew food was expensive on the road. Nicole and I took a microwave to cook with, along with a small TV and DVD player with some movies. The time had come, and we were ready to go pick up our rig and be on our way. We dropped the girls off at their dad's house, Nicole gave her girls a kiss, and we both said goodbye."

"Aaron, it still amazes me how you and Nicole met, managed the things going on in your lives, and the way you loved one another."

"Why is that, Johnathon?"

"Because you and Nicole had a love that is rare. I mean, you were both battling evil, had battled CPS, were attentive parents and working with doctors, and handling medications and some psychiatric illnesses. I would say that you and your wife were two very strong individuals."

"We were, Johnathon. Nicole always said we were TNT, dynamite."

With a smile on her face, Bridgett speaks up and says "you both were."

"Aaron? Can you feel that?"

"Feel what, Johnathon?"

"There is a storm coming our way."

"How do you know that, Johnathon?"

"I can feel it, Aaron."

Just as Aaron stands up to go look through the window, he hears thunder in the distance. Approaching the window in the sitting room, he sees flashes of light engulf the cabin. The first drops of rain can be heard hitting the roof on the front porch.

"Johnathon, you were right, and I think this is going to be a bad storm."

"Aaron, we might want to close the shutters before the rain comes down too hard."

"Good idea, Johnathon."

Bridgett stands and says she will help. As everyone steps outside, the wind is picking up, the lightning is everywhere, and the rain is coming down in sheets.

"Johnathon, I will go in the back and get those shutters closed."

"Sounds good, Aaron."

"Bridgett, can you help me?"

"Yes, Johnathon, I am coming."

Hail starts dropping from the sky, intensifying the need for all to work together to finish closing the shutters outside. Once their task is accomplished, and soaked from head to toe, they meet back on the porch, under the cover of the roof and try to shake off the cold rain. Walking back into the cabin, everyone takes off their boots and heads for the closet to grab a towel to dry off with. As Johnathon and Bridgett move back into the sitting room, Aaron goes to the kitchen to get everyone hot coffee. Johnathon finishes putting a log on the fire, while Bridgett wraps her towel around her shoulders to help keep her warm."

"Bridgett, can I get you a blanket?"

"I would like that, Aaron, thank you."

Setting his coffee cup down, Aaron heads upstairs to grab a blanket. Just as he nears the bed, he notices a picture that wasn't there before. He hollers for Bridgett.

"Yes, Aaron, what is it?"

"Would you come upstairs for a minute?"

Bridgett rises out of her chair and walks upstairs with Johnathon right behind her.

"What's wrong, Aaron?"

"Can you explain this?!"

As Bridgett starts to ask, 'Explain what...' Aaron pulls a picture out from behind him. "Bridgett, this picture was on the mantle above the fireplace."

"Aaron, I don't know what to say."

"Johnathon, can you explain this picture?"

"Aaron, Bridgett and I are brother and sister."

"Why didn't you tell me that, and how did it get here when neither one of you have left

this cabin?"

"You will start to see more, as time goes on, but for now you must trust Bridgett and me."

"Johnathon, I want to know now!"

"We can't tell you right now, Aaron, but please trust us. What I can tell you is this; the reed goes deep into the ground and love is the root that binds all living things."

"More riddles, Johnathon?"

"Don't be mad, Aaron."

"I'm not mad, Bridgett, just confused."

"Let's just go back downstairs and stay warm, and you can tell us about you and Nicole driving over the road."

"That's fine, Johnathon, but the time is coming when I will ask for real answers."

Johnathon and Bridgett begin moving back to the sitting room. Aaron knows they are hiding something from him; something bigger than any of the moments they've shared together. Looking back on his journey to this place that has no name, Aaron starts remembering that the eagles disappeared, how Johnathon showed up out of nowhere, and that Bridgett just happened to hear about a man traveling and staying in a cabin. He wonders, now more than ever, if he truly is in Heaven.

Chapter Twenty-Three
Thankful

*A*aron and his two friends find their seats in the sitting room while the storm hammers the cabin with hail and rain.

"How were you and Nicole going to continue to see the psychiatrist when you both were going to be driving over the road?" Bridgett wondered.

"We scheduled the appointments with him once a month. Her doctor was fine with that and so were we."

"Aaron, you were telling Bridgett and me about dropping the girls off and picking up the semi."

"I remember, Johnathon. When we pulled into the lot, our semi was sitting next to the shop. We sat in the car for a few minutes and just looked at how beautiful the rig was. Nicole smiled and asked me if I was ready to start a new journey. I told her I was, and we both got out of the car and loaded up the compartments in the semi. I remember she was wearing a gray Nike sweatshirt and sweat pants with her K-Swiss shoes, and I was wearing bib overalls."

"Just like me, Aaron," Johnathon said, smiling.

"Yes, just like you are wearing. After we loaded up the semi we both went into the office and were dispatched to get a load from a packing plant up north. We jumped in the rig and headed down the highway to the plant. When Nicole and I arrived, I hooked up to the trailer and scaled out."

"Aaron, where were you two going and what were you hauling?

"We were going to Oakland, California, and our load was meat. I remember it like it was yesterday. Nicole always laughed because our trailer was a refrigerated unit."

"Why was that funny, Aaron?"

"In short , when someone asked us what we hauled, Nicole would always say we ran reefer."

Johnathon replied, "Oh, I get it, Aaron."

"As Nicole and I drove out to Oakland with the load of meat, I made sure to stop in every state, so she could get her shot glass. She smiled every time she bought a new one. I loved seeing her smile. We took a lot of pictures of us in the different states and I love the pictures of her standing by the semi. I remember one time the rain set in as I was driving, and I looked over and Nicole stuck her head out the window and just felt the rain on her face."

"Was it hard driving and dealing with the evil, Aaron?"

"I will say this, Bridgett. The angels were always with us, we had our Bibles and the evil was losing. Because, as Nicole's faith in Father grew, the Devil was losing his grasp on her. She fought hard, right alongside of me and the angels. It's hard to explain, but I will say that, as time went on, the demons that did come out were stronger and more powerful than the ones before. I always told Nicole that the Devil will try harder than before to gain back the footing he has lost on her. She would tell me she was scared, but having me by her side made everything all right. Yet, we would have many more obstacles to overcome."

Bridgett asked, "What do you mean, Aaron?"

"Once Nicole and I arrived in Oakland, she wanted to see some of the sights. I told her after we drop the load and hook up again, we would be driving down the grapevine."

"What is the grapevine, Aaron?"

"Johnathon, it was a run through southern California. The land along that route was some of the most beautiful we had ever seen, with gorgeous mountain regions that made a spectacular backdrop on both sides of the road. The next morning, I dropped the load off and we went on our way, but before we left Oakland I found a nice restaurant and we sat down to eat."

"I bet Nicole loved that, didn't she, Aaron?"

"Bridgett, she always liked me taking her to restaurants, as it made her feel like someone cared for her. We experienced one adventure after another in the truck together, despite the evil that followed her and me. I remember one year it was Christmas, and Nicole and I were running down Interstate 10. The Christmas music was playing, and we sang together all night long."

"Did you two have a favorite song, Aaron?"

"We loved a lot of songs Johnathon and had plenty of time to listen to them together, but our favorite was 'O Holy Night.'"

"I know that song, Aaron, and it is one of my favorite songs, too, and I know Johnathon loves hearing it, don't you?" Bridgett said, turning to him with a smile."

"I certainly do. It has a special place in my heart."

"As Nicole and I were headed back to Iowa to see the girls for Christmas, we went through St. Louis. The traffic was detoured the day before Christmas because a husband and wife had jumped off a bridge together. They were together that morning when a semi was running down the road."

"I can't imagine how the trucker felt after that happened."

"Neither can I, Bridgett. We said a prayer for them as we sat in traffic, waiting our turn to exit and take the detour."

With a somber look on Bridgett's face she softly says, "That makes me sad to hear, Aaron."

"We were sad, too, and that morning I told Nicole how thankful I was to have her as my wife. I remember her telling me, after seeing the couple take their own lives, that she was thankful more than ever for the smallest of things in life and for having me as her husband."

"Aaron, did you and Nicole always give each other compliments?"

"Yes, Johnathon and we always told each other almost every day how much we loved each other."

"If I may ask, Aaron, how was Christmas for you and Nicole's daughters?"

"Johnathon, Christmas was good, and we all had a wonderful meal together. The children received many gifts and I gave Nicole her gift."

"What was the gift, Aaron?"

"Bridgett, I gave her a diamond ring to go with her wedding ring. She said she felt like she was on top of the world and held on to me with her two arms wrapped around me as she smiled with all her heart. It was a good feeling to see the children and Nicole laugh and enjoy each second that passed by that Christmas morning, and every day after that. There was another time when Nicole and I were out west, and we detoured for a little while to go see the ocean. When we arrived at the ocean, we both got out of the truck and sat in the sand, just listening to the waves as the sun was setting. The wind was softly blowing and, with our shoes off, we felt the sand beneath our feet. I remember singing to Nicole that evening and as she smiled her eyes seemed to sparkle."

"Aaron, that sounds very romantic. What did you sing to her?"

"Bridgett, I sang a song by the band called Journey 'After All These Years.' It was romantic and relaxing for both of us. I told Nicole, before we left the beach, the light that shimmers across the ocean is our love that will always dance in the night. She smiled, kissed me, and we gave each other a hug. When we left the sandy beach, we walked together with our hands clutched tightly. We didn't want to leave but we knew we had to. Soon, we were back on the road with another amazing memory we shared. We also made sure to get her daughters a gift as often as we could."

"Aaron, that sounds wonderful. And I want to hear more. But do you mind if we go to bed?"

"I don't mind at all, Johnathon. Are you tired Bridgett?"

"I am, Aaron. I would love to hear more tomorrow."

Aaron decides to tend to the fire. Bridgett gets the bedding and Johnathon walks to the kitchen to empty the pot of coffee and make sure the wood stove is out. As Aaron tends to the fire, he can still hear the thunder and the rain coming down on the roof of the cabin. Bridgett makes the bed and Johnathon grabs a few extra blankets after returning from the kitchen."

"Johnathon, I am going to step outside on the porch and smoke."

"We will be in here, Aaron."

Aaron walks to the entryway, puts on his boots and grabs his coat. On his way outside, he thinks about Nicole and how she loved being on the road. As the door opens, the wind rushes in and he quickly shuts the door behind him. He lights his cigarette, finds the rocker, and looks out upon the land. He watches the lightning flash, lighting up the sky and Mother Earth. The rain smells different in this place he is in, and the thunder is extremely loud. He smiles at the lightning, as the light show in the Heavens above causes the angel statue to glow. He remembers how Nicole would step out into the rain on those days a storm would come. She always said the rain was God cleansing the Earth.

Taking the last drag of the cigarette, he decides to walk down off the porch and step into the rain, just as Nicole did in the past. He steps into the rain, extends his arms, and lays his head back with his eyes closed and lets the water run down his body. As every drop of rain trails his flesh, he softly speaks and says, "For you, Nicole, my love" before turning around and walking back into the cabin, happily drenched from the rain. As he enters, Bridgett and Johnathon are surprised to see him dripping from the rainstorm.

"What happened to you, Aaron?" Johnathon asked.

"I stepped into the rain and just felt the water from Mother Nature coming down from the Heavens."

After Aaron gets dried off, he lays down on the floor, where Bridgett and Johnathon are already nestled in for the night, with an extra blanket by their sides in case they need it. The storm continues, but Johnathon, Bridgett and Aaron sleep peacefully through the night. In the morning Aaron finds himself in an odd situation. He looks to his right and sees Johnathon next to him, and turns his head to the left to find Bridgett there. He looks back and forth a few times at both of them and smiles.

When they both wake up, Bridgett sees Aaron looking at her and asks, "What's wrong, Aaron?"

"Nothing is wrong, Bridgett, but I am curious why you two are sleeping next to me."

Holding her head down with a subtle smile, Bridgett replies, "Aaron, the storm was ferocious last night, and the floor seemed like the safest place to be."

"I see, Bridgett, but may I ask why you are next to me Johnathon."

Johnathon, somewhat sheepishly, replies "Well, I just thought that, since Bridgett was down here, I might as well be, too."

Smiling, Aaron says, "But Johnathon, you were already on the floor."

"I know, but…"

"It's okay, and I understand. Nicole used to press herself against me and hold me when the thunder and lightning raged in the night. It made her feel safe."

As they all get up to start the day, Johnathon picks up the bedding while Aaron and Bridgett make fresh coffee for everyone. The storm has passed and Johnathon steps outside and opens the shutters to let the morning sun cascade into the cabin as the coffee brews.

"Bridgett, I think this morning I am going to have some cream and sugar with my coffee."

"I will, too, Aaron."

Johnathon comes back in from outside and catches the conversation between Aaron and Bridgett. "Hey, you two, what about me?"

Smiling Aaron replies, "Would you like cream and sugar in your coffee, Johnathon?"

"I would, thank you very much."

"Are you feeling a little left out, Johnathon?" Bridgett asked.

Both Bridgett and Aaron smile at each other as Johnathon has an almost pouting look on his face."

"Johnathon, here is your coffee and Bridgett, there is your cup. The creamer is on the counter with the sugar."

After all three have their fresh coffee, they move to the sitting room, where Johnathon asks Aaron to tell them more about Nicole and himself.

"Would you both like to hear what Nicole's favorite Bible verse was?"

"We would love to hear it, Aaron" Bridgett replies on behalf of both of them.

"In the book of Luke, 15:3, there is the parable of the lost sheep, which goes as follows:

Luke 15:3

"What man among you, having a hundred sheep and losing one of them, would not leave the ninety-nine in the desert and go after the lost one until he finds it? And when he does find the sheep, he sets it on his shoulders with great joy and, upon his arrival home, he calls together his neighbors and says to them, rejoice, rejoice, for I have found the lost sheep. I tell you, in just the same way, there will be more joy in Heaven over one sinner who repents, than over the ninety-nine righteous people who have no need of repentance."

"Aaron, that's a beautiful Bible verse that has a lot of meaning."

"I would agree, Bridgett."

"Aaron, I think that verse suits Nicole very well. And, if I may say, teaching her faith was a blessing from Heaven. And by your hands, God found the lost sheep wandering in the desert."

"I wouldn't go that far, Bridgett, but thank you. I did what my heart told me to do and that was love Nicole as best as I could. That's all I did."

"Aaron, love is a great and powerful thing, both in this world and in Heaven. Without love, Christ would not have died on the cross for our sins. And people on Earth would never have known the feeling of love without our Father's desire to share his heart with every man, woman and child."

Chapter Twenty-Four

Visions of Heaven and Hell

"I believe every word of that is true, Bridgett."

"Can we hear more, Aaron?"

"Sure, Johnathon. Nicole and I were on the road for several years. We made sure to visit the children every weekend, even as we were still fighting the demons that resided within her soul. She and I, along with many more angels we met, fought hard in our crusade to fight the Devil. I was able to see everything that Nicole saw by looking behind the glass for quite some time. The images of what she was seeing I wouldn't wish upon anyone and, as one demon was destroyed, another unclean spirit would come forward. I remember one time we had come home from driving over the road. It was a Sunday morning and I was awakened by the sounds of something unnatural."

"What was happening, Aaron?"

"Before I opened my eyes, I heard people screaming as if they were being tortured. It was a sound I had never heard before and, when I opened my eyes, I could see the fire in the pits of Hell and those within it were burning. It was the souls claimed by the Devil as he ravaged each spirit. This layer of Hell had a multitude of souls burning in Lucifer's breast. The blackened demons raged against the souls and seemed to slowly take away any sense of reason they had left. Would you two like to hear something I wrote about that experience?"

"We would appreciate hearing it," Johnathon replies.

"Okay, it's called:

Awakening in death, I lay

in a room filled with demons.

Screams cry out

from the underworld, haunting my ears

as the mutilated, dark distortions

begin raping the souls of many.

The reaper slowly clutches

their shell-less bodies, dragging every soul

the Devil marks into the pits of Hell –

only to burn

in the Devil's breast.

I wrote that poem many years after I had seen the vision of Hell. To this day, the vision of what I had seen remains burnt upon my flesh. Sometimes, I wish I could wipe away what I've seen, but I can't."

"Aaron, it's hard to understand what you and Nicole went through."

"It was hard for both of us, Bridgett. I remember when I wrote 'Damnation,' my professor in college asked me where I came up with the idea to write that poem. I told him that, since our assignment was to write a poem inspired by the periodic table of elements, I chose the element of fire. But I didn't tell him the truth that day because I kept the real reason a secret."

"Aaron, I think your professor would understand why you didn't tell him the real reason. And I think you have seen more than you have told Johnathon and me."

"You would be correct, Bridgett."

"What happened next, Aaron?"

"Johnathon, when I looked for Nicole, I saw this black altar made from stone with chains that were binding her down. The demons had her on the altar and I saw the seven-headed beast standing in front of her. The crucifix was upside down and the only light around was blood-red. The fire raged and, with the sounds of those in Hell being tortured by the Devil's demons, I could see Nicole feeling the torment as I felt it myself. Her hands and feet were bound in chains. I remember, as I looked upon the Devil and his demons surrounding her, that they were torturing her with every instrument they could. As I stood there, watching and listening, the beast looked at me with his cold, dead, blackened eyes, and I could feel his fury. At that moment, I cried out to Nicole and told her I was there. I began praying to Father in Heaven. I prayed for St. Michael, the archangel, to pull her from Lucifer's grips. And from Nicole's lips, she also cried out, 'please save me from the wrath of Satan.' At that moment the light shined down, and Nicole and I watched the angels ascend from Heaven and lift her up from the depths of Hell. And that wasn't the first time the Devil made me watch his torment of Nicole."

"Aaron, have you ever told anyone these things you are telling Bridgett and me?"

"For the most part, I haven't told anyone, Johnathon, but some people do know a little."

"Can you tell Johnathon and I more about that Sunday?"

"Bridgett, as I watched the angels come down from Heaven and bring forth Nicole from Hell, I was also brought out of the vision. When we laid there together, afterwards, I stood up and looked at her. I saw cuts all over her, and on her left forearm there were markings."

"What were the markings, Aaron?"

"Johnathon, the markings were of the Devil. It was the sign of the beast. I dressed Nicole's wounds as she cried, and as I wiped her tears an angel came down and told her that her heart would be saved by the hands of Christ in the end. The angel spoke to her again and said, 'Nicole, your torment on Earth will not be forgotten to those in Heaven.'"

"Did the angel tell you anything else?"

"Yes, Johnathon, she did. The angel turned and looked at me and said, 'Aaron, you are the guardian of Nicole and strength is in you.' I told the angel that I was not this man you think I am. The angel replied, 'faithful is the servant to God the Father and the sword you carry, Aaron, has the markings made from the finger of God. You are the watcher, Aaron.' And just like that, the angel was gone. After she left there was peace in the apartment for both of us. It was like we were surrounded by angels that helped keep the evil away."

"Aaron, I am confused,"

"What about, Bridgett?"

"You said this was a vision, but when you and Nicole came out of the vision, she had markings inlaid upon her and she was hurt. How does that happen?"

"Bridgett, the Devil is powerful, and his reach is great. Just as God can do many things, the Devil can, too. Much of what I knew, and what I had seen over the years, I cannot explain. But I know that what happened in the years Nicole and I were together was real."

"I believe you Aaron. I was just confused."

"Bridgett, it was very confusing to me, too."

Johnathon, with a thoughtful expression on his face, added

"I believe that, Aaron, because Job was a prime example of what the Devil can do to someone, and Nicole's life was no different than Job's."

"Well, I also know this: the Devil may be able to make people suffer on Earth, but he is also governed by God regarding what he can and cannot do beyond this world," Aaron shared.

"So, what happened after that?"

"Johnathon, I hated seeing Nicole hurting and I did the best I could for her. We read the Bible together for a while and then we watched one of her favorite movies."

"What was the movie, Aaron?"

"Bridgett, we watched *The Last of the Mohicans*."

"Why did Nicole like that movie?"

"First, Bridgett it's a great love story, and secondly, she was a half-blooded Indian. She loved the movie and it gave her peace by taking her mind off what was going on. I remember how she and I would listen to tribal music with the sounds of nature in the background. I loved hearing the music, as well, and together we embraced the meaning of what the music stood for. Bridgett and Johnathon, I am going to step outside to smoke a cigarette. I will be right back."

With that memory once again fresh in his mind, Aaron makes his way to the front door and walks outside to find the sun shining down on him. The birds are singing and the sky is as blue as the Pacific Ocean. He lights the cigarette and takes his first drag, but as he begins smoking, he is taken off guard by a man standing by the corner of the cabin. Aaron looks and the man smiles."

Aaron asks, "Who are you?"

The man replies, "My name is Trenton and you must be Aaron."

"How do you know my name, Trenton?" Aaron asks, walking down off the porch toward the man.

"Aaron, may I shake your hand?"

"Yes, you may, Trenton, but why?"

"I just wanted to shake your hand and say hello."

"How did you hear about me?"

Trenton smiles and says to Aaron. "Your wife, Nicole, told me to tell you she loves you and misses you."

"How could she have told you to tell me that when she has passed away? Hang on, Trenton, I will be right back."

Aaron puts his cigarette out and runs into the cabin to get Johnathon and Bridgett.

"Hey, please come outside. There is a man here named Trenton, and he said that Nicole told him to tell me she loves me and misses me."

When Johnathon, Bridgett and Aaron hurry back outside, the man is gone.

"He was right here, Johnathon."

"Aaron, are you okay?"

"I am, Bridgett, and I know what I saw and heard."

"Aaron, many things happen for a reason."

"He said he knew my wife, Johnathon."

"Aaron, let's go back inside."

"Alright, Bridgett. But Trenton was real and he was here."

Making their way back into the cabin, Johnathon and Bridgett smile at each other as Aaron walks in front of them. Aaron is puzzled and thought-laden, but finds his seat in the sitting room. Bridgett gets him a fresh cup of coffee and Johnathon puts a log on the fire.

"Aaron, it will be okay."

"I know, Johnathon, but this place I am in is so confusing."

Bridgett replies, "It can be, Aaron. Are you able to tell us more about you and Nicole?"

"I guess there is no sense in over-thinking what I just saw outside, so, yes, I can tell you more. The spiritual conflict went on like it had been for us for many years. The only difference in Nicole's life and mine was the intensity of everything. She and I stopped driving over the road and I went to work at another place. We moved from the apartment because we needed more room, so together, as a family, we moved into a home on the south side of town. It was simple and we both loved it. We lived there for several years with the children."

"Aaron, I thought Dick had the kids at this time."

"He did, Bridgett, but when Nicole and I stopped driving over the road the girls came back home. So, the house was ours and we did what we could to fix it up, but then we started noticing the floor sinking in certain places."

"What was wrong with the house, Aaron?"

"Well, Johnathon, when we bought it the old owner never told us about the termites."

"How were you able to buy a house?"

"Nicole and I bought the house on contract, Bridgett. We didn't have the amount of money needed to fix the walls, flooring and the roof. Structurally, the house was not safe because the termites were in every wall and the main support beams. So, we ended up moving into another place in the west end of town."

"Aaron, did the old owners of the house you and Nicole bought give anything back for your troubles?"

"No, they did not, Johnathon. The couple that sold us the house didn't care, and we felt the owners were dishonest, so we just cut our losses at that point. This other place we bought on contract had four lots attached to it, with three bedrooms with a back porch, a garage, and a shed. I worked it out with the owner and we inspected everything before we bought it. We loved the house and Nicole's daughters loved the yard because they had room to play. After we moved from our old house into the new one, Nicole and I talked about trying to get her on disability."

"What was going on with Nicole, Aaron?"

"Her body was getting weaker, Bridgett. She was having a hard time getting up out of bed, and with her diagnoses from the psychiatrist, she couldn't work. So, we hired a disability attorney and filed the claim with the Social Security Administration. Nicole was on fifteen different medications from the psychiatrist, which is a lot under any circumstances."

"Why so many, Aaron?"

"Johnathon, with everything going on in her life, the doctor was trying to control her symptoms, which included, among other things, breaking down emotionally and trying many times to commit suicide. She was cutting on herself and the constant battles with evil spirits were taking a toll on her."

"How long had you and Nicole been together at this point in your life?"

"Seven years had passed, Johnathon."

"Aaron, what would you do when Nicole would try and take her life?"

Chapter Twenty-Five
Lost in Time

"*B*ridgett, during the times when Nicole would attempt suicide, I would use F.M.L.A., the family medical leave act, to stay with her and make sure she was okay. As I told you, there was a mix of the psychological and spiritual issues going on with her."

"Did you ever admit Nicole into the hospital for suicidal tendencies through the years, Aaron?"

"I did several times, Johnathon, but then I stopped admitting her and dealt with her issues myself – with the help of the psychiatric doctor."

"Why did you stop admitting her into the hospital?"

"For several reasons, Johnathon. I remember the way Nicole struggled with almost everything: her dreams; her memories of the abuse; being around people; not seeing her sisters and brother. Sometimes, she would even slip back in time to her early childhood years."

"How old would Nicole be, Aaron, when she reverted to be a child?"

"She would be six or seven years old."

"Johnathon," Bridgett said somewhat nervously. "Please just let Aaron talk."

Aaron smiles a little at Bridgett, and continued with, "Here are a few reasons why I stopped taking Nicole to hospitals. One time, I drove her to the hospital after talking with the psychiatric doctor about the issues she was experiencing. The doctor thought I should take Nicole to this hospital that was in another town. I was hopeful this would be a good facility, but it wasn't. The hardest part of this, for me, was taking her to get admitted."

"Why was it hard, Aaron?"

"Johnathon, it was hard because I loved her so much, and I hated seeing her hurt and being sad most of the time. I drove Nicole two and a half hours to this place and I cried the whole way there."

"Why were you crying, Aaron?"

"Sometimes, Bridgett, after Nicole would revert to her childhood years, or when she would see demons, she would attempt to take her own life. There were always a lot of triggers for her at almost every turn. When we were on the road, the little girl inside of her would say, over and over, 'Daddy, why are you trying to get rid of me? Daddy, don't leave me alone. Don't you love me anymore?' The little girl inside of her would cry the whole way up to the hospital. I would cry, too, and I would ask Father in Heaven for strength. The little girl inside Nicole begged me not to 'go bye-bye.'"

"Aaron, why would she think you were her dad?"

"Bridgett, I am not sure, but if I was to guess, I would say that her biological dad was taken from her, her adoptive dad abused her, and I was another male figure that she misconstrued as wanting to get rid of her because I was driving her to another hospital to be admitted. She couldn't understand, when she was in that state of mind, that I loved her and was only trying to do what was right. All Nicole could see was that she was a little girl being taken away."

"That is so sad, Aaron."

"I know, Bridgett, and it was hard on her and me both. Now, remember, I said I thought this would be a good facility?"

"Yes, I remember, Aaron."

"Well, I am here to tell you I was completely wrong."

"What do you mean you were wrong?" Bridgett inquired.

"When Nicole and I got to the hospital, I took her to admitting, where three men came out to escort us inside. Those three men, who worked in the ward, triggered Nicole's anger. I could see her switch. And noticed that those men were arrogant, rude, and had no concept of compassion. I even overheard one of the men laugh and tell another worker, 'Thank God for padded rooms.' Nicole's defense mechanisms inside suppressed the little girl and, as we entered the corridor, Nicole grabbed a butter knife off of the tray that was sitting in the hallway. Immediately, the staff wanted to disarm her, and I did, too, but the men were very aggressive in their body language. I shut the doors to keep the staff out. Because there were two doors leading into the ward with glass windows, I told the staff members, through the glass, 'If you all come through that door and try and take her down, I will stop you all.' I told them to back off or there would be Hell to pay."

"What happened next, Aaron?"

"Bridgett, I disarmed Nicole and the staff stayed out until I did."

"How did you disarm her, Aaron?"

"She trusted me and I told her I was going to take her back home and I would not leave her there. That's when she started crying and handed me the butter knife. I told the doctor I was taking Nicole home after I had seen how the staff was towards her. The doctor tried to tell me that I was not taking her home. With a few choice words, I told him I was taking her, A.M.A., against medical advice. I called the psychiatrist that she was seeing in our town, and he told me on the phone that he supported me and had faith in my decision. He also worked with me by teaching me what to do and how to handle certain situations."

"Oh, my goodness, Aaron! That psychiatrist sounds like he really respected you and Nicole."

"He did, Bridgett, and it was helpful to have one person understand what we were going through, or at least have an idea of our struggles. After I signed the A.M.A. papers, I took Nicole home and worked with her every moment."

"Aaron, it sounds like you changed your mind on the spot at the hospital when the staff wanted to come at Nicole. Is that a fair statement?

"It is, Johnathon, and that experience did change me. My heart is a dragon's heart and, whenever I felt like someone had bad intentions with Nicole, I was ready to protect her at any cost. That was just one example of mistreatment that she went through when she was admitted into the hospitals. We were already dealing with a lot, and it always pissed me off when those who were supposed to help never did."

"Aaron, unfortunately, the world has changed its outlook regarding the care for the elderly and the disabled."

"Oh, I would agree, Johnathon, despite the fact that there are also a lot of good men and women who do care about what they do for a living. It just seemed like, in one instance after another, we would run into those who didn't care. After that incident at the hospital, I never did admit Nicole into another hospital again. The psychiatric doctor always stood up for me, even to his own staff."

"What do you mean, Aaron?"

"Well, Bridgett, I called the doctor's office another time and talked with his nurse and explained that Nicole was having psychological issues. The nurse said I needed to admit her and I told her I wasn't going to do that again. The nurse tried to explain that I had no choice, due to Nicole's suicidal thoughts, so I asked to speak with the psychiatric doctor. When he got on the phone, he said, 'Aaron, just keep Nicole home and watch over her.' He told me to call him on his personal cell phone number, or his home phone number, if I need anything. He also said he would call me every day to check in on us."

"It's amazing that he did that for you two, Aaron?"

"Yes, Bridgett, and to this day I know that he was an angel that watched over us. Looking back, I had to keep Nicole home, away from the hospitals at all costs."

"Why was that, Aaron?" Bridgett asked with a confused look on her face.

"Because, I could give her what the hospitals couldn't:

love, understanding, compassion, and faith. Plus, having Nicole's psychiatric doctor by our side meant that I didn't have to admit her any more. There were many times I had to walk her through life using trigger points because she would slip back."

"What are trigger points, Aaron?" Bridgett asked, confused by the phrase.

"Trigger points are specific times in Nicole's life that I had to remember, from everything she told me through the years. They could be birthdays, events, and specific times in her life that I knew she could recognize, even in the state she was in. I was careful not to suggest anything during these times when she would slip back because I didn't want to alter any of her memories. Oftentimes, I would assume an identity other than myself, because Nicole did not know who I was, due to her being in a different state of mind. Sometimes, it would take me three to four hours to bring her back, but eventually she would return. There were other ways, though, to bring her back to the present day."

"How would you do that, Aaron?"

"Sometimes, Bridgett, when Nicole would slip back to a young age, I would ask the little child inside of her to listen to my voice. It was usually when her mind would take her back in time to that scared little child who was terrified of what her adoptive father would do to her. I would hear everything she went through as a child, but somehow she could see and hear me there. She wouldn't know who I was, but she knew she could trust me. I would tell her to listen to my voice and take my hand, after which I would tell her to close her eyes. "

"Would Nicole close her eyes, Aaron, and trust you, despite feeling that anxiety and dread?"

"Yes, Bridgett, she would hold my hand and, with her eyes closed, I would count to three and then smash a glass against the wall."

"Why would you do that, Aaron?"

"Johnathon, I would smash the glass because the unexpected noise would bring Nicole out of where she was in time."

"Would she remember what happened, Aaron?"

"During those times, no, she wouldn't, Johnathon. But she would ask me how I broke the glass when she came back to present day."

"Do you remember how many times you had to walk Nicole through time, Aaron?"

"Through the years we were together, Johnathon, I can say I walked her through time on many occasions."

"You and she had so much to deal with. Now I understand how there was a mix of psychological and spiritual issues going on and why Nicole filed for disability," said Bridgett.

"There was not a day that went by that Nicole wasn't going through something. Her life, as I have told you, was plagued by the Devil."

"And it sounds like the Devil really used his servants here on earth to try and hurt her," Johnathon added.

"Yes, he certainly did, and my anger for him continues and will continue until it's time."

"Aaron, I think Nicole was a very tough lady to withstand all of the abuse, multiple types of trauma, and the evil that came at her and through her all those years."

"Yes, Bridgett, she was a survivor and I know her heart was a lion's heart filled with strength."

As Aaron speaks of Nicole and what they went through together, Bridgett and Johnathon notice his eyes beginning to fill with sadness.

"What's wrong, Aaron? Why are you crying?"

"Bridgett, I just miss her so much and I wish I was with her now."

Johnathon replies, in an effort to comfort Aaron, "It will be okay."

Bridgett comes over and wipes his tears, as Johnathon holds him.

"I failed her in so many ways. I just miss my wife."

"Aaron, I am going to get you a cup of coffee."

"Thank you, Bridgett, that is very kind of you, but I don't feel like a cup of coffee."

"I know I have asked this before, but why do you think you failed Nicole?"

"All I can say is that I did, Johnathon, and I don't want to talk about it right now."

"I understand, Aaron," Bridgett replies. "Why don't we take a break?"

"I do need a break."

As nighttime approaches, Johnathon throws a log on the fire and Bridgett gets the bedding ready for bedtime. Aaron's heart breaks every moment that passes, and his soul cries out for Nicole.

When Johnathon and Bridgett return, Bridgett asks, "Aaron, are you feeling any better?"

"My heart hurts right now, Bridgett, and I feel so lonely."

Bridgett replies, "I am sorry, Aaron. I tell you what. How about if I throw a blanket on the floor in front of the fireplace in the sitting room, and you and Johnathon and I sit there and just hang out together?"

"I would like that, Bridgett."

They move in front of the fireplace and everyone grabs a pillow to sit on the floor of the cabin.

"Thank you both so much for being my friends."

Bridgett replies, "You are welcome, Aaron."

"Bridgett and I love you, Aaron, and you are welcome," Johnathon tenderly admits.

"I love you both, too. Would you like to hear something I wrote for Nicole? It's called:

Nightfall

Tenderly, the night's apparition emerges.

Moving evenly over the sea, the swoon shadows

her existence. Gazing into the night, I hear

her thoughts, heavily laden with loneliness.

Whispers echo, internally and externally. She falls

behind the glass. A tear flails against her flesh.

Wanting to be loved, she clutches

the strands of green. Recessing,

on the meadow's tier, coolness

surrounds her soul, gushing with emotions.

A soft, No 3, *Moonlight Sonata* plays through the cords, wrapped in bark.

Limbs move away, as the cello uplifts her.

Unveiled, a hand reaches out, floating

her cheek, up then down, as the air embraces her forgivingly.

Her thoughts flourish with listlessness.

The wind churns around her hand, drawing her

along the lavish landscape.

An undertoned voice embeds in her mind,

longing to comfort her, searching for the seeds.

Planted in the minced terrain of desire,

unearthing the planted Black Rose, I go deep

into the abyss. The tentacles run deep,

entangling her every wish, cutting to the surface.

I manifest my visionless body into the thorns.

Bleeding with every razor upon the Rose,

hanging on, wrenching out the threads of green,

the black, dark-petaled flower gives way.

As she dredges the words, outwardly, into the night,

listening to the unspoken, between the lines, I hear

her red, velvet lips sing a soft tone, ringing in

my ears. Sweetly she smiles, and her eyes glisten.

Upon her breast, beauty falls, the wind fades,

and the cello calms. Her life begins.

Wanting more, lastingness brings the tide, high

and low, helping her understand, she is loveliness.

Glazing the soil, her heart mends tenderly.

Knowing a harvestable life draws near, she stands

reposed, somewhere in the midst of Mother Nature.

The warmth surrounds her elegant, beautiful skin.

A fire burns of confidence and strength,

and a light cresting on the horizon builds,

emanating a perfectly cut diamond.

I smile, looking within, at The Eighth Wonder of the World,

hoping I made a difference, as the burnt, auburn orb

spells nightfall, effortlessly in time, as the silhouette of

the garden sprouts lilies in the field.

I begin to fade. The stage I set upon dissipates,

like the morning dew. Happiness she now has,

turning back, once more. I look,

pondering her thoughts, walking away,

The crossroads call me home,

lonely again.

Chapter Twenty-Six
Walking with Angels

"*I* wrote 'Nightfall' when Nicole and I were together. I could see her heart and the pain she was in all the time, mentally, physically and spiritually. The other reason I wrote the poem for her was because I spent so much time within her soul, fighting right beside her, to wrench out the demons that plagued her."

"Bridgett replies, "Aaron, you and Nicole are very special people but, if I may say, I can see pain inside of you. I don't want to over step my bounds, but your heart seems broken."

Johnathon adds, "I can, too, Aaron, and I also agree with Bridgett."

"You are both right. I do hurt all the time because I miss Nicole, my son, and my mother. I look back and realize that the love Nicole gave me through the years was stronger than the ties that bind, and her love was also greater than the mountains that were formed by Father in Heaven. After years of being with her, she taught me so much, especially about the angels. She taught me to see the soul within the flesh of people."

"What do you mean, Aaron?"

"Johnathon, every time I would look at Nicole, or myself, or someone else, she would remind me to look deep within people. If I opened my eyes, and looked hard enough, I could see the soul bound in the flesh, until God the Father says it's time to come home to Heaven."

"Aaron, we are all bound in flesh on Earth."

"I understand that, Johnathon, but sometimes it gets frustrating, being so close to Heaven and having to remain on Earth. Nicole could see the soul in other people and would be frustrated just like I was."

"Why was she frustrated, Aaron?"

"Bridgett, Nicole told me many times that she loved walking with the angels, but she would get frustrated because she would have to return."

"Return, in what sense, Aaron?"

"She loved being in Heaven, Bridgett, but being on Earth was an anchor that weighed her down with grief and depression. She explained to me one time when we were sitting on the porch. Returning home from being at Father's side always made her sad because Heaven was always so peaceful. The anchor was the living existence on Earth. She would tell me that Heaven was within us, and when she crossed the plane into God's kingdom, the chains bound to her flesh made up the anchor that sinks within the soiled lands."

"Aaron, I think Nicole knew how close Heaven was and she was blessed to be able to go deep within and see it in all its glory."

"Johnathon, in so many ways she was blessed by our Lord in Heaven, but she was also plagued by the Devil. I remember that she always said our hearts together were like the stars in the night sky, lighting the Heavens for all the angels to see. She would smile and tell me when she walked in Heaven she could look down and see the stars shining bright and she knew our hearts were beating as one."

Bridgett looks over at Aaron and asks, "Why are you smiling?"

"I was just thinking about Romans, 8:9, in the Bible, 'But you are not in flesh, but in the spirit, if so be that the spirit of God dwell in you. Now if any man or woman have not the spirit of Christ, he or she is none of his.'"

"Aaron, Nicole's faith grew so much, and Christ did fill her heart," Johnathon said assuredly. "And that verse from the Bible says it all."

"Aaron, do you think a person can have too much?" asked Bridgett.

"I don't believe that, but in this world, the one we live in, one can find the darkness of the seeds tainted by Satan. Worldly goods seem to have more value to many, rather than their faith in God. And the Devil knows how to feed the hunger for greed.

"Aaron, sometimes people forget the things that matter the most and fall into that trap."

"Johnathon, you are right about that, as I know I have fallen into that trap, as you will later learn. But back to where we left off, when Nicole would walk in Heaven, she would tell me about the peace she felt and how she would walk with Our Lady, Mother Mary. She always said that Mother Mary would tell her that the wounds she suffers from on Earth is in the eyes of her Son and will not be forgotten in Heaven. She would also tell me how Mother Mary would tell her, 'Nicole, your conversion to faith is the trumpets sounding in the ears of those who walk in the barren-less lands, bringing joy and knowing the lost sheep was found.' Nicole would cry and tell me she didn't understand what Mother Mary was saying. I told her that I didn't know for sure, but if I was to say, Mother Mary was talking about the parable of the lost sheep."

"Wasn't that Nicole's favorite Bible verse?"

"Yes, it was, Bridgett. She loved that verse years before she walked with Mother Mary."

Johnathon, speculating, says, "That is really something, Aaron. It's as if Mother Mary knew that was Nicole's favorite verse."

"I believe you're right. So, after Nicole's spirit would return within her flesh, she would endure everything she didn't feel in Heaven. Her body hurt, and the torment of the demons, her abuse, and everything else she went through made her long for Heaven every day. I love my wife and it hurt me to see my very special lady wanting to leave this world, but I understood why. As Father in Heaven said, Nicole was his daughter and he loved her, and we always knew we were different."

"What do you mean by different, Aaron?"

"Bridgett, when Nicole and I were together, she and I always said that, sometimes when we would walk down the street, we would see someone just like us. When we would look at the person, we would smile and he or she would always smile back. Without saying a word, Nicole and I knew we weren't the only ones. We knew we didn't walk this Earth alone and so did the others we crossed paths with. To this day, I can see those who our Father in Heaven has sent to help others. It was a good feeling to know that we were not alone."

"Aaron, did you always know that Nicole was your soul mate?"

"I believed that from the day I met her, Bridgett."

"I have heard of people being soul mates, and having a special connection to the one he or she was meant to be with and other planes of existence. And I believe we can do many things, like looking inward and seeing that we are not just flesh and blood here on earth, but we are more than that. We are a symbol of what God the Father created."

"I would agree, Johnathon, and God the Father knows that evil exists, as well as good, and he does not forsake us."

"No, He does not, Aaron."

Bridgett adds, "In the Bible, there is a verse that touches me, in John, 3:16. 'For God so loved the world, as to give His only begotten son; that whosoever believeth in Him, may not perish, but may have life everlasting.'"

"Bridgett, thank you so much for reciting that Bible verse."

"You are welcome, Aaron."

Johnathon, connecting their discussion to past conversations, remembers something important.

"Aaron, thinking back to some of your writings, you reference Mother Nature, falling curled like a newborn baby, and in swaddling clothes."

"Yes, Johnathon, and thank you for listening so closely."

"Aaron and Bridgett, based on what I've heard, then, please tell me what you think."

Bridgett replies, "I will, Johnathon, but what are you

thinking?"

"Well, when a mother carries her child within the womb, that child grows within the mother, within the world unseen. But when the child is born into the world, the child becomes the seen. But we are still the newborn, even after birth – growing, learning, loving and teaching within God's womb in the seen, in this world. It's an understanding that our hearts are just what Samuel said to you, Aaron, the other night in the cabin. The human heart is the voice closest to God and love is the reed that feeds the soul.

"I would agree, Johnathon, and I would add that angels are always in Heaven, but there are times when angels appear to people on Earth, much like the angels that always helped and stood by Nicole and me. The angels go beyond the boundaries of Heaven, just as she was able to walk with our Father in Heaven, as well as the angels and Mother Mary."

"Guys?"

Aaron replies, "What is it, Bridgett?"

"How about we get some sleep?"

"Absolutely. We could all use the rest."

"Aaron, if you want to go smoke a cigarette, Johnathon and I will get the bedding out and take care of the fireplace."

"I would like that, Bridgett, thank you."

Aaron heads to the cabin door and opens it, the night air is calming while Johnathon and Bridgett begin taking care of everything in the cabin before they all sleep. Outside, he lights the cigarette and sits in the rocking chair. The rocker creaks back and forth as the moon shines brightly over the land. In the distance, Aaron hears two owls talking with one another and the wildlife rustles through the dark timbers. He smiles, looks at the angel statue glowing from the rays of the moonlight, and sees a fawn lying next to the fountain the angel stands atop. He can also hear the current from the river running down through the mountain. The wind blows softly, and he can smell the pine trees in the air. He thinks to himself that he could fall asleep right here in this chair. Even after he finishes his cigarette, he decides to relax a few more minutes outside. After about twenty minutes, Bridgett and Johnathon decide to check on him. Stepping outside, they find

Aaron asleep and they smile at each other.

"Johnathon, I am going to get Aaron a blanket and cover him up."

"Should we let him sleep out here?"

"Why not, Johnathon?"

"He can't be comfortable, Bridgett."

"But he is sleeping so peacefully. How could he not be comfortable?"

"All right, I see what you are saying, Bridgett."

Bridgett goes in the cabin and gets Aaron a blanket and returns to cover him up. Afterwards, both Johnathon and Bridgett give Aaron a soft kiss on the cheek and whisper in his ear, "We love you, dad, and mom loves you, too, with all her heart." Then they quietly go back in the cabin and bed down for the night as Aaron sleeps peacefully on the porch in his rocking chair. The night passes slowly and gently, with everyone in their rightful place.

As the morning sun rises, and the rays give warmth to Aaron's body, his eyes open. Looking around, he sees the blanket on him and smiles. Just then, he feels something at his feet and looks down. The fawn he had seen last night by the angel fountain is fast asleep at his feet, curled up in his blanket. He gently talks to the fawn, "Hey there, little fella, how are you?"

The fawn looks up at Aaron and stands. The two look at each other and then the fawn comes around the chair and rubs his nose against Aaron's cheek. Aaron kisses the fawn on the forehead and watches it walk off the porch and disappear into the wilderness. His mind flashes to how he and Nicole used to give each other Eskimo kisses almost every day. Smiling again, he looks around and then hears the cabin door open.

"Good morning, Bridgett."

"Good morning, Aaron, how are you? Did you sleep well out here?"

"I actually did, Bridgett, and you?"

"I did as well, Aaron. Here is some coffee."

"Thank you, Bridgett. You knew what my mind was thinking."

"What's that, Aaron?"

"That I needed coffee with my cigarette." Seeing Bridgett smile, he continues, "And I have to say, your coffee is always good. The coffee you and Johnathon make always tastes like the coffee Nicole always made me."

"Well, thank you, Aaron. That is a kind compliment."

 Aaron and Bridgett both embrace the moment, Mother Nature, and the morning sun that shines down."

"It's so peaceful here, Bridgett. Was Johnathon still sleeping when you got up?"

"Yes, he was, Aaron, so I didn't bother waking him. Aaron…I can really see how you and Nicole struggled with everything you both went through."

"It was tough for us through the years; that's for sure."

"And even though I now know there was a lot of psychological stuff going on with Nicole, I have to say that the Devil created all the problems she went through. If it weren't for the Devil, she could have been happy in life."

"Bridgett, she was happy when she was with me, and in life to a certain extent."

"I know, Aaron, but I am just saying that what she went through was a long, hard road and you can't blame yourself for her death."

"Bridgett, thank you, but I don't want to talk about that topic right now."

"I am sorry, Aaron."

"Don't be sorry, Bridgett. It's okay. Hey, this morning I had a beautiful fawn sleeping at my feet, all curled up in the blanket."

"Aww, Aaron, that's so sweet!"

"Yep, the fawn got up and rubbed his nose on my cheek and I gave him a kiss on his forehead."

"Aaron, you are a good man and, as a friend of mine tells me all the time, you have a heart of gold, and if Heaven won't take you, then I won't choose Heaven."

"Bridgett, who told you that?"

"Why do you ask, Aaron?"

"Because there are only two people that know that saying. One of those people is me and the other is a man I respect."

"Umm, he is just a friend, Aaron."

"No, Bridgett, tell me. I want to know."

"His name is Marcus."

"Marcus. Huh, Bridgett, that name is familiar to me. I suppose you know John Paul, Lucas James and Daniel."

"Aaron, I might, but I am not positive. Who are they?"

"They are friends of mine and I call them family. Bridgett, you are full of surprises."

As Aaron talks more with Bridgett, Johnathon steps outside with a cup of coffee in his hand. Sitting down, Johnathon sips on his coffee and enjoys the morning with Aaron and Bridgett.

"Aaron, can we hear more about you and Nicole today?"

"Yes, you can, as I was just talking with Bridgett about her. As you both know, she was dealing with many different issues, including the effects of the psychotropic medications, the demons, her psychological issues, the children, getting disability, and her ex-husband."

"Aaron, where would the children go when you wouldn't admit Nicole into the hospital?"

"They would stay with their dad, Johnathon. Dick had temporarily proven himself to be okay, but I was seeing a slight change in his attitude."

"What was it about his demeanor, Aaron?"

"It was mild, Bridgett, but Nicole and I still had to let the girls stay with him during those times we were struggling to fight her tendencies."

Chapter Twenty-Seven
The Rite

So, Nicole and I decided to go talk with the priest about the evil we were fighting. The priest recommended this man within the church, a monsignor of the Catholic Church, to be exact. The priest called the monsignor and we met him the next morning. He sat with us for some time, evaluating Nicole and her demeanor. The monsignor felt that she was afflicted by the Devil and recommended us to some people who could perform a rite to cleanse those with spiritual afflictions. Before we left him, he gave us two large crosses to wear around our necks and told us they would protect us. The crosses were blessed and had writing in Latin on them. They were St. Benedict XVI crosses."

"What does that mean, Aaron?"

"St. Benedict XVI was an exorcist, priest, and a saint. The Latin language inlaid upon the cross meant 'purity of the soul is upon you through Jesus Christ.' The monsignor told Nicole and I to go and he would call and let the people know we were coming. When we arrived to meet the people who were going to administer the exorcism, we got out of the car and were greeted with kindness."

"Aaron, how is an exorcism granted?"

"In the Catholic Church, Bridgett, an exorcism must be approved by the Bishop. Then the person believed to be possessed must go through the documentation by the church. Once it is believed the person is afflicted by demonic possession, then the exorcist will be called out to perform the rite of expulsion."

"Did you and Nicole have to do that, Aaron?"

"We didn't have to go through the traditional process, Johnathon. The day we met with the monsignor, he informed us that the church had changed and, 'as you both know, the Devil hides in the shadows. He has corrupted many things in this world and has blinded the eyes of many, as he blots out the sun.' The monsignor went on to say that Pope Paul VI once declared, 'the smoke of Satan has entered the church.' For this reason, he sent us out to his trusted people. But, in other religions, the rite of an exorcism is granted in different ways."

"Aaron, where was this place you and Nicole went to?"

"Bridgett, we were asked to keep silent of those who were present and where it took place, and we have all these years. When we went into this place, there were four people waiting: one to read the Bible, one to hold the crucifix, one to use the Holy water, and one to cleanse her soul and oversee the rite."

"Was this an exorcism, Aaron?"

"It was, Johnathon. I had been researching exorcisms and was aware of how they were performed. Nicole was scared, naturally, so I told her I would be at her side the whole time. She made me promise I wouldn't leave her, and I didn't. As the exorcism started and throughout, I have to say it was like nothing I had ever seen before. It wasn't like the movies at all. Even though I had been reading about how they were to be performed, having textbook knowledge is nothing like seeing it firsthand. It was different and what went on in that room was intense."

"What happened, Aaron?"

"Well, a lot of things happened that day, Johnathon, but one aspect that blew my mind was the darkness that filled the room. The apparition, if you will, was pure evil and the sounds were not of this world."

"Did the exorcism work, Aaron?" Bridgett wondered with great anticipation.

"No, and Nicole and I were told that cleansing the soul might take several attempts to be successful. I asked the people why that was the case, and the one man spoke up and said there are many different demons in this world and some of them are many. We were disappointed when we left, but having others experience what we been going through provided some relief."

"Why was that, Aaron?"

"Bridgett, it was just the fact that the people performing the exorcism were able to see what we had been dealing with and battling for quite some time. Even though Nicole and I had been living with the reality of her afflictions, and had seen her different identities manifested in her, it was also sometimes hard to believe."

"I see, Aaron, and I can't say I know what you are feeling, or can even imagine it, but I'm glad it gave you a sense of relief."

"I appreciate that, Bridgett. After going through the intensity of that experience, we were both exhausted, so when we got home we decided to lay down and try and rest. We rested peacefully for a while..."

"What disturbed your sleep, Aaron?" Johnathon inquired.

"I woke up to a knife to my throat and was told if Nicole and I ever did that shit again, I would be dead."

"Oh, dear God, Aaron! Who was it that came out of her?"

"He wouldn't give his name, Bridgett, but the unclean spirit did say to us that, since we tried destroying them, they would destroy us. Then the demon was gone and Nicole was back. Afterwards, the angels came down to protect her. She said she had this feeling of fear inside of her. I told her and the angels what happened."

"What did they say, Aaron?"

"Johnathon, Nicole was too scared to say much of anything, and the angels said it will be all right, for Father in Heaven will be with us always. As we laid in bed, Nicole said she could feel and see Jesus with her and me. We heard this calm voice say, 'Sleep, for the angels will watch over you and rest will be given unto thee.'"

"Were you finally able to rest without other incidents, Aaron?"

"Yes, Bridgett, we got some much-needed sleep. With everything that had been going on, we were more exhausted than we usually were when we had to overcome the evil that emerged from Nicole. Then, a few days later, I received a call from Dick, who told me he was behind in his child support and wanted it forgiven so he could get his driver's license back and be able to file his taxes and get a return. I told him that it wasn't my problem, nor were his problems Nicole's."

"How did he take your response, Aaron?"

"Not very well Bridgett, because he told me that I better get Nicole to forgive the child support debt, and give him custody, or I would spend the next twenty years in prison. I asked Dick how he was going to put me in prison for twenty years. I even laughed a little and told him that I would have to commit a crime first. Then I told him he could take his threats and go to Hell. I also told Dick; I will not be backed into a corner. I will not let Nicole be bullied or threatened. I will not succumb to threats of violence. Many have tried and many have failed because I have always stood in one voice, of one mind and with one heart. I will defend Nicole and fight any entity such as yourself, as I have stood against CPS, and the Devil. No-matter what you try to do I will stand steadfast always. Dick called me a few choice words and then hung up the phone."

"Aaron, I can see how you always stood your ground, but why would Dick want custody now, Aaron?"

"Johnathon, if he didn't get custody of the two girls, then the child support would continue to accrue – even if Nicole forgave the debt. The other reason he wanted custody was that the laws state if a person is so far behind in child support, he can be put in jail for a period of time. What Dick didn't know, however, is that I was recording the conversation, just as I had done in the past due to not trusting him."

"Could you legally record him without his consent, Aaron?"

"Yes, Bridgett, it was allowable under the one-person consent law. After I got off the phone with him, I let Nicole listen to the recording. She told me that Dick could go to Hell and nothing would be forgiven, nor would he ever get custody of her girls. So, we went about our business and let the matter go. We were still going to the psychiatrist, dealing with the evil, and just trying to enjoy life as much as we could as a family. Months had passed and our routine hadn't changed any. Nicole, the children and I were all getting along great. Nicole wanted to get an eighteen-foot, four-foot-deep pool to swim in for her and the girls while I was working. She was tired of being cooped up in the house while I was away at work. So I bought a pool and we put it under a tree so Nicole wouldn't have the sun coming down on her during the day."

"Did you ever hear any more from Dick?"

"Yes, Johnathon, unfortunately we did, or I should say we were blindsided by him. It was mid to late summer and I was working as a route driver. The days were very long, as I was up around four in the morning and left the house around five a.m. every day, six days a week. Then, every night when I got home from work, I was setting up medications, cooking dinner and helping Nicole through her struggles. But there was one day that seemed different when I was driving my route. I noticed that Christ had fallen off my St. Benedict crucifix onto the floor of the truck. I reached down and picked up Christ and put him in my binder that held all my paperwork. Later that afternoon I remember the rain was coming down hard. The sky became pitch black. The lightning streaked across the sky, thunder shook the ground around me, and hail mixed with the heavy rain came in wind-driven sheets that blew fiercely across the road. It was one of the most powerful storms I had ever seen. Streets were flooding, the river was rising, and the fields were getting washed out."

"How late in the day was this, Aaron?"

"It was about three o'clock in the afternoon, Bridgett. We lived right on the city limits in the west end of town, and the river was only a mile and a half behind our house. There was a levy there to stop the water from flooding the houses, which gave us some peace of mind. Anyway, I came home from work in the blinding rain, and had only been home for about a half hour when there was a knock at the door. When I opened the door, there was an officer with a child protective worker. They asked to come in the house, and I obliged, wondering about the nature of their visit. I asked the officer and the worker what was going on, and the CPS worker told me there was a sexual abuse complaint filed regarding me and the middle daughter. At that moment, the middle daughter explained to the CPS worker and the officer that their oldest sister and father were going to make the accusation against me. The officer asked the middle daughter how she knew that, and she replied that their dad had been coming to the school and meeting with her. So Dick had been telling her that he wanted custody and he was going to get what he wanted. The middle daughter was told by him that the only way he could get rid of me was to get me out of the house. The middle daughter also stated her older sister and her dad would make this allegation out of hatred. The officer asked her about our relationship, and she informed them that nothing had ever happened regarding any abuse, and that I was a good stepfather.

Despite that fact, the worker told me I had to leave until the investigation was over. The officer looked at the worker and told her she would document everything that was said. The officer even told the social worker she would write in the first initial contact that this was planned by the oldest daughter and the father."

"Did you leave, Aaron?"

"I had to, Johnathon. Even though the allegations against me by Dick were preposterous, causing trouble with the investigating authorities wasn't going to help the situation any, nor would the added stress be good for Nicole or her daughters."

"Was this the same worker as before, Aaron?"

"No, Bridgett, it was a different CPS worker that I had heard about, but never encountered. However, Nicole and this particular CPS worker hated each other from past encounters that took place before Nicole and I were together."

"Aaron, did you know her?"

"Like I said Bridgett, I had heard many distasteful things about her and how she would destroy families. She was known for falsifying documents and abusing her authority."

"Aaron, I think I can see where this is going."

"You would be right, Johnathon. I left that night in the storm and stayed in a motel room. The next morning, I called an attorney and explained everything that was going on and that had transpired. I even let the attorney listen to the recording from Dick."

"What did he think about the situation, Aaron?"

"He was confused and didn't understand why the state would

even continue the investigation. However, he did pick up the case on my behalf. During this time, Nicole would call me and tell me she was sorry for what Dick and her oldest daughter were doing. I told her that it wasn't her fault and she had nothing to apologize for. Ironically, the CPS worker that I told I would sue for harassment, and the one that said she would like to get her hands on the girls, is the one that took over the case."

"Are you kidding, Aaron?"

"I wish I was, Johnathon. When Nicole and I heard that she was taking over the case, we both knew this wouldn't be about the truth. It would be about exerting power over us and exacting revenge. Since the girls knew that Nicole needed me by her side, they decided to go back with their father. I was able to move back in and my attorney told me it would be fine in the end. He also tried to reassure Nicole not to worry, but that was easier said than done with these cases and her fragile disposition. We were both trying to hold our emotions in check, despite being extremely angry with Dick. The attorney worked hard on the case and told me the state was going to set up an interview with the middle daughter, along with another investigator to conduct the interview. I told him what I figured the CPS worker was going to try to do, and that I could only control my own actions. Finally, he was informed that the time was set for the interview and we would get copies of what transpired when it was over."

Chapter Twenty-Eight
Colliding Storms

"A few weeks later the attorney called and said that the middle daughter had now changed her story. Nicole and I told him, sarcastically, how convenient that was for her to alter her original story. When he asked what we meant by that, I told him that it always seemed like everything was fine until the girls go live with their dad. Then everything changes. The attorney told us that, in many cases, one parent or the other can influence a child in order to get their way. And in this case, the attorney stated after listening to the audio recording, it sounds like Dick uses manipulation and threats to obtain what he desires."

"That's so unjust, Aaron."

"I agree, Bridgett. It's called coercion, and Nicole and I risked losing everything at this point because some derelict piece of work was destroying what we had worked to have. He was just looking out for himself, and was willing to do literally anything to get out of paying child support."

"Were you upset with the middle daughter, Aaron?"

"No, I wasn't Bridgett, because I knew that this wasn't her

fault. It's the work of a man who had no soul – the same man who made Nicole sleep outside in the winter and physically beat on her all the time."

"I am going to say it, Aaron. Dick is a complete jerk. How did you not find him and lay him out again?"

"Believe me, Johnathon I wanted to, but I couldn't because Nicole and I already had a lot on our plate. In fact, after the middle daughter changed her story and the CPS worker founded the accusations against me, it led to the state picking up the case criminally. My attorney told the CPS worker that she couldn't make her case based on the evidence presented and the statements from the middle daughter made against Dick. He received the transcripts from the night the officer was at the house and everything that transpired and was said, but the lady from CPS was not interested. Nor did she want to hear the digital recording of what Dick said, which collaborates the night the middle daughter told the officer and the CPS worker of his plan. My attorney told Nicole and me that the CPS worker didn't want to listen to anything he had to say, not even the tape of Dick threatening me with prison and what he wanted. She said she didn't care, and that she said she could do anything she wanted because she had the power and authority, which Nicole said was typical for her. We were both so angry with how everything was transpiring."

"Aaron, that is pure arrogance on her part."

"We were not at all shocked by her statement to my attorney, Johnathon, as she had a history of abusing her authority. Just think about how many families had their lives ruined by this lady. But I will tell you, Johnathon and Bridgett, that her comment and her actions ended up biting her in the ass later in the investigation – right along with the falsified documentation and the papers that came up missing, but that were later found by my attorney."

"What papers came up missing?" Johnathon asked.

"The first issue that CPS created was the initial first contact report, which was falsified by the CPS worker. The second issue that arose was that she failed to investigate the biological father and what he had said in the recording. It was evident, at this point, that nothing mattered to her except exercising her control over Nicole and me."

"Aaron, what was going through your mind when all this was

going on?"

"I was more worried about Nicole because I knew many people get railroaded in the court system all the time. Despite the evidence I had, I also knew that CPS was a powerful entity. But there was no way in Hell I was going to lay down and let this lady, or any other person like Dick, try and ruin my life, or Nicole's. I was fighting for my freedom against a man who was out only for himself. But I was also fighting against an organization that destroys families every day. I am not saying every person that works at CPS is bad, because there are a lot of good people that I know who work for the state. But it only takes a few bad people with power to destroy lives. As my old criminal justice professor said when I was in college. Every day, across the United States there is case after case where CPS invades, terminates parental rights, and continues to use their power to manifest cases against families to increase their Federal funding. The more cases they create, the more money CPS earns."

"Aaron, the Devil works in the same manner."

"Yes he does, Bridgett, and after what I've experienced with Nicole, who's to say why certain people decide to try to create chaos and destroy harmony? At any rate, the middle daughter changed her story on a whim. It was a few days later, after the CPS worker founded her investigation on me, that I was arrested on two counts of sexual abuse, which were a class C felony."

"Aaron, what was the basis for her making the accusations founded?"

"They do not have to follow the same rules as the court system, Bridgett. As each case is investigated, it's the CPS worker that is solely responsible for determining what they believe to be true or not true."

"So, Aaron, let me get this straight. The CPS worker, whom you and Nicole had issues with and fought against when Nicole was in the rehab center – along with the other one that showed up that night to investigate – were the ones who determined the findings?!"

"That's correct, Bridgett."

"Wasn't that a conflict of interest?"

"That is what my attorney said, Bridgett, but they didn't care, and they were the ones with the authority."

"Aaron, both workers at CPS sound like they need a full-time job with the Devil."

"Johnathon, they already were working for him. So, since the worker founded the report, I was now in the heart of a storm that Nicole and I didn't need. With each count punishable of up to ten years in prison, we spent many nights worrying about the future and also trying to enjoy our time together in case the worst happened. When the officers arrested me, it was around three in the morning. Nicole and I lost our home, having to sell off as much stuff as we could to pay for the attorney."

"Where were you picked up, Aaron?"

"We had moved to a park and were living in a camper."

"Oh, Aaron, that's terrible!" a deeply saddened Johnathon replied. "It sounds like many forces were trying to get rid of you and destroy Nicole at the same time."

"It's funny you should say that, Johnathon, because my attorney often said; I was being crucified by someone who hates me, and by a state organization that blatantly and egregiously attacks those with a voice."

"Who do you think he was referring to, Aaron?"

"He was talking about the CPS workers and Dick who always wanted to destroy Nicole in one way or the other. He shared with us that, in all the years he had been practicing law, he had seen them destroy families by not following the laws as they should. Nicole asked him how that is even possible that they can try and destroy the life of this man with no-prior convictions in his past. The attorney told us that some people like to use the court system and CPS for revenge against those they want to hurt. The sad part about that is people's lives can get ruined because of childish games."

"Aaron, after you were arrested, how did people treat you?"

"Bridgett, some of my friends who knew me stuck by my side, while others would not speak to me and some even spit on me. After that, I decided to have the mentality that those who wanted to spit on me could go to Hell. I didn't need them and neither did Nicole."

"That's so awful, Aaron."

"Unfortunately, that's life nowadays. Many people are quick to judge and convict without knowing the whole circumstances. Much like Nicole was judged her entire life. But there are also those who, thankfully, choose to listen before judging. I am going to go get some more coffee. Would you and Bridgett like some, too?"

"We would, Aaron, and I will help you."

"Thank you, Johnathon."

On their way to the cabin for more coffee, Bridgett looks out at the land and embraces the beauty before her. Her mind wonders what made the Devil choose Nicole to torment and try and destroy. She also tries to fathom how Aaron and Nicole withstood so much. As she ponders those questions, she remembers what John had told Aaron when they were talking about God and the Devil. Aaron and Johnathon return to the porch and Bridgett gets up out of her chair to open the door for them with a smile on her face.

"Here is your coffee, Bridgett."

"Thank you, Aaron. Will you please tell us more? I know the story can be difficult to tell, but we would love to hear the rest of what you are willing to share."

"That's no problem, Bridgett. After I was arrested on two felony counts, my attorney told me that the arraignment was waived, and I didn't have to appear in court. As time passed, and Nicole and I had caught wind that the stepmother had written out what the middle daughter was to say during the interview, we let the attorney know."

"How did you hear about the letter, Aaron?"

"Someone who knew Dick and his wife, and that didn't like them, told us about it. We immediately called the attorney and explained to him about the letter. He was able to track down and subpoena the letter. Several months had passed, and every court hearing was delayed. After four more months had passed, it was deposition time."

"What is a deposition, Aaron?"

"Johnathon, depositions are taken to get statements from everyone involved, and each statement is used in court to keep the stories straight. Therefore, the CPS worker was questioned regarding why the initial visit to the house was never submitted to their investigation. Then she was also asked why her supervisor told her to lie during depositions."

"What?!" Bridgett and Johnathon utter in unison.

"I will get to that in a minute. So, she couldn't answer why her supervisor chose to act as

she did and, as for the visitation paperwork, she said that it must have gotten lost. I smiled when my attorney told her that it is against the law to withhold evidence and falsify documents. After he was done, the CPS worker stormed out of the office. When the second officer came and was questioned, she was very honest and told the same scenario as the middle daughter did on the first night they were at the house. She was asked if she was told to lie about what the daughter initially said, and if she was aware that the story had changed four different times. The officer responded and said, yes, she was told to omit certain details and statements of what was said that night. Additionally, she noted in depositions that she told the CPS worker and her supervisor she would not lie under oath and commit perjury.

After the depositions were over, some time passed and I had yet to step into the courtroom. It was delay after delay, and then finally my attorney called me into his office. When Nicole and I got there, he told us that he had turned over all the evidence to the county attorney. After reviewing the discovery evidence, the county attorney said they would offer two years' probation for two counts of aggravated misdemeanor assaults, court costs and attorney fees."

"Aaron, I thought you and Nicole paid the attorney?"

"We had, Johnathon, but we ran out of money and had to petition the courts for a court-appointed attorney. It just so happened that the same attorney who we paid, stayed on the case. So, after hearing what he said, Nicole and I both asked why there was two years' probation. The lawyer responded that, since this case has dragged on for sixteen months, and despite the truth and the evidence, 'all a crying young girl has to do is gain the jury's sympathy and Aaron is gone from your life Nicole.' He said he had seen it many times before. Nicole spoke up and said, 'Aaron, it's your decision but this whole situation is wrong.' I told the attorney I would have to think about it, and we left the lawyer's office."

"What did the attorney say, Aaron?"

"He informed us that we had forty-eight hours to decide, Bridgett, and then the offer was off the table. After we left his office, I made a phone call to another attorney in Chicago."

"Aaron, why did you do that?" Bridgett asked with a puzzled look on her face.

"I was pissed and so was Nicole. The company I drove truck for had 'on call' attorneys that I could seek advice from, so I figured asking a second lawyer couldn't hurt in this situation.

When I called the attorney in Chicago and explained everything that was going on with the case, he (who was also certified to practice law in Iowa) stated that there was no reason why the case shouldn't be dropped. I asked him why the state would even proceed, and he informed me that there were several possible reasons why the state wouldn't drop the charges. Then he offered his legal opinion."

Frustrated, Johnathon asked, "What were his thoughts, Aaron?"

"The attorney told Nicole and me, on speaker phone, that he believed my attorney in Iowa was not experienced enough or that he might have taken a sideline deal – not to mention there were court costs and attorney fees that needed to be paid back. So I asked him what he meant by 'a sideline deal' and he shared that oftentimes a prosecuting attorney and a defense attorney will work out a deal that concerns scratching each other's back. Essentially, they work out a deal to help each other on different cases in order to get the desired outcome they want."

"So, in other words, Aaron, the attorneys get the desired outcome they want by getting a lesser conviction for a greater one down the road by using unconstitutional methods. Even if a man with no-prior convictions is innocent?"

"Yes, Johnathon, that is what he was saying."

"Then what separates the county attorneys from the defense attorneys?" Bridgett inquired.

"Nothing, because many of them work as a team, have drinks together, and socialize often."

"Nothing like having someone in their back pocket. It's no wonder that attorneys have the stereotype of being crooked," Bridgett stated angrily.

"Ultimately, near the end of our conversation, I asked the attorney from Chicago what makes the difference regarding the court costs and court-appointed attorney fees. He told me the state does not like to take a loss of time and money. Therefore, he suggested to Nicole and me that if I fired my attorney, I would be screwed, and if I didn't take the deal, he felt my attorney would not fight as he should. I told him that I had always thought my attorney was working hard for me. He replied that he may have been, but also to remember that perceptions given can be an illusion. He told me I should take the deal, do two years' probation and walk away. Any other choice will just burn me in the end. Lastly, he added that the state likes to give time limits as a tactic to scare people into doing things they normally wouldn't do, and this case is a prime example of your lawyer and the state working a back alley deal. I told this attorney I didn't want the deal. He explained, Aaron, if you think for a minute that fighting CPS will allow you to win if you go to court, you are wrong. CPS proceeded in your case with evidence that proved this was retaliation from Dick and the CPS workers. Furthermore, fighting the state would prove to be a failure because you have witnessed how CPS lies and manipulates. Many people have tried fighting CPS and the state and have lost. Take the deal Aaron and walk away and continue to take care of Nicole, she needs you. He wished me luck and told Nicole and I that his prayers would be with us."

"Aaron, is the court system that corrupt?"

"I will say this, Bridgett. A good friend of mine, who was an attorney for twenty-five years, said the criminal justice system – combined with the court system – is a multi-billion-dollar entity and that both of these systems love to make money, as other state entities do, too."

"Aaron, that says it all."

"Yes, it does Bridgett. After Nicole and I got off the phone with the attorney from Chicago, I told her I loved her and, if it meant two years' probation for a crime I didn't commit, at least I knew I would be by her side. I trusted the advice I received from the attorney in Chicago and what he said made sense. We were at a huge crossroads and I couldn't risk being away from her and not being able to help her with her medications, her emerging demons, and the ongoing threats to her safety and mental health. Nicole said she loved me and said that she and I would make it through the storm. The next day we went to the attorney's office to sign the deal. The attorney told me the judge would have to sign off on the plea agreement and then I could move on with my life.

Chapter Twenty-Nine

Moving Forward

"Weren't you upset, Aaron?"

"I was, Johnathon, but the court system isn't perfect, and I didn't trust the power that CPS had, nor did I trust the courts. As the attorney told me, he had seen many people be convicted of crimes they didn't commit."

"But, Aaron, the daughter changed her story four times, the stepmother wrote out what the middle daughter was supposed to say, the CPS workers lied, and you had the officer who admitted the truth about the workers."

"All true, Bridgett, but again, being able to take care of Nicole was of primary importance. I didn't want to be, as the Chicago attorney put it, another statistic. I listened to him because he made the most sense and fighting the state was futile. And that was the first time I truly opened my eyes to see the world and the justice system as it is, filled with politics and deception."

"That is tragic Aaron."

"Nevertheless, Bridgett, it continues to happen, In the end,

Nicole forgave Dick's child support, which was in the thousands of dollars, he got custody of the kids, and never had to worry again about his taxes being taken for back child support. Although that was a tough pill to swallow, not every outcome was all bad. The supervisor at CPS in our town was suspended for two weeks for withholding evidence. The other CPS worker was written up and it was put in her jacket that she wanted the officer to lie under oath."

"How did that happen, Aaron?"

"Interestingly, Bridgett, when the case was closed, my attorney filed papers against the two CPS workers and pressed the issue."

"Good for him, Aaron. Maybe he had your back, after all. Those two CPS workers should have been arrested and each one deserved more than what they got, but something is better than nothing."

"You know, Bridgett, I still see the supervisor every now and then. She tries to talk to me like nothing ever happened, but I keep it short and sweet and always will. You know, the more I think about it, everyone lost in the game Dick played. Nicole loved her daughters, but she had a hard time forgiving them for listening to him. Nicole and I lost everything, and we were homeless for seven months. Everything was destroyed, including families, friends, and a home. The only thing that was constant was anger. And the only winner out of this, unbelievably, was Dick, and he received everything he wanted from the time he made that phone call to me."

Visibly seething, Johnathon replies, "I am going to say it again, Aaron, and Father in Heaven please forgive me, but Dick is a worthless human being."

"Johnathon, I agree with you, but I also know when the man named James came and said if I helped Nicole, he would destroy everything I hold dear, he wasn't kidding."

"Did the judge sign off on the plea deal, Aaron?"

"My attorney, Nicole and I walked into the courtroom to have the judge sign off on the deal. Everyone waited as she read the court documents. After reading the evidence and the plea deal, the judge looked at the county attorney and my attorney and said, 'there is something seriously wrong with this picture.' The county attorney asked the judge what was wrong. She replied, to everyone in the room,

'Either you two (meaning my attorney and the county attorney) are trying to railroad this man, or you both are covering up something. Then she told everyone she wouldn't sign a deal that could potentially harm her career."

"Aaron, she saw right through both attorneys. So, what happened next?"

"Bridgett, both attorneys finally found another judge to accept the deal and I did two years' probation. I remember my probation officer said to me, after she read the case file in one of my visits, 'Aaron, you were thrown in a pile of shit that never should have happened.' I told her 'amen to that!'"

"You said the convictions were for aggravated misdemeanors?"

"That's right, Bridgett, a lesser class of convictions."

"How did you and Nicole recover financially from losing everything?"

"Well, Johnathon, I worked as much as I could and still took care of Nicole. We lived in the park until we could afford another place. It wasn't too long after that when my dad and mom helped us move into a place, with the help of a lady who had rental properties. Dad and mom knew about how we would go pop-can hunting for extra money. Almost every night Nicole and I were pop-can hunting and we had fun. We were doing everything we could to start over. I know I had to have a permanent address while I was on probation and, looking back, I think dad, mom, and our new landlord wanted to see us get back on track."

"Aaron, do you mind if we go inside? It's getting late in the day?"

"I am okay with that, Johnathon. Bridgett, would you like to go inside?"

"Why thank you for asking, Aaron."

"You are welcome, Bridgett."

"Aaron, sometimes Johnathon doesn't have any manners."

Aaron laughs and Johnathon has a playfully hurt look on his face.

"Bridgett, I have manners."

"Sometimes, Aaron" she continues to tease me."

As Aaron reaches for the latch on the front door, Bridgett and Johnathon follow. The rocking chairs tick back and forth as everyone enters the cabin. Bridgett heads for the kitchen with Aaron to make some fresh coffee, while Johnathon moves toward the sitting room to start the fire, turn on the oil lamps, and throw a blanket with some pillows on the floor for everyone to sit down on. Aaron and Bridgett return from the kitchen and find Johnathon comfortable on the floor by the fireplace. Once they are all comfortably sipping their fresh coffee, Bridgett asks Aaron to tell her about Nicole's passing.

"Why do you want to know?"

"I didn't upset you, did I, Aaron?"

"No, you didn't, Bridgett."

"It's okay, Aaron, you don't have to tell us. I was just curious."

"I will read you and Jonathon something I wrote but, as for the rest of the story, I am not ready to travel down that road yet."

"I understand, Aaron. What did you write?"

"Johnathon, it's called:

Emotions

Tears fall from her eyes as she asks why

her life had to end so soon.

The hands of the clock move slowly

as her life begins to drift away into the night.

I gently lift her hand and grasp it

with all the love I have and softly

tell her only Father in Heaven

knows why. The seconds seem like hours

and hours seem like days

as my heart knows the time is coming

when the final beat will give way to silence.

Sitting by her side, I wonder

if I will be strong when the pin drops.

I wonder if she will remember me

when I get to Heaven. My heart aches,

and my soul is drowning in the flood,

but I cannot show it. She asked me to be strong.

Sitting by her side, I hear, I feel

the drum beat soften. My armor weakens.

The flood comes, and I cannot hold it back

any longer. Silence creeps in. The clock stops.

The chains are broken, the earth quakes,

and my soul screams into the night.

Fallen, I have.

A cool breeze flails against my flesh.

My Angel, my love, peace she now has.

And Father embraces my wife,

my Nicole.

Aaron starts crying as the last words are read to Johnathon and Bridgett.

"It's still so hard. I miss her so much."

Bridgett starts crying and reaches for him.

"Aaron, it will be okay. Nicole loves you very much. I know you are in her heart always."

But he doesn't respond. The tears fall from his eyes and run down his cheek like the flooding waters in the middle of a storm. Johnathon also tries to tell him that it will be okay. Both Johnathon and Bridgett wrap their arms around him in an effort to comfort him.

"Aaron, I am so sorry for asking you about Nicole's passing."

"It's not your fault, Bridgett. Every day since she has been gone, I put a fake smile on my face and pretend everything is okay and it's not."

"Johnathon and I are here for you always," Bridgett adds, holding back her own tears.

"Thank you both, and I appreciate that. But what happens when I must leave this place that has no name?"

Bridgett softly replies, "Aaron, all of us will be here for you, no matter what."

"But how will you both feel when I am gone?"

"You must believe Johnathon and me when we tell you it will be okay, and we will always be with you."

Aaron wipes his tears and hugs Johnathon and Bridgett.

"Would you both like to hear one of Nicole's favorite songs?"

Smiling, and a twinkle in Bridgett's eyes, she responds, "We would love to, Aaron."

"The song is called 'The Secret Garden.'"

Aaron rises and moves to the bench in front of the piano. The fallboard and housing are opened, and he stretches his hands before playing. As he begins to play the piano, he whispers softly into the night, "Nicole, I love you so much and I am sorry I failed you. Please forgive me, my love."

Johnathon and Bridgett hear the words he spoke and tears fall from their eyes. As Aaron plays the song, the moonlight shines in through the window, lighting the piano where he sits, as if he is glowing. The music continues, and Johnathon and Bridgett hold each other, as they can feel the love that Aaron has for Nicole. After the last key is struck, he turns to see tears running down the cheeks of his two friends.

"Bridgett and Johnathon, how about we go to bed? I am suddenly very tired."

Bridgett, on behalf of Johnathon, replies "We are tired, too, Aaron."

But then Johnathon asks, "Aaron, can you, Bridgett and me all sleep here on the floor by the fireplace?"

"I am okay with that, Johnathon, as long as Bridgett doesn't mind."

"It will be like a slumber party, but without the party and just some good sleep," she says, yawning already.

Johnathon, Bridgett and Aaron get the rest of the bedding and put the stove out. Everyone feels the emotions running through their minds and bodies. A few minutes pass and, with everyone bedded down for the night, Bridgett asks, "Aaron, is it all right if we say a prayer?"

"I don't mind at all."

Bridgett begins to pray...

"Dear Lord,

Be with Aaron, Johnathon and me on this night and every night to come. I would like to say thanks to you Jesus, God, Mother Mary, the angels, the archangels, our guardian angels, and the disciples for always being there for us. Dear Father in Heaven, please watch over Nicole, all of Aaron and Nicole's children in Heaven, Aaron's mother, and all the angels that walk the earth in your name. We all love you and, in your name, Amen."

"That was beautiful, Bridgett."

"Thank you, Aaron."

Johnathon replies, "It was very nice, Bridgett."

They all say goodnight, and Aaron reaches up and turns out the oil lamp. As they rest peacefully, the sounds of Mother Nature outside are soothing. The storms have temporarily passed, both the ones that blew down the mountainside earlier in the week and the ones that still rage in Aaron's soul.

Early in the morning, Aaron wakes up and decides to start making coffee. Quietly and softly, removing Johnathon and Bridgett's arms from his chest, he moves carefully toward the kitchen to start the stove for their coffee. He looks out into the darkness of morning and softly whispers, "I love you, Nicole." Sitting at the table by the window, he waits for the coffee to be done. The smell of fresh coffee is amazing, and after twenty minutes Aaron rises and fills his cup. He steps back through the cabin quietly, trying not to wake Johnathon and Bridgett, until he reaches the front door and steps outside. He shuts the cabin door, breathing in deeply, and smells the pine trees and all that the crisp, high altitude air has to offer.

Moving to the rocking chair, he sits and enjoys his coffee, and reaches for a morning smoke. Lighting the cigarette, he looks at the sun beginning to rise in the east. The angel water fountain begins to shine brightly and woodland animals begin stirring in the forest. Startled by a soft voice, Aaron turns his head and looks to the north side of the cabin.

"Aaron, how are you?"

"Trenton?!"

"Yes, it's me, Aaron."

"Why did you leave when I went to get Bridgett and Johnathon the other day?"

"I had to go, Aaron."

"Why?"

"I just needed to, and I don't have long now, but I wanted to see you again."

"What is going on, Trenton?"

"Aaron, you are a good man and many people love you."

"I hope so."

"They do. I also want to tell you that you must look harder within the place you are, for you will see much."

"What do you mean, Trenton?"

"Aaron, you must look."

"I will."

"I must go for now, Aaron."

Trenton turns and walks back around the north side of the cabin. Aaron gets up and walks down off the porch. Moving toward where Trenton was heading, he turns the corner and sees no one. His mind wonders, again, where Trenton has gone. It's like he just disappeared.

Chapter Thirty
Our New Home

Aaron looks around in disbelief, then raises his head heavenward and prays: Father in Heaven, please guide me and help me understand what is going on in this place that has no name. The wind slowly grazes his body and a calm voice echoes in his mind, telling him it will be okay. He walks back to the front porch and up the stairs to find his rocking chair. His mind still reeling from what he thought was a visit from Trenton, he tries to piece things together. About ten minutes after his encounter, the cabin door opens.

"Good morning, Aaron. How are you?

"I am okay, Johnathon. How did you sleep?"

"Very well, thank you. Aaron. You look confused."

"That's because I am. Do you remember when I told you about the man that was on the side of the cabin?"

"Yes, I remember, Aaron. Why?"

"Well, he was back this morning and he told me, very directly, that I must look harder at the place I am in."

"What do you think that is supposed to mean, Aaron? Did he say anything else?"

"Just that he wanted to see me again. Johnathon, do you know who Trenton is?"

"Aaron, who can tell?"

"What do you mean by that?"

"I just mean that many people watch over and care about you. Let's drink our coffee and embrace the beauty God has given us on this day, as he gives every day."

"I'm not sure your answer suits me, Johnathon, but having coffee and looking at this amazing scenery is something I'll always take you up on."

While they enjoy their coffee, Johnathon thinks about Nicole and Aaron's life, and what it must have been like for both of them to fight the unseen, Nicole's disabilities, the corruption of the court system, Dick's sabotage of Aaron's character and well-being, and everything else that reared its ugly head.

"Aaron, how was Nicole's health, after all of the struggles you two went through with

your court fiasco?"

"She was on eighteen different medications from the doctors."

"Oh my word. Why so many?"

"Since I kept track of them closely, I can tell you that two of the medications helped with

Nicole's memory loss, some helped her sleep, and others helped her anxiety. The other prescriptions helped control her bi-polar, depression, schizophrenia and anger disorders. On top of all of that, she had trouble walking sometimes, due to diabetic neuropathy, and other medications prescribed by another physician which only relieved some of her pain."

"Wasn't she too young for memory loss?"

"You would think so, Johnathon. But remember when I told you about Nicole being gang raped at a young age, and how the men beat her head into the concrete?"

"Yes, unfortunately, Aaron, and again I am very sorry she suffered so much."

"Well, with that incident and the abuse from her stepfather, over the years Nicole developed short-term memory loss. The doctors told us that sometimes it can take years for the symptoms to be noticed."

"I can certainly understand that there was a lot she would want to forget, Aaron. How bad was her memory loss?"

"Some days were better than others. She was taking nine-hundred milligrams (mgs) of Seroquel at night to help her sleep, two milligrams of Xanax four times a day, twenty milligrams of Aricept, and one-hundred and twenty milligrams of methylphenidate, which was designed to wake her up from the Seroquel the night before. Nicole had so many medications and it seemed like every one of them had side-effects."

"That is an unusually large number of different drugs to take, Aaron, and especially for someone who was a recovering addict. Nicole sure was one tough lady, and I admire and love her with all my heart."

"I do, too, Johnathon. I am going to get some more coffee. Would you like some?"

"Yes, I would, Aaron, but can I get the coffee for you."

"Why thank you, Johnathon. Maybe Bridgett would like some, too, if she's awake."

Aaron, deep in thought about Nicole, waits while Johnathon goes into the cabin for more coffee. When he returns, Bridgett is right behind him."

"Good morning, Bridgett. I was wondering if you were going to join us soon."

"Good morning, Aaron, how are you?"

"I am okay, and you?"

"Just a little tired, that's all. This gorgeous morning is helping with that already."

"I hope Johnathon didn't wake you."

"He did, Aaron, but it's fine. I needed to get up anyway."

With everyone together outside, they sit and enjoy the coffee, Mother Nature's blessings, and the feeling of family between them.

"Aaron, you were telling me about Nicole and her numerous medications."

"Right. They were definitely taking a toll on her, as her body hurt almost every day. Some days I would have to bathe her, but for the most part she did the best she could, despite the side-effects of all the pharmaceuticals. I remember one of the medications messed up the pigmentation in her skin, which made it extremely sensitive to heat and sunlight. If she stayed in the sun too long, her skin would burn to a dark purple color, and the heat would completely wipe her out."

"Aaron, I hate the Devil and what happened to Nicole."

"So do I, Bridgett. Every day, I recite these words in Latin. 'In nomine Christi, ego sum venio diabolus, et gladio meus per fidem meam.'"

"What does that mean?"

"Johnathon, it means 'In the name of Christ, I am coming, Devil, with my sword and my faith.' It's reckoning that I want. The Devil should have kept his word to me and stayed away from Nicole in the end. But, with his arrogance and deceit, Lucifer couldn't do that. And, as I have thought every day since Nicole's passing, I would rather die and burn in Hell knowing that I fought the Devil than to live in Heaven, knowing I didn't raise my sword to Lucifer for what he did to my wife throughout her years and at the end of her life."

"Aaron, what do you mean when you say that the Devil should have kept his word?"

"Bridgett, just as James, the unclean spirit, came to me in the beginning, he also came to me at the end of the war. But that is for another time…"

"I am starting to see why your hatred runs so deep for the Devil. I have heard about so much destruction that you and Nicole went through. What you endured together would be a nightmare for anybody."

"It was hard on both of us, Johnathon, especially mentally and physically. Nicole didn't deserve to be treated the way she was, but many times society's pitfalls found Nicole, and the Devil was attached to them in one form or another."

"From what you've told us, I would agree," Bridgett replied. "Aaron will you tell us what happened when you got to your new house?"

"Yes, mom, dad and the landlord had made it possible for us to rent the house. It was small, with one bedroom, a kitchen, a bathroom and living room. We didn't have much to move, except little things like pictures, her shot glasses from driving over the road, and our clothing. We had each other and that's all that mattered. I remember we slept on the floor for the longest time. I was working as much as I could, and Nicole was still fighting for her disability claim."

"Aaron, was the evil still coming out?"

"Oh yes, Bridgett. Nicole and I were still being mocked by the Devil, but held on steadfastly to our faith. And, because of our allegiance to Father, the occurrences of evil showing up in our lives were slowing down."

"Why are you smiling, Aaron?"

"I just remembered how Nicole always said this verse from the Bible, 'Upon this rock I shall build my church.' She said Peter from the Bible was the rock that held the foundation to her faith."

"That says it all, doesn't it?" Bridgett shared with her own smile.

"With it only being the two of us in the house, it made it easier to start over again. Several months had passed and Nicole's disability finally came through."

"How did that happen, Aaron?"

"Johnathon, Nicole had been fighting the Social Security Administration for years and her lawyer called us one day and said the judge had an offer."

"Hopefully, this offer was better than the one your lawyer offered you when you were dealing with Dick and his daughter's lies," Bridgett said protectively.

"The attorney told us that, if we forgave the past accounting that was acquired from the time Nicole filed the claim, he would grant her disability."

"What does that mean, Aaron? Was this another back-alley deal?"

"No, Bridgett, it just meant that, from the time a person files a claim for disability, he or she may receive back disability pay from that time, which could be in the thousands of dollars."

"I understand, Aaron, so what did you and Nicole decide to do?"

"We thought it was better to forgive the back pay and have her on disability, rather than to continue fighting it any longer. After all, Nicole's medications were being covered by Medicaid and, by having Medicare with her other insurance, it helped a lot. Furthermore, she would be getting an income, as well, and that helped us greatly."

"Just out of curiosity, Aaron, what did Nicole's medications cost annually, if I may ask?"

"Her medications cost, on the average, fifty-four thousand dollars a year."

"Jumping Jehoshaphat, Aaron! That's a ton of money."

"There's no doubt about it, Bridgett."

"Please continue, Aaron."

"Right after Nicole's disability came through, the holidays were approaching, and we finally had furniture in the house and it looked like a home. It was right before Thanksgiving and her middle daughter called us and asked if she and her sisters could come visit us for the holiday. We were hesitant at first, but then decided that it was okay."

"Aaron, you must be kidding me? After they tried to destroy you and ruin your and Nicole's lives, and left you with nothing while providing Dick with a way out of paying child support?! Oh, I am at a loss for words..."

"Please calm down, Bridgett."

"I am calm, Johnathon. Didn't the girls know their mom loved them with all her heart and what they did was a load of horse manure?"

"Bridgett, there were many forces at work in our life when Nicole and I were together."

"I know, Aaron, but still…"

"Bridgett, the Devil doesn't present himself out in the open. He is slow moving, he is subtle, and he entices and makes the perception that his way is the only way."

"So, Aaron, you and Nicole agreed that the girls could come down for Thanksgiving."

"Yes, Johnathon, we told them they could join us. Despite what had happened, we thought it would be best to try and move forward with forgiveness."

"How did that go for both of you?" asked Bridgett, regaining her composure.

"The night before Thanksgiving, I borrowed a smoker from a friend and smoked the turkey with applewood and did an injection for twelve hours. We borrowed some tables from our neighbor and I cooked all night long. Nicole was happy, but didn't completely trust her daughters like she used to."

Bridgett replies, "Who can blame her for not trusting them?"

"I agree with you, but sometimes we must forgive those who trespass against us," Johnathon spoke out. "Bridgett, it's hard to forgive, but Aaron and Nicole were right to let her daughters come over for the holiday."

"I understand the value of forgiveness, Johnathon. It's just that, in Aaron's case, it would be incredibly difficult to forgive."

"Yes, it was, Bridgett, but forgiveness shames the Devil every time. But, before I continue, do you mind if I have a cigarette."

"It's all right with us, Aaron. We are ready to listen," Johnathon replied.

As Aaron reaches for the pack of cigarettes by his chair on the front porch, Johnathon and Bridgett smile at each other.

"The next morning, which was Thanksgiving Day, the girls showed up at our house around nine o'clock in the morning. I could feel some tension throughout the house, but it seemed to dissipate over time. As the day went on the girls, Nicole and I laughed and had a nice dinner. I watched Nicole and her daughters hug each other."

"How were you feeling, Aaron?"

"I was okay, Johnathon. The girls joked with me, as well, and complimented me on my cooking skills. I was surprised that all three daughters gave me a hug, too, before they left that night."

"That must have felt awkward for you, Aaron."

"It was a little uncomfortable, Bridgett, but my main concern was seeing Nicole smile. After a good day for our family, she slept peacefully in bed that night."

"Were you still staying up, watching her sleep?"

"Yes, I was, Johnathon. I always tried to stay up as late as I could to make sure she was okay."

"Aaron, it's an understatement that you really did a lot for Nicole."

"Thank you, Bridgett. I remember, during my months off from working, we would pass the time by listening to music. There were a lot of times Nicole would ask me to sing to her."

"What would you sing, Aaron?" asked Bridgett.

"I would sing Johnny Cash, Alabama, and other songs to her. She would smile from ear to ear when I sang to her. But, as time went on, her body was hurting even more, and then I had my own little accident."

A worried Bridgett asks, "What happened?"

"Bridgett, I would get up early and go to work and service grocery stores by stocking shelves. On one occasion, I had worked a long day and my boss called me and asked me if I could cover a shift for someone. I asked Nicole if it was okay and told her that Christmas was upon us and I wanted to make sure we had a good holiday. Nicole said that was fine, so I called my boss back and agreed to work. I woke up that morning around three a.m. and started driving to Centerville, which was a town about an hour away from where we lived. It was snowing and the roads weren't the best, but I kept driving. As I was coming into the town of Centerville, I fell asleep at the wheel. By the time I woke up, I had rear-ended an SUV. All I remember was this flash of light and this feeling of peace all around me."

"Oh, my dear heavens, Aaron! How bad was the wreck?" Bridgett gasped.

"On impact, the witnesses said in the report that the windows shattered, the front fenders curled up and the engine was halfway through the dashboard. When I was at the hospital, the state patrol officer said I hit the SUV so hard the car I was driving spun backwards three times."

"How did he know that, Aaron?"

"Bridgett, he had witness reports and there were markings on the road."

"How badly were you injured, Aaron?"

"Johnathon, I was up walking around four hours later."

Chapter Thirty-One

A Guardian Angel

"I had a mild concussion, and the doctor told me to rest for the next two days. Nicole was there for me, every step of the way. It was a role reversal and, even though I appreciated her watching over me, I was stubborn and didn't rest much. I was just so used to being the one that took care of her. When I was in the emergency room, the patrol officer and the doctor both agreed that someone was watching out for me because I shouldn't have been up walking around that soon after the accident. The officer added that I shouldn't even be alive by the looks of my car."

"Aaron, God the Father must have thought your work on Earth wasn't done."

"That might be, Johnathon, but the accident scared Nicole something fierce."

Looking like she almost lost her own father, Bridgett replied, "I bet that was very difficult for her, because not only did she almost lose the love of her life, but also her shield and watchman. It seems like, no matter what you did, that old Devil really wanted you gone."

"I would say so, Bridgett. I don't believe in coincidences;

however, I do believe that the Devil hates Nicole and me as much as we despise and hate him. I remember, about a week after the accident, we stayed up late one night watching a movie. As the night moved on, we decided to lay on the floor and cuddle. Eventually, we fell asleep, and at about three a.m. I felt something crawling on my body. I slowly woke up and then I woke Nicole up."

"What was it that you felt, Aaron?"

"Johnathon, after Nicole and I were awakened, we both stood up and I turned on the lights. When we gazed at the floor, there were hundreds of maggots crawling everywhere. Our house was completely clean, and there was no garbage anywhere and no rotting food in the house. All we could do is stare at the writhing spectacle, and I remember Nicole said, "In the name of Christ our Father in Heaven, be gone evil spirits!"

"What happened, Aaron?"

"The maggots were gone, as if they were never there."

"It sounds like you and Nicole didn't get much rest through the years."

"No, we didn't, Bridgett, but things were slowing down somewhat in the war between good and evil, and the fight over Nicole's soul would soon be over. I will say that, throughout the darkness we went through, which was seemingly endless at times, Father in Heaven always made sure to shed light into our lives, which allowed us to live, laugh and love."

"Were you and Nicole still seeing the psychiatrist, Aaron?"

"Yes Johnathon, and the doctor remained a positive figure in our lives, as well as a good friend to us. He really liked us, and there wasn't a day that went by that we felt like he didn't care about us. It was refreshing for Nicole and I to know that her psychiatrist cared enough to keep us both in his prayers. He always told Nicole that, out of all his clients, she was the queen and stood at the top of the mountain because she was so strong. Looking back now, I am able to more clearly see the struggles she faced every day in her life and it makes my heart hurt."

"Aaron, not to change the subject, but how was your Christmas that year?"

"Johnathon, Nicole and I had a good Christmas. Our tree was placed in the living room, in front of the picture window. The angel stood tall on the top of it, and the two of us also decorated the outside of the house. Although I made a lot of decisions for us, when it came time to putting up our decorations, Nicole told me where to put them and I listened."

Bridgett and Johnathon both smile.

"Nicole was the boss, huh, Aaron?"

"Yes, she was, Bridgett, and I wasn't going to try to interfere with her expertise where Christmas decorations were concerned. As time went on, though, we needed additional help."

"Help with what, Aaron?" Bridgett inquired.

"With me working and Nicole being at home, we needed a home health aide to help take care of Nicole. We contacted a lady at CPS who handled in-home health care workers. She knew of a program that was state-run, which allowed nurses or people to come into the home and help take care of those with disabilities. The state hired people and Nicole needed someone while I was away at work. So, I called the lady at CPS who oversaw the health program and we set up an appointment for her to come over to the house."

"What was the lady's name that came?"

"Johnathon, do you remember the night right before you and I went to sleep, and we had been talking about God sending angels on earth to help us."

"I do, and you told me about a lady named Heather."

"Yes, that was this lady from CPS. We didn't realize that she would be our angel until the end. Heather set up the workers to come in and always watched over Nicole and me. She made her visits every three months. She checked in on us and always went above and beyond for Nicole. When we needed a ride to a doctor's visit outside of town, Heather made sure we had a ride when our car wasn't running the best. She was truly a blessing sent from God and, over time, she became very close to Nicole. We were visiting with her daughters again and things seemed to be okay between all of us. Johnathon and Bridgett, the clouds are getting darker and I can smell rain in the air. Off in the distance the clouds are building."

"Aaron, do you want to go inside?"

"I think we all should, Johnathon."

About that time, thunder crashed and lightning was flashing in the Heavens. As the clouds roll in, Johnathon, Bridgett and Aaron move inside the cabin. Johnathon heads towards the fireplace and Bridgett moves into the kitchen to make a fresh pot of coffee. Aaron gets some blankets so everyone can cover up to stay warm. In the sitting room, as Aaron waits for fresh coffee, he decides to play the piano. Sitting at the bench, he first stretches his fingers. Johnathon turns his head and looks at Aaron.

"What are you going to play, Aaron?"

"Johnathon, Nicole always listened to a song by Josh Groban and Celine Deion called 'The Prayer.'"

Aaron begins to play and Johnathon grabs a blanket and covers up in the chair. Bridgett comes in with coffee for everyone and sits down to cover up, too. Johnathon and Bridgett listen as the ivory keys are pressed. Aaron looks at Johnathon and Bridgett as they smile. The rain patters against the cabin, while the thunder and the lightning crack in the sky. As Aaron plays, everyone can feel the emotions of the song. The love for Nicole can be heard in every note, and Johnathon whispers to Bridgett, "Mom is here with us." Bridgett smiles and agrees with him. Aaron finishes as he remembers how beautiful Nicole was and the love she had for him.

"Aaron, I loved it."

"Thank you, Bridgett. What did you think, Johnathon?"

"That song was as beautiful as Nicole's heart is the rose that blooms in the meadow's field."

Aaron rises and gives Johnathon and Bridgett a hug and then sits down with a blanket to cover up with. He takes a sip of his coffee and can genuinely feel contentment in his soul.

Eager to hear more about Nicole, Johnathon asked, "Aaron, tell us more."

"The worker that Heather allowed into the home to help take care of Nicole was her oldest daughter. The county nurse was set to come in once a month to oversee Nicole's general health care. Since she was talking to her daughters and things seemed to be okay, she thought her oldest daughter could do the job and get paid from the state. I was okay with it at first."

"What do you mean, Aaron, 'at first'?"

"Bridgett, as her oldest daughter was taking care of Nicole, I started to notice her attitude changing. Nicole was asking me to stay home more and wanted me to tell her oldest daughter not to come over. I asked her why and, after a little prying, she told me what was going on."

Bridgett replies to Aaron and Johnathon, "Get the straps and strap me down because my gut tells me I am not going to like this."

"Please continue, Aaron," Johnathon uttered calmly.

"Nicole told me her daughter was threatening her, hitting her and not feeding her. The oldest daughter would tell her mom that, if she didn't take her medications, there would be no eating breakfast or lunch. Other times, the oldest daughter would slap Nicole in the face and there were even days where she would let her lay on the floor after she fell."

Bridgett chimes in, "Aaron, I tell you, I am so mad right now! The oldest daughter, all of Nicole's daughters, are lower than the dirt that Satan slithers on."

"Bridgett, I was very upset, and I called the oldest daughter over to the house. When she arrived at the house, I let her come in and sit down and I explained to her what her mom had told me, and her response was that Nicole was lying. I told her that she was fired and she stood up, offered a few choice words to her mom and me, and left in a huff. After she left, Nicole and I didn't hear anything from her children for the longest time. I decided to quit my job and start college at the age of thirty-five. By becoming a full-time student, I could go to school and be home enough to take care of Nicole, but I still needed someone to help her while I was at school. She was proud of me and I was proud of her, but when I told her that, she always asked me why. I told her I was proud of her for learning faith; for having the strength to find other ways of dealing with her pain than cutting on herself; for telling me what her oldest daughter was doing to her; for fighting the Devil, and for loving me and being a survivor. She started crying and told me I was her angel sent by God to guard and watch over her as her protector. I told her thank you for the compliment, but it was God the

Father who is her protector, not me. She told me I was wrong, and that I was her guardian sent by God, and I should believe in myself more."

"Aaron, did Nicole still talk with Father in Heaven?"

"Many times, God came to her and told her she was His daughter and she is loved by Him. And I always told her that those who hear the truth shall hear His voice."

"That is so true," Johnathon replied.

"Bridgett, you are awfully quiet. Are you okay?"

"I am upset with the fact her daughters did that to their mother."

"I was, too, Bridgett, but we corrected the problem and I can't change what happened. All we could do is move on, so I started school and we brought another lady into the home to help Nicole. My days at school were about six hours long and I wasn't that far away from home if she needed me for something. The in-home health care lady was nice, and Nicole seemed to be happy. To cut expenses, I rode a bicycle everywhere, which took some financial stress off of me because it was helping us save money. And, with a living expense check from my school tuition, we were able to make ends meet. I was still on probation, but my officer was good to me and I didn't worry about a thing. Every now and then, Nicole would sit on the floor and play with her stuffed animals and would ask me if I would play, too."

"Would you play with her and her stuffed animals, Aaron?"

"I would, Bridgett, because through the years she would slip back in time, and at those moments it seemed to help her if I would join in and play. When these moments occurred, it was only for a short time, but I also knew that it would happen again. I remember two angels that came down during those times and Nicole always recognized them when she was in that state of mind. When the angels watched us playing with the stuffed animals, there was a joy that I cannot explain in Nicole. The angels kept peace all around us and she would laugh without a care in the world."

"What were their names, Aaron?"

"Johnathon, the angels were Keith and Kyle. It seemed, at the time, that the war was almost over with the grasp that the Devil had on Nicole. Many of God's heavenly hosts fought hard and died, and just as many demons died throughout the thirteen years that Nicole and I were together."

"Aaron, I don't know what to say."

"Bridgett, to this day, I am still trying to find the words for everything that happened with the angels, the demons, God and the Devil, and Nicole and me. Several weeks had passed and, shortly before the end of the war, I remember Nicole was in her rocking chair and I was on the love seat. I looked over at her and immediately recognized that she was not herself."

"Who was she, Aaron?" Bridgett asked with worry in her voice.

"She was a little girl. When I asked her who she was, the little girl replied, 'My name is Amy.' I asked Amy where Nicole went, and she said Nicole is in Heaven with the angels, visiting. Then the little girl asked me if I would play with her and the stuffed animals. I told Amy that I would for a while, but Nicole needed to come home. Amy told me that it wasn't time for her to come home."

"What did you say, Aaron?"

"Bridgett, I told her it was okay, and that she could stay."

"Aaron, if I may ask, why do you say Nicole slipped back to her younger years when these children seemed to be from Heaven?"

"Bridgett, because some may believe it was psychological and others may believe the children were actually from Heaven. I believe the children were angels, but people have a right to believe what they want to believe. For me, it's an understanding that everyone has free will to choose what to think and feel."

"I understand, Aaron" Bridgett stated, appeased.

"Amy would ask me if she was bothering me and I told her, 'Heavens no.' As the night went on, Amy and I played, watched television and laughed. Through the years I used to tell Nicole stories every night at bedtime. She always said it relaxed her and gave her peace. That night, Amy asked me if I would tuck her in bed and tell her a story."

"Aaron, that is very sweet."

"Thank you, Bridgett, but I only did what I had to do through the years for Nicole because I loved her. So, that night, I tucked Amy in and told her a story. I slept on the floor next to where she was sleeping and I thought, by morning, that Nicole would be back, but she wasn't. Amy was still present, so I asked her again where Nicole was, and she told me Nicole was with Father and Mother Mary in Heaven. I asked Amy if she was hungry and she told me she was, so I cooked her breakfast and we ate together. Later that day I took her to the store and bought her treats and ice cream. By the time Amy and I got back home, the ice cream was gone and she was happy. She had a smile on her face from ear to ear."

"Aaron, what were you thinking during all this?"

"Well, Bridgett, I knew Nicole would slip back to herself again, or another child would come down from Heaven. As I told you both, she always talked about how she could walk with the angels in Heaven. To me, it was like she had this gift, by the grace of God, to walk in places never seen before by the living. Amy was an angel and I know she was, just as I know the things Nicole and I saw and heard were real. I guess I just went with the flow and treated Amy as I would want to be treated. I took care of her for three days and it was a Sunday night when she started crying as she sat in Nicole's recliner."

"Aaron, why was Amy crying?"

"I asked her what was wrong, Johnathon, and she looked at me with tears flowing and said she had to leave. I asked her why she had to go and she replied that she was sad, and then she said, 'I know now that all daddies aren't bad people and I love you.' Amy cried hard that night and, as she got up out of the chair and gave me a hug, she whispered in my ear, 'You will be my daddy from now on and I must go.' Before she left, she told me, 'Love is the reed that feeds the soul and I am the reed in the river that flows in many hearts.'"

Chapter Thirty-Two
The Three Messengers

"*I* started crying, as I held her in my arms, and then Nicole was back and Amy was gone. When Nicole came back from Heaven and walking with the angels, she asked me why I was crying, and I told her my tears were happy tears. She wiped my tears and said she had this feeling of peace throughout her soul. She smiled, thanked me, and whispered, 'I love you, Aaron.' She talked about Heaven, the angels, Mother Mary, Father, and how beautiful it would be for her and me when it's our time. Peace seemed to be on our doorstep and we embraced the peace with love."

Aaron looks at Bridgett and sees her crying.

"Bridgett, are you okay?"

"Aaron, that is sad, but joyous, too, in many ways."

"Bridgett, it was joyous to see Nicole feel so much peace in that moment. But that was the night when everything changed."

"What do you mean, Aaron?"

"Do you both remember when I told you about the crosses Nicole and I wore around our necks?"

"Yes, we remember, Aaron."

"Well, we laid down in bed together and during the night I was visited by three of the most beautiful angels I had ever seen. In this vision I was standing in this field with lilies all around me and there was this rose bush blossoming. The three angels had long, curly hair past their neckline and were draped in fine garments. Their voices were soft and very soothing, and when they approached me, the one angel spoke and said, 'We must take your cross to Heaven, for it's in the hands of God that shall seal the ties that bind.' At that moment the other angel took her hands and reached around my neck and uncoupled the cross from my neck. The three angels smiled, and the third angel said, 'Blessings are upon you and Nicole, always.' She then took my hand and showed me the seal that God had put upon the Devil."

"Aaron, what was the seal?"

"I remember, Johnathon, that the angel told me, 'Behold the power of our Father in Heaven, for this is the seal that binds the Devil – the faith Nicole has and forever shall have until the end. As I looked at what the third angel showed me, I saw Hell, and then this light appeared that was beautiful. But it was also a light that was a seal through which Lucifer could not pass. The third angel took my hand and I was back in the meadowed field with the blooming rose bush. After returning to the field, the first angel kissed my forehead and then all three angels were gone. When I woke up my cross was gone. I asked Nicole if she had my cross that I wore around my neck and she said no. I looked everywhere, but couldn't find it. I told Nicole about my dream, and she smiled and said, 'Aaron, when I walked in Heaven with Mother Mary and Father, they both told me it would be over, and that three angels would come to take up our cross.' I asked her why she didn't tell me that when she returned from Heaven, and she told me Father in Heaven said she couldn't tell me until the waters flow across the sea, for it is that time when I would stand in the meadowed field with the lilies. So Nicole knew about the three angels and how I would be visited."

"Did the angels come back, Aaron?"

"Johnathon, after that night, Nicole and I had silence. It was just the two of us. The demons were gone, the angels were gone, and we had peace.'"

"How long had it been, at that time, since you and Nicole first met?"

"Johnathon, it was in 2000, and the war didn't finish until 2013."

"Bridgett replied, "So, for thirteen years you and Nicole fought this battle and every other battle that came your way."

"We had no choice but to fight. I wasn't going to let the Devil consume her life as he had done in years past, before I met her, and neither was Nicole. I remember she asked me how I was able to stay strong throughout the years. I told her it was the faith that my mother and father instilled in me that made it possible. I asked her the same question, given all of the abuse and torment she faced since she was a little girl. She smiled and said she made it through the years hoping she would meet a man like me. Nicole also told me that night, when she was a little girl lying in bed, crying and praying to Father in Heaven for help, that she always thought that God wasn't listening, but now she knew better. Then she told me, 'Father in Heaven sent you, Aaron, to me, your wife. It may have taken some time, but father was not blind nor deaf to my cries, and I love you, Aaron, for following the path that He set you upon.' I told her that I loved her, too, and that I would do my best to remain steadfast on the road God had made for me."

"Aaron, I don't know what to say."

"There were many moments that Nicole and I had together, Johnathon – both good and bad – that left me speechless. Mostly, though, I remember the pain she went through all her life, the angels who died and went to God's special place, as well as the ones who survived the battle. I was thankful that Nicole could finally have peace, and we had a lot of support over those thirteen years we were together. I owe much thanks to our Father in Heaven, his Father, Mother Mary, the disciples, St. Mathew, St. Mark, St. John, St. Luke, St. Isiah, St. Samuel, the archangels, St. Michael, St. Uriel, St. Gabriel, St. Raphael, and St. Amintiel. There are also the children in Heaven that called Nicole and me mother and father: Mattie, Amber, Joshua, Lucas James, John Paul, Samuel, Dan, Marcus, Amy and Christina. Thanks also to Bill, Luke, Joyce, Maurice, Doug, George, Ed, Eddy, Leo, Ron, Gilbert and Edward."

"That is a lot of names Aaron."

"And that's not even all of them, Johnathon. The night the

angels came for the cross and showed me the vision was the last day Nicole and I talked with them for a long time. There was a piece of both of us that was sad because we both felt like we lost our friends. We reminded each other that Heaven is within us, and all who hear the truth shall hear God the Father and his angels. But, for some reason, it just wasn't quite the same. Johnathon and Bridgett, I am going to step out on the deck and smoke a cigarette."

"We will wait hear for you, Aaron."

Aaron gets up out of his chair with tears running down his face as he thinks about Nicole, and everyone else in Heaven that he misses. With the wind and the rain coming down, Aaron puts his boots and coat on before stepping outside. He reaches for the latch and steps outside with this feeling that he soon will be leaving this place that has no name. Saddened by his thoughts, he lights the cigarette as the storm intensifies. Thinking back, he remembers when Nicole always said that rain is the cleansing of Mother Earth, and each drop of rain is a tear of joy and sadness from Heaven above. He takes his time smoking the cigarette and knows his new friends, Johnathon and Bridgett, will go away, too. While his thoughts weigh him down as if the Earth was on his shoulders, a calm voice echoes in the wind, "I love you, Aaron." He stands up and runs down off the porch. Again, he hears the lady's voice in the wind, "Aaron, I love you with all my heart."

He yells back, "I love you too, honey! I love you, my wife, and I am sorry I failed you."

Tears fall as Aaron drops to his knees, repeating these words, "I love you Nicole. I love you."

Johnathon and Bridgett come outside and see Aaron in the mud, on his knees, crying. They come down off of the porch and help him up out of the rain. Bridgett tells him, "It's okay, whatever you are feeling right now."

"Don't be sad any longer," Johnathon adds. "Let's go back inside and get you into something warm."

On their way back to the cabin, Aaron asks, "Did you hear a lady's voice?"

"Both Johnathon and Bridgett reply, "We did, Aaron."

"I hurt so much. I miss Nicole and my heart aches every day."

Bridgett replies, "I know, Aaron, and I can see your heart is broken."

"Aaron, Nicole is with Father in Heaven," Johnathon says in an attempt to comfort him. "It's Nicole's voice in the wind that calls from above and very few people in this world can hear the cries from beyond the plains."

"Aaron," says Bridgett gently, "go change your clothes in the room and when you come out. I will have some fresh coffee and a warm blanket for you."

Making his way into the downstairs bedroom to change his clothes, Aaron looks at the curio cabinet that holds the same bears as he has, as well as the two roses and the shamrock Irish blessing. He wonders when he will see his love again....

Back in the sitting room, which is filled with silence, Aaron covers up with the blanket and takes a sip of coffee. The fire in the fireplace crackles and emits a life-affirming glow, and the rainfall hits the cabin like the pitter-pattering of a squirrel racing across the roof. Johnathon, Bridgett and Aaron can hear the wind blowing through the pine trees in the wilderness.

"Aaron, are you okay?"

"Bridgett, I wish I could say yes, but I can't. Since I have been in this place that has no name, so many things have happened, and I still don't understand any of it."

"Aaron, I promise you it will be okay in the end."

"As much as I love you both, and all of us have been on a journey together, sometimes a heart cannot be mended. I wish it could, but this heart, my heart, is not the same any more since Nicole passed away. I have tried to express how losing her has torn me apart inside. Would you both like to hear this poem called:

Broken

The threads of time still hold the past

in my existence, in my heart

and in my life. I wander in darkness

looking for absolution, for peace. I pray

to be filled once again with wholeness.

But I know some things can never mend

a broken heart. Still, I move quietly

into the darkness of night.

Mother Nature pulls me close

to her breast as I walk

in the shaded moonlight. My mind escapes

into the yesteryears, yearning

for that moment when I held my love,

once again, in my arms. I fall

to the wilderness floor as the tears

trail my body. I fall to the soiled land,

and leaves embrace my flesh

as if I was a child filled with innocence.

A cool breeze swirls around me,

a calming sensation flows softly within.

I gaze upon the dark night sky.

A white-feathered owl approaches,

perching himself high above the land.

Our eyes meet and I breathe slowly.

The picture fades before me,

as I remember how beautiful my Nicole was

and forever shall be.

"Aaron, that was beautiful."

"Thank you, Bridgett. When I can't take the pain from my memories, I try to put my emotions on the canvas of white so that they have somewhere to go."

Johnathon replies, "Aaron, there is no doubt in my heart you loved Nicole with all of yours."

"I did, Johnathon, but there is also that part of my heart and soul that is filled with regret."

"Aaron, what regrets do you have? You were there for Nicole and you taught her so much over the years."

"Johnathon, you don't understand now, but you will in the end, why Nicole's death was my fault and why I failed her."

"Aaron! please…"

"No, Johnathon, her death was my fault. Now, if you will both excuse me, I would like to go smoke a cigarette."

"Aaron, I understand. Bridgett and I will wait here for you."

Aaron wraps his blanket around him and steps outside. He finds his place in the rocking chair and lights the cigarette. The air is a little chilly, the rain is coming down and the wind has a fresh scent. With each drag of the cigarette he takes, he looks at the angel fountain and still wonders who the stone cutter was that carved the angel so beautifully. The fountain never dulls and seems to reflect a continual glimmer – both in the light of day and in the darkness of night. Aaron sees a fawn slowly walking toward the porch, seeking shelter from the rain. He wonders if this is the same fawn that slept at his feet a few nights ago. The fawn walks up to the porch and up the stairs, approaching him. The fawn's nose once again nuzzles Aaron, and once again his mind goes back to the Eskimo kisses Nicole always gave him. As soon as the memory becomes almost real again, the fawn turns and runs off into the woods. Aaron smiles and feels comforted by one of God's creations.

Chapter Thirty-Three
Nicole's Bedtime Story

*B*ridgett peeks out the cabin window to check on Aaron and sees that he is okay. Aaron smokes his cigarette and, as he takes his last drag, he rises out of the chair. The wind is cold, and the rain is falling steadily. He re-enters the cabin and finds his seat in the sitting room. The cabin is warm from the fire and, with the blanket wrapped around him, he feels cozy.

"Aaron, you were telling Bridgett and me about the stories you told Nicole before bedtime."

"I did tell her stories almost every night."

"Can Bridgett and I hear one of your stories you told Nicole?"

"You may Johnathon, if you both really want to hear one?"

"We do," they tell Aaron.

"After I would tuck Nicole in every night, I would sit up in bed and run my fingers through her hair. She would look at me and tell me she wanted to hear about:

The Little Lost Girl

Many years ago, when the land was free, there was a mother, father and daughter who lived on the plains out west. The father had built a log cabin with his wife. There were woods, a small stream, and plenty of green grass growing everywhere. The father stood six feet two inches tall, and had a grey beard and short hair. The mother was five feet ten inches tall, and she always wore a white dress and a ribbon in her hair. The little girl was nine years old. She wore a grey dress and had long, black hair. Now, the little girl had no one to play with except her mother and father, and sometimes she played by herself. She would find sticks or pretend she had friends. The family was happy and had faith, and they held their own church service in their cabin upon the beauty that God created. Then, one day, the little girl decided to wander into the woods. Mind you, Nicole, the mother and father told their daughter not to play so far away in the woods. (Nicole would always stop me there, Bridgett and Johnathon, and say, 'what happened?' and I would smile at her and tell her to let me finish. She would say 'okay' and I would continue…). The parents knew their daughter would get lost, but the little girl didn't listen and went into the woods to play. The little girl laughed, played, and enjoyed herself without a care in the world. But, as the day went on, she noticed that the sun was setting. The little girl looked around and she knew she was lost. She had no idea where she was and became scared, with a feeling of helplessness. (I would always smile because Nicole would whisper, 'What did she do, Aaron?' and I would tell her, 'I am getting to it, hang on'…). So, after the little girl knew she was lost, she started crying and calling for daddy and momma, but her parents couldn't hear her. The sun was almost down, and the little lost girl sat below an old tree and cried. Then she saw this little white, fluffy bunny coming towards her. The bunny stopped and stared. The little girl stared back at the bunny.

The little girl spoke to the bunny, as she sniffled and tears fell, 'It's okay. I won't hurt you.' The bunny must have understood what she said, because the bunny hopped right up to her. The little lost girl pet the fluffy bunny and then she heard the bunny say, 'What's wrong?' and the little girl replied to the bunny, 'I am lost, and I don't know how to get back home to my ma and pa.' About that time, the little girl sees a papa deer, mamma dear, and a baby fawn come out of the shadows. The papa deer says to the little girl, 'What's wrong?' and the bunny replies to the papa deer, 'She is lost and can't find her way home.' The little girl says to the papa deer, 'I am scared,' and then the tears flow heavily from her eyes. Then, papa deer looks at mamma deer and mamma deer nudges papa deer. Papa deer walks over to the little girl. The fluffy bunny hops off the little girl's lap, as papa deer grabs her shirt with his mouth and flings her on his back.

The little girl, not knowing where she is going, asked the woodland creature where they were headed. Hearing no response, the little girl rides calmly on the back of papa deer. Then she sees light from the moonlight that is no longer shadowed by the woods. As the woods clear, the mamma deer, papa deer, baby doe, the bunny, and the little girl leave the woods and all stop on a hilltop. The little girl hops down and sees her cabin down below and hears her ma and pa yelling her name. She turns and hugs all the deer and the little bunny, and then begins to run to her parents. As the little girl reaches her parents, her dad picks her up and holds her tight with her ma. The father asks his daughter, 'How did you get home?' and the little girl tells her parents about the papa deer, momma deer, baby fawn, and the bunny, and how the woodland animals brought her out of the darkness. Both ma and pa look at each other with disbelief. The little girl says, 'Look pa, look ma,' and, as the little girl's parents look at the top of the hill, they see the deer and the bunny standing with the moonlight shining down on them."

"At this point in the story, Nicole would be smiling, and I would smile, too. I would ask her what the moral of the story was, and she would say 'I don't know, tell me honey.' I would say, 'Nicole, sometimes in life, a person gets lost in the world, and when he or she becomes the feather floating upon the wind, the breath that flows from the unseen will let the light shine through and the darkness is no more.' She would ask why and I would tell her, 'Just like the deer and the rabbit found the little lost girl in the woods and carried her home again, Father in Heaven is always watching, guiding and leading the way home for all those who are lost. Nicole would smile and about ten minutes later she was asleep."

"Aaron, that is an amazing story and I love it!"

"Thank you, Bridgett."

Johnathon, also smiling from the story about the story, replies, "Aaron, that is a story I have never heard before, and it was very well-spoken. How many stories did you tell Nicole over the years?"

"I have about thirty different stories I told her, and she loved every one of them."

"So, Aaron, how was it going with you and Nicole when you enrolled in college?"

"As time went on, Johnathon, I was still taking classes and on probation, but she and I were okay. She was regularly going to the psychiatrist and taking her numerous medications. The one thing I started noticing with her, though, was that she was starting to take her methylphenidate medication more than she should. This was a medication that acted like speed and would amp her up if she took too much. Over time, she complained that she needed more of it to get her motivated. I was concerned about her becoming addicted to her Xanax, methylphenidate, and other medications, but I was not the doctor. I told her she needed to slow down but, by the time I mentioned it, she would have already taken her month's supply of methylphenidate in four days."

"Aaron, how much was she prescribed for the month?"

"Bridgett, she was given one hundred and twenty mgs daily, and they were twenty mgs pills. She would color her pictures for hours and hours while she was on methylphenidate. The other seventeen pills were set on a daily schedule of three times per day."

"Aaron, why wasn't the methylphenidate on a set schedule?"

"Because pills like Xanax and methylphenidate, Bridgett, were to be taken at certain times, but those medications are also deemed 'as needed.' I would get frustrated when Nicole would take all the methylphenidate pills."

"What would she do while being on the pills?"

"Johnathon, most of the time she wouldn't talk and just colored pictures. My frustration came when she was out of the pills and asked me to get her more. I would tell her I couldn't, and then her frustration kicked in and there wasn't anything I could do for her withdrawals every month. Some days were better than others for her and, as you both know, her health wasn't the greatest. She was now addicted to the prescription pills and all I could do was try and comfort her. She would ask me to sit with her and read the poetry I had written. She always said my voice was soothing, and it relaxed her and took her mind off the withdrawal symptoms she was experiencing."

"Aaron, were those pills fast-acting and short-lasting?"

"Yes, Bridgett, between the Xanax and methylphenidate, Nicole needed them to function and the pills were very addicting. After years of being on eighteen different medications, I hated what the pills had done to her body."

Johnathon replies, "Aaron, I can't begin to understand how Nicole and you felt. It seems there was one thing after another for you two."

"The struggles were never far away, and it was mentally difficult for both of us. I was getting to my breaking point, but I was hanging in there, just as Nicole was."

So, what happened next?"

"Bridgett, I think Johnathon told you I had a second son, didn't he?"

"Yes, he did, but he also said you and your son didn't speak any more."

"That's right, Bridgett. I remember Nicole and me talking about my son, Isaac, as we were sitting in our living room. We both wanted to see him again and, for years we tried keeping track of his whereabouts. But, as I told you, Johnathon, my ex-wife lived in five different states and had twenty-eight residences. She was always bouncing around."

"Aaron, didn't you say you were still paying child support without being able to see Isaac."

"I was, Johnathon, and even though Nicole and I were dealing with our many challenges, we still looked for Isaac."

Johnathon, somewhat hesitantly, asks, "Are you going to tell us why you and Isaac don't speak any more?"

"I will do that, along with telling you what we went through when he came to live with us. It was in the spring of 2014 when Nicole and I located my ex-wife and Isaac. They were living one state over from Iowa, in Nebraska. When we found this out, we hired an attorney in Iowa and another one in Nebraska. Nicole and I wanted custody and, after about six months of court hearings, we were finally granted it. Isaac came to live with us and we were all happy at first."

"What happened, Aaron?"

With a smile, Aaron replies, "Hang on, Bridgett, I am getting there. I have to say, you and Nicole would have gotten along great."

"Why is that, Aaron?" Bridgett asked, somewhat flattered.

"Nicole would be impatient and want me to hurry up with what I was talking about. So you two are a lot alike."

Bridgett smiles, "Why, thank you, Aaron. That is a very kind compliment."

Johnathon whispers in Bridgett's ear, "I told you, Bridgett."

"When Isaac came to live with us, we took him shopping for new clothes because my ex-wife wouldn't give us his clothing. She was being obstinate, due to our dislike for each other, so she withheld the clothes out of principle. Anyway, Isaac was home, and Nicole and I enjoyed our time with him. However, things changed about a month later. Once, when we were sleeping, I felt this presence standing over our bed. Isaac was watching us sleep, and when I woke up, he had this look on his face that was completely blank. It was a cold, dead stare and he didn't move. I asked him what was wrong and he didn't respond. I sat up out of bed, after I woke Nicole up, and asked Isaac, again, what was wrong. That time he responded, but only to say that nothing was wrong. I told him he needed to go back to bed and get some sleep. Nicole and I laid back down and Isaac went back to bed, as well, but as I laid in bed that night my mind knew something was off with him. I had seen that look before."

"What do you mean, Aaron?"

"Bridgett, in years past, when Nicole and I were dealing with the unclean spirits, she would stare at me just like Isaac was staring at us that night."

"Aaron, are you saying…?"

"I wasn't sure, at that point, Bridgett. I blew it off, but I remembered what the unclean spirit had told me about destroying everything I held dear to me in my life. It wasn't long after that episode that Nicole and I were talking and thought it would be best if Isaac went to a therapist to be assessed. I had a good friend, named Pam, who had great credentials in therapy and we trusted her expertise. We took Isaac to see Pam and, after he was assessed, she brought us into her office and told us she believed Isaac had sustained some abuse, but she didn't know to what extent. Nicole, Isaac and I left and went back home. Later that night, Isaac started telling us how he could weigh out marijuana, cocaine and make mixed alcohol drinks."

"How old was Isaac, Aaron?" a concerned Johnathon asked.

"He was fourteen years old when he came to live with us. I remember Nicole asking him questions about the drugs because she knew quite a bit about them from her past addictions. As she asked Isaac certain questions, he knew (to a tee) everything she was talking about. The next morning we called Pam and told her what he had shared with us. Pam asked us to bring Isaac back to her for another assessment."

"Aaron, I don't like the way this is going."

"Well, Bridgett, neither did Nicole and me."

Chapter Thirty-Four
Gone Away Inside

"After Pam assessed Isaac again, she told Nicole and me that she believed he had been severely traumatized, but again she didn't know what type the abuse was. Once again, we all left her office, but Isaac had to come back twice a week for therapy. When we got back home, Nicole started watching television. I went to my desk to do homework and I told Isaac to do his chores. As I sat down at my desk and began working on my Composition paper, I noticed Isaac out of the corner of my eye. I turned my head and he was standing there with the same blank look he had that night when he was standing over us while we were sleeping. This time, though, he had a knife in his hand, and said, 'Look at what I got, dad. The next time you tell me to do my chores, I will find this knife a new home' and then started laughing. I told Isaac that, before he threatens me with a knife, he better be ready to use it, because threats don't scare me. Nicole was standing in the doorway, watching, and Isaac put the knife down and went back to doing dishes. Nicole pulled me to the side and said she was a little scared. I told her it would be okay, but I also told her I needed to watch Isaac very closely, and that she should, too."

"Aaron, what was going on with him?"

"Johnathon, I think you know. As time went on, Pam told Nicole and I to have Isaac journal his thoughts and every week we were to bring his journals in with him so she could read the book. As Isaac started journaling, he time-stamped, dated and signed every page with precision."

What did Isaac talk about in his journals, Aaron?"

"At first, it was simple stuff, Bridgett, like what he did at school or who he played with, but that all changed."

Both Johnathon and Bridgett tell Aaron they would like more coffee.

"Aaron, would you like some fresh coffee?

"I would, Bridgett. If you are going to get some coffee, I'm going to step outside and smoke a cigarette."

Johnathon and Bridgett head for the kitchen and Aaron goes outside to smoke. With Aaron outside, Johnathon and Bridgett have an opportunity to talk.

"Bridgett, can you believe everything that has gone on in Aaron and Nicole's lives?"

"I can, Johnathon, just as I know you can, too. The Devil is everywhere in the world and, unfortunately, they were amid destruction for thirteen years."

"Bridgett, it breaks my heart to know mom went through all that, and then to know Aaron suffered, too."

"Johnathon, all I can say is that God was with them. I am curious, though, as to what else happened with Isaac."

"So am I, Bridgett."

After refilling their coffees, Johnathon and Bridgett return to the sitting room and Aaron comes back in from outside. Finding their seats, they all sit back down and take a sip of coffee.

"Aaron, you were telling Bridgett and me about Isaac."

"Yes, as you both know, something wasn't right with him. I remember Nicole and I were in the living room when I noticed him standing in front of the picture window, clutching a backpack in his arms. I thought it was strange and I asked him what he was doing.

Isaac replied, 'Nothing, dad.' I told him to bring me the pack so I could look inside, but he wouldn't hand it over, so I got up and grabbed it from him."

"What was in the pack, Aaron?"

"Johnathon, when Nicole and I opened the backpack, I found a utility razor knife, some rope, one cigarette, a lighter, duct tape and a cloth."

"What was all that for, Aaron?"

"Johnathon, when Nicole and I questioned Isaac, he wouldn't tell us at first. But then he said the stuff was for 'his first victim.' We were shocked and had no idea what he planned to do. We immediately called Pam and told her what was going on, and she urged us to take him to the emergency room for evaluation. We followed her advice, and after admitting him, we went back into a room with the doctor. Isaac told the doctor, after a few minutes, the stuff in the backpack was, again, for his first victim. The doctor asked him who his first victim was and what he planned to do. He responded by saying that, 'When Freddy gets done teaching him how to hunt, he will become the most perfect serial killer this world has ever seen.' Isaac then said his first victim was a friend he knew from across the street. He told the doctor he was going to take the girl, strap her down, cut on her for a while, stop and smoke a cigarette and then cut on her some more. Then he added, 'Right before she dies, I will hurt her one last time before the life leaves her eyes.' That night, Nicole, the doctor and I stepped back and looked at each other."

"Oh, my dear heavens, Aaron, Isaac sounds..."

"Yes, I know Bridgett..."

"It was Isaac's first time being sent to a hospital for psychological treatment. He spent three days under observation and then was released. When he got home, Nicole and I called Pam to discuss what the doctors told us. Pam thought it would be a good idea if we informed our friends across the street about what was happening with Isaac."

"Why did Pam want you to do that, Aaron?" Bridgett asked, puzzled.

"It was for safety, primarily. Just in case we needed help, our neighbors would know about our situation."

"How big was Isaac, Aaron?"

"He stood six feet three inches tall and weighed one hundred and fifty-five pounds, Johnathon."

"That's a big boy."

"Yes, he was, Bridgett. Isaac started his medications to control his tendencies and, for the most part, they were working. Nicole and I were trying to work with him as much as we could, and Pam was still seeing him twice a week. I remember I was making his bed one day and was changing his sheets. I lifted the mattress and found more journals he had written. I sat down at the table and began reading them and could not believe what I found."

"What was in the book, Aaron?"

"Bridgett, Isaac had never lived with Nicole and me in the thirteen years we fought the Devil and went through all of the things we did. But, in his journals, he talked about the altar, Hell, and other things that were associated with our struggles."

"You must be kidding, Aaron?! How is that even possible?" Johnathon inquired, mystified. "Was there anything else in the journals he wrote about, like things that happened in his past?"

"Isaac talked about how his biological mother was into drugs and alcohol. He also explained in his journals how he was hurt by the men his mother had in their house. He wrote about a time he was pinned down to his bed and the male figure hurt him as he watched pornographic materials on television."

"Oh, my lord, Aaron!" Bridgett blurted out.

"Another time, he wrote about how he slept on the roof of his house to keep away from his mother's boyfriends while they drank alcohol and did drugs. When he woke up the next morning, hungry, he went looking for his mom and found her passed out with two other men. Isaac stated that there was cocaine, marijuana and alcohol bottles everywhere. So, he went looking for food on the streets, in dumpsters, and while searching for food, he was beaten up by multiple attackers. Nicole and I took the journals to Pam and let her read what Isaac had written. When she read the journals, she advised us to bring CPS into the picture."

"Why did Pam want CPS involved, Aaron, and did she know anything about your past experiences with them?"

"No, she didn't, Bridgett, but she thought it would be best if Isaac was placed in what the state calls 'child in need of assistance,' or C.H.I.N.A. By having the state come into our home, Pam thought the state could aid in getting the help Isaac needed since he was a danger to himself and others. We were not thrilled about calling CPS to help us, but we both thought, along with Pam, that he should be institutionalized. When the state was contacted, and we asked for help, the county office where Nicole and I lived wouldn't accept the case. We were all stunned. The worker for CPS said Isaac was getting the therapy he needed and being looked out for in a positive manner. So, we continued trying to help him in every way possible, but then he changed even more. Shortly thereafter, Isaac went into the kitchen while Nicole was in the living room and I was at my desk doing homework. That's when I saw him coming at me with a butcher's knife. I stood up and began trying to get the knife away from him, and Nicole immediately called the neighbors and told them what was going on. The husband from across the street came over and helped me get the knife away from Isaac.

That day, I called the authorities out to the house and explained what happened. The officer told me, Nicole, and the neighbor there wasn't much the police could do except take Isaac to the hospital for psychiatric evaluation. I asked the officer about juvenile hall until something could be figured out, and he said he could take Isaac, but he would be released within twenty-four hours. Once again, we took him back to the emergency room and he was admitted and transported to a hospital in another town."

Aaron, how long was Isaac in the hospital this time?"

"He spent five days in the psychiatric ward and then was released, Johnathon. Nicole and I had to pull him out of school and began to home school him because of his tendencies."

"With everything that was going on with Nicole, you were also dealing with Isaac full-time at home?"

"We had no choice, Bridgett. Despite his emerging psychological problems, we loved him and just wanted everyone to be safe."

"I can understand that, Aaron."

"It was hard for Nicole and me, but we managed. The school system thought it was for the best that Isaac was not in classes. Pam also deemed it best, in her professional opinion, for him to not be tempted to hurt other classmates. We tried to get the state involved, but they would not have any part of helping Isaac or helping Nicole and me."

"So, the state did nothing for Nicole and Isaac. At least they were consistent."

"Sometimes, it's the organization that fails people, Johnathon, and sometimes it's the people working within the organization. And, at other times, like with the House with the Dove, it's both."

"Which 'house,' Aaron," Bridgett asked.

"Oh, I will explain that at a later time, although you won't like to hear about it. At any rate, the final time Isaac was admitted into the hospital was for fourteen days. Nicole and I were sitting down and watching television when we got the call from the hospital. The doctor told us he had to be isolated in his own room. I asked the doctor why and he explained that Isaac was brushing up against other girls his age and then would go into his room and violently masturbate."

"Oh, Aaron! Why did he do that?" Bridgett, visibly rattled asked.

"Apparently, Isaac was acting out the violent thoughts in his head. I told the doctor that we had tried getting help from the state, but with no success, and that Nicole and I would like to have him institutionalized so he could have around-the-clock care and better odds of not hurting himself or others. The doctor at the hospital called Pam and they discussed what should happen. Somehow, the two of them persuaded CPS to help us, but they did so by going above the jurisdiction of the county office and calling their head office. I bet you can about guess what I am going to tell you next..."

"Oh, please don't tell me that the same person..."

"That's right, Bridgett," Aaron confirmed before she even finished her sentence. "Nicole and I were stunned to see the same worker that we had dealt with in the past."

"This can't be good, Aaron" Bridgett said anxiously.

"You could bet on that. This is the same CPS worker that took over our previous case – the one that said she would like to get her hands on Nicole's daughters."

"Aaron, so you encountered the Devil's right hand once again," Johnathon pointed out.

"I would agree with that statement. When the CPS worker came into the house and talked with Nicole and me, she didn't seem very concerned. I expressed to her that Isaac needed to be institutionalized because he was a danger to himself and others. We had the documented reports from the hospital, the psychiatrist, and Pam regarding his behavior, the content in his journal entries, and the violent fantasies he had shared with me. But none of it mattered, if you can imagine that. The lady from CPS didn't take any of it seriously, nor did she listen to Nicole, Pam, the psychiatrist or me, but she had to open the case because her supervisor in the state office gave the directive."

"Aaron, what did the state worker finally do for you?"

"Well, Johnathon, the CPS worker whom Nicole and I had such a horrific experience with, due to her blatant disregard for the laws, read through the file and came back with a decision. But before I finish, you both look tired. Would you like me to finish this story tomorrow?"

Both Bridgett and Johnathon nod in agreement, "We are tired, Aaron. But we also want to know what happened with Isaac."

Bridgett tells Aaron and Johnathon she will put the wood stove out and dump the coffee. Johnathon throws another log in the fireplace and Aaron makes the beds. Bridgett still sleeps on the couch, and Johnathon and Aaron sleep on the floor in the living room. Everyone settles in for the night, under their covers, and the cabin is peaceful. The only sounds to be heard are the lulling songs of insects along the mountainside.

"Aaron, are you afraid of leaving this place?"

"Admittedly, I am, Bridgett. As I have gotten to know you both, I feel something inside of me that says you are close to me in some way. I don't know any other way to describe this feeling I have. It's like you both are very special."

Johnathon replies, "Aaron, a gut instinct is usually right."

"The other reason I fear leaving this place that has no name is because I have no one and nothing to return to – only the memories of the ones I hold dear in my heart."

"Before drifting off to sleep. Bridgett whispers, "Aaron, if you have memories, you are never truly alone."

Chapter Thirty-Five
The Loft

*W*ith Bridgett and Johnathon sleeping comfortably, Aaron's mind can't stop thinking about Bridgett's question about leaving here – wherever this is. His eyes open as he hears the crackling of the fire. Outside, the wind has picked up, and he can hear the tree limbs swaying from the strong gusts. He thinks to himself how the weather outside almost always matches the storms inside his head – sometimes just a calm breeze, and other times a tempest of turmoil. He decides to walk upstairs and, as he quietly reaches the loft, he lights the oil lamp that sits next to the book called *A Love Story*. He relaxes in the rocking chair by the bed and stares at the fireplace mantle. Rocking back and forth, he remembers how Nicole would do the same to calm herself after she was hurt as a little girl. With sadness upon his heart, Aaron's mind flashes to the stories he listened to from Nicole for all those years. The imagery in Aaron's mind is intense and his soul cries out in the wilderness.

From his rocker, he notices the mattress on the bed across the room, with the comforter that says, "*I Love You*." He looks again and there seems to be a slight hump under the pillows. Confused, he rises out of the chair and places his hand where the hump is on the mattress. Moving the pillows and pulling the quilt back just a little bit, he finds a wooden box with a latch on the front. The top of the box reads, "Forever." He raises the wooden box to his face and can smell the pine from which it was crafted. He returns to the rocker and closes his eyes, afraid to open the box. Just as his eyes close, he hears a calm, tender voice say, "I am here, my love." He whispers back, "I love you, honey." With new-found courage, he slowly pulls the latch up on the pine box and begins to open the lid. Before him is a picture of himself with Nicole. He remembers the time when they had the picture taken by a sketch artist in a gallery. As he takes the picture out, he sees a sealed envelope beneath it.

Tears begin to fall from his face as he sets the picture down and reads the front of the envelope. Just then, he hears footsteps on the staircase and quickly puts everything back inside the wooden box and returns it to where he found it on the bed. As he wipes his tears, Bridgett enters the room.

"Aaron, what are you doing?"

"Nothing, Bridgett, I couldn't sleep after you asked me about leaving this place with no name. I thought you were asleep."

"I woke up and you weren't there, so I came looking for you. Were you crying?"

"I'm okay, Bridgett. I was just revisiting some of those memories I mentioned at bedtime."

Bridgett sits on the corner of the bed. "Aaron, can I tell you a story?"

"Sure, Bridgett. A role reversal would be refreshing, thank you."

"Aaron, first let me say that love is a very powerful thing between two people. And that love swings like a pendulum. With the good times, there will also be a shift to bad times, and sometimes the two people who love each other will need time away for many different reasons. I want to tell you this story about a young man and a young lady. Then I will explain why I told you this story. It's called:

Runaway Cafe

"Sometimes, in our life, we dream of the perfect mate, and aspire to make the oath of friendship and love come true. Love is not easy, dauntless, or kind. In fact, it can be rather tough on the mind. The first date seems hard, as we don't really know what to do. '*Does she want this?*' or '*Does she want that?*' Both the man and woman are nervous about the unknown, but are also ready for anything to rise or fall. The young man who ventures out on his new journey trembles inside with questions and fear. But, pierced by the prospect of affection, he looks upon their distance, and hopes to someday draw her near.

So, at the young age of twenty, he wonders if this could be the one. He finds himself outside, feeling the freedom of the wall-less lands. Envisioning her tonight, he tells Mother Nature, '*I'll be all right.*' Late in the day, he realizes that time is passing him by quickly. He follows the same path that he had taken earlier and finally makes it back home. Walking up the stairs to his bedroom, he wonders what he will wear tonight. Sifting through his closet, he pulls out his best suit. Slowly dressing in front of the image, he looks at himself and hopes that tonight he will shine.

He leaves his room and his mother hears his steps upon the stairs and comes to see. She smiles at her son and says, '*I'm proud of thee.*' The reservations have been set at the café. All prepared, he clutches the keys and drives down the road to meet that beautiful woman named Rose. He arrives and enters the doors. Sitting at the table, Rose smiles with her red velvet lips, and stands as her man catches a glimpse. Wearing a blue silk dress that follows every curve of the lay, she wonders if this is enough to make him stay.

Intimidated by how beautiful she looks, he humbly makes his way to the table. As he draws near, she notices how handsome he is, '*so slender*' and '*so sleek.*' Their bodies embrace; both feel the intense fire that's burning between them. Rose kisses him softly on the lips. They sit, and the waiter pushes their chairs in. The evening seems perfect. They inch closer together as the night moves along. Wondering what the other desires is the only question they each have for one another.

Silently, as they gaze into each other's eyes, the answer is clear. They rise from their seats and step out into the moonlight. He reaches for her hand as they walk upon the land. Softly, she whispers in his ear and asks if he will draw her near. His desire has come true as he holds her tight, both of them walking step in step on this perfect night. They stop at the loch he calls his own. The swoon shimmers on the lake, and a cool breeze tingles upon their flesh. Their passion heats as they fall to the ground, and their bodies engage, caressing each other as they become one. Silence sets in after their love has been shown. They turn their heads to one another and smile, and all that is said is '*Forever.*' Holding each other, they feel that this is their first memory. Not wanting to let go, they hold on tighter and tighter to each other. This time, he whispers in her ear, '*Marry me, my perfect dear.*' The sun slowly rises upon the land as he clutches the golden band."

"Aaron, I tell you that story because love can be exciting, but what many of us do not realize is that, with love, there are also hardships that can arise at a moment's notice. It is those hardships that can make us stay, or leave, the ones we love. When things happen, we react in different ways and sometimes the euphoric feelings we have make us blind to what may come. In some cases, the two who love each other lose sight of what brought them together, or one of them may pass away, but the love will always continue. It is our actions in the end, not in the beginning, that defines us, and the love we have for one another is the water that flows beneath the stars in Heaven. The young man who found his one true love in the story made lasting memories with her.

You, Aaron, of all people, know that we forget the little things that make us love and it is hard to find them sometimes, but when a person does find that special feeling again, it might be too late. What I am trying to say is this: the love that you and Nicole had was the love of two soulmates and was a very special love. Both of you had good hearts and wanted the best for each other. Hang on to the memories of what you two shared, for that will be your greatest reward."

"Bridgett, thank you for the wonderful story. It's just hard, sometimes, and the guilt I harbor for her death rages within me like the strongest storms."

"Aaron, I don't believe you caused Nicole's death, nor do I believe you failed her."

"Well, thank you, for those kind words."

"Can I also tell you something else, if you don't mind?"

"I don't mind, Bridgett."

"A man or woman can walk this Earth for years and never find his or her treasure, their true love. And when he or she never finds their true love, his or her heart becomes filled with emptiness and sorrow. Another man or woman can walk this Earth for years searching for the treasure he or she longs for, and he or she may find their true love. But when he or she finds their true love, the man or woman may lose sight of what brought him or her together. And, over time, like sand sifting through one's fingers, his or her love is gone. Finally, there are those who find their treasure and embrace it, cherish it, and hold the treasure within their heart for a lifetime. I tell you this, Aaron, because there is something in your heart that cries silently – that very few people see or hear. And I want you to know that I see and hear the cries of your heart and soul with the unspoken words you project outwardly. I know, Aaron, in time you will tell Johnathon and me some of those unspoken words, but for now please give me a hug. Then, let's go wake my brother up and make some coffee."

Aaron smiles and gives Bridgett a hug. As they head downstairs, his mind wonders what the letter says in the wooden box, and how the picture of Nicole and him got inside it. While Bridgett wakes Johnathon, Aaron looks out the cabin window and sees the sun cresting in the east. Everyone in the cabin is awake, and after their good mornings, they fill their cups with fresh-brewed coffee and head to the front porch. Last night's winds have died down, and the cool morning breeze is refreshing. The sound of the river is peaceful, and the sky is filled with every color imaginable. Aaron breathes in deeply and fills his soul with the gifts of Mother Nature and from the Heavens above. He reaches down for his cigarettes and lights one before sitting down to relax. Johnathon and Bridgett smile at each other and the morning seems wonderful.

"So, Aaron, you were telling Bridgett and me about how the CPS worker had made a decision regarding Isaac."

"Right, Johnathon, she had to do as she was told by her supervisor from the state office, so she brought Isaac into the court system. But little did I, Nicole, Pam, or the psychiatrist know what she was about to do behind our backs."

"Oh, no!" Bridgett replied. "What did she do, Aaron?"

"The CPS worker contacted Isaac's biological mom, my ex-wife, who was living in Florida. Once she heard what was happening with her son, she was afforded a plane ticket and transportation by the state."

"Aaron, I thought your ex-wife lived in Nebraska?"

"She did, Bridgett, but then she moved again when I got custody. So, when she arrived from Florida, Nicole and I, along with Pam, the psychiatric doctor and Isaac, had a court hearing to decide what to do with him."

Nervously, Bridgett interrupts, "My gut tells me this lady from CPS is about to do something incredibly stupid."

"Please, just listen to Aaron," Johnathon instructed Bridgett.

"After the judge heard that Isaac was a danger to himself and the people around him, as well as what the doctors had stated, she told everyone in the courtroom that the biological mother created the problem and she could deal with Isaac back where she lives. The judge took custody away from Nicole and me, and gave custody of Isaac back to my ex-wife. We all told her that, if she decried this, Isaac will offend within six months of being with his mother."

"What did the judge say?"

"Bridgett, she told everyone in the courtroom that it was not her problem and the state will not institutionalize Isaac. She also stated that Isaac needed to be far away from Iowa. It was clear that the CPS worker wanted to just get rid of the situation and not help my son, and she used the judge to carry out her wish."

Angered, Bridgett interjected, "What is the matter with society?! To let a child be neglected from getting help is simply pathetic."

"There is no doubt about it, Bridgett. But just look at Nicole's life and how the state neglected to help her during her nightmarish childhood years. It happens every day to children, the elderly, and those who are deemed unfit to contribute to society. I remember, right before we all left the courtroom, I told the judge that if Isaac offends and hurts someone and I am notified, I will tell whomever it may be that you knew my son was a danger and complete liability is on CPS and the court system."

"What did she say, Aaron?"

"Not much, Johnathon. She asked us to leave, my son went with his mother, and that was the last time I saw Isaac. Just over two months later, I got a phone call from the state of Florida. When I answered the phone, I was at the college. It was a prosecutor in Florida calling to tell me Isaac had offended. He asked me if I could fly down there on behalf of my son. When I asked what Isaac had done, the prosecutor told me that Isaac had assaulted two females. I explained to him what had happened regarding the state and the courts in Iowa, and told him there was nothing more I could do for him. I called Pam once I got home and explained to her what had happened with Isaac and what I told the prosecutor.

She told me I made the right decision and that the son I knew as a baby was gone. As Pam and I talked, she also said, 'Aaron, the court system and the CPS worker have made it impossible for you to help Isaac' and she was sorry. I told her that maybe I could have fought harder, and she responded by telling me that I fought more than most people would have in a situation like mine, and I had nothing to feel bad about."

Chapter Thirty-Six

Sorrow

"*I* remember how devastated Nicole and I were because we both knew the Devil was still at work. Even though things were sealed, Lucifer's servants were still prowling around."

"Aaron, in the book of Job, chapter seven, verse one, 'The life of man and woman upon this earth is a warfare, and his and her days are like the days of a hireling,'" Johnathon quoted.

"Johnathon and Bridgett, Nicole loved Isaac as I did, and we didn't understand how the ones who represent the state could be so blind to the severity of the situation. But we also knew that Lucifer, the father of lies, had enough demons walking this earth to turn daylight into darkness, and that his evil ones would never stop working at destroying lives. Nevertheless, we were alone again, and we managed. We took car rides together, listened to music, and enjoyed our time as much as we could. But it was hard for both of us to deal with so much hurt. I was still in college and Nicole was always telling me she was proud of her man, but I didn't feel proud. I felt like a failure."

Johnathon replies, "Aaron, if I may say, the tragedy of the situation you and Nicole were in was a failure of society. In the Bible, in the first book of John, chapter two, verse ten through eleven, it states:

He that loveth his brother or sister, abideth in the light, and there is no scandal in him or her. But he or she that hateth his brother or sister, is in darkness, and walketh in darkness, and knoweth not whither he or she goeth; because darkness hath blinded his brother and sister's eyes."

"Aaron, I tell you what John wrote because too many times the sight of society has gone dim and, in the absence of light, corruption sets in and consumes the better sense of many, even the strong and those with faith. You and Nicole found corruption in the darkness of society and the destruction was horrific. Nicole went through life plagued by the hands of the Devil, who tried, in every way possible, to fill her with torment, abuse and loss. And you, Aaron, who once leaned against your old 1979 pick-up truck, asking Father to show you more and guide you in your journey, found the lost sheep Christ was searching for on this Earth. But you also found the lion that prowls the earth, seeking to destroy God's most cherished gifts. When James, the unclean spirit, came to you and asked if you were going to make your mark, you stood tall in the name of Father in Heaven and chose to fight, just as Nicole made her choice to fight."

"Thank you, Bridgett. Despite being told that the Devil would destroy everything I held dear to my heart, Nicole and I chose to love our Lord and we chose to love each other."

"I know, Aaron, but one cannot have one without the other. If one believes in Heaven, then one must believe there is a Hell. Just as people love, they will come to know pain and hurt. In the midst of still waters our eyes can become devoid of sight, as the waters become engulfed with the blood that bleeds from the sands upon the flesh. Aaron, can I read you something?"

"Of course, Bridgett."

"Okay, Aaron, it's called:

Silence

"Why does God stand in the silence of the trees to watch those who walk upon the land?

I say this to you! One must first consume the bark of the wood to digest the leaves that bring life. Without the veins of the roots below the surface of the trees, one cannot hear the voice echoing in the distance. It is not God that stands silently in the wilderness to watch, but the living whose eyes are blind to what we see. If one can consume the bark of the trees and digest the leaves that bring life, then the blind can truly see our Lord God standing upon the land above the breast of Mother Nature.

Aaron, I believe that Johnathon told you that walking in different planes of existence, or having dreams about Heaven and Hell, are a gift and should be embraced – just as love is a gift between two people, like you and Nicole. Many times, our Lord God has warned his children on Earth about the Devil and his cohorts tempting man and woman. And He has also taught his children to love thy brother and sister. But I also know, Aaron, that many people love their possessions on Earth more than they love God the Father. Don't get me wrong. There are those who love our Lord in Heaven, and not everyone prides themselves on material acquisitions, but greed is at the heart of much of our soul's discontentment."

"Bridgett, our Lord is good, and I know God has watched over Nicole and me through the years, and she and I love him with all our hearts."

"I am grateful for the gift of your and Nicole's faith, Aaron," said Bridgett.

"So, did you ever hear from Isaac again?"

"Not in any traditional sense, Johnathon...but if you two don't mind, let's get some coffee. Would you both like some?"

"We would, Aaron, and I will help you."

As Aaron and Johnathon walk into the cabin to get fresh coffee, Bridgett rocks in the chair. The wind is subtle and the light from the sun is warm. Bridgett notices the baby fawn coming around the north corner of the cabin. Their eyes meet and the fawn stands still, just looking at Bridgett, who smiles and begins to silently pray.

"My Father in Heaven, I come to you my Lord, God of Abraham, to ask that you help Aaron through this time. For his soul cries silently in the shadows of light, and his flesh is marred from the fangs of the Devil. My Father, God of Abraham, help him, for he has fallen in the brush that feeds the lands. I beseech thee and pray for the light upon his soul. Amen."

Just as Bridgett finishes her prayer, Johnathon and Aaron walk out the cabin door with fresh coffee. Aaron lights a cigarette and, savoring the first drag, notices an eagle in the distance, soaring high in the heavens. Johnathon and Bridgett smile as they look at Aaron and hear the white-tailed eagle's piercing cry through the skies.

"Johnathon, do you see the eagle?"

"I do, Aaron."

"Isn't she beautiful, Bridgett?"

At just exactly the same time as Aaron poses his question, the eagle flies away into the canyon. Aaron rises and walks down off the porch, with his cigarette in one hand and his coffee cup in the other.

"What are you looking for," Johnathon asked.

"I wanted to see where the eagle went. Everything that comes into my life has a way of disappearing."

Bridgett and Johnathon smile from ear to ear as they look at Aaron. After a few moments, he begins to walk up the stairs to find his seat and get comfortable.

"So, Aaron, where were we?"

"We left off where Nicole and I had the worker coming into our home to help us and I was learning as much as I could in school. Being a 'nontraditional' college student made me feel a little uncomfortable, but I continued with my studies. I remember one of my professors in college that I had for a speech class I took. He had a Ph.D. in literature and was very intelligent. He walked up to me one day and said, 'Aaron, I need you to do me a favor.' I replied, 'What favor do you need from me?' and my professor responded, 'I want you to take a poetry class of mine.' I told him I hated poetry and I didn't want to. He confidently replied, 'Take one class of poetry with me as your instructor, and if you don't like the class, I won't try to persuade you to take another poetry class again.' I told him I would try it out and he told me I wouldn't regret it. When I asked my professor why he wanted me to take the class, he answered by saying, 'Aaron, your voice is deep, your stance is tall, and I believe you yearn for avenues of expression in your life.' He also told me, 'One day you will write, and when you write your voice will carry.' I thanked my professor for the kind words and told him I would sign up for his class."

"Is his class where you learned how to write?"

"Yes, Bridgett, my professor showed me the way to paint on the canvasses of white by using words."

"What was his name, Aaron?"

"His name was Immanuel, Bridgett, but I always called him 'doctor.'"

"Why did you call him doctor, Aaron?"

"It was a sign of respect and because he earned his Ph.D. He was different than most instructors. In my eyes he was a warrior, peacemaker, and philosopher."

"You must have really respected your professor."

"I did, Bridgett, and I still do. As I would write poetry, Nicole would listen to my every word without fail. She always said my voice was relaxing and the words I spoke were beautiful. She would listen to me for hours as I read to her."

Bridgett, looking perplexed, asked, "Not to change the subject, Aaron, but what guilt lays on your shoulders that cries silently?"

"Why do you ask, Bridgett?"

Suddenly, Johnathon notices a man walking in the distance. Aaron stands up and sees Trenton coming towards the cabin. When he gets to where they are sitting, Aaron introduces him to Johnathon and Bridgett.

"Trenton, we have an extra chair. Would you like to sit down?"

"I would, Aaron. Thank you."

Johnathon looks at Bridgett with a smile and asked Trenton, "What are you doing here?"

"I came to see all of you."

"Do you know Johnathon and Bridgett?" Aaron asked.

"I do know them, Aaron."

"Johnathon and Bridgett, how come you didn't tell me you knew Trenton when I told you about him coming to the cabin?"

They look at each other and Bridgett replies, "We thought it would be best if we didn't say anything to you at that point."

"Help me understand why you wouldn't say anything."

Trenton speaks up, "Aaron, I asked them not to say anything. I wanted you to get to know them first."

"Trenton, Johnathon and Bridgett are like family to me and I love them as my own."

"I am glad to hear that, Aaron."

"What are you doing here?"

"Aaron, I came like the eagle upon the wind to say that you are not alone. I stood by the white marble angel statue when Johnathon and Bridgett didn't know where you were. I sit now with you to whisper of the time when you read the Bible to your first born, Nicole, and those whom you and Nicole called your own. Many hearts were filled with joy and sadness as the waters parted in the end. My love grew as I listened to the spoken and unspoken words from your lips and your soul, from behind the glass. I found a heart within the brush that grows upon the desolate land in the heat of day. I remember your heart was a dragon's heart, Aaron, and even though the waters parted from above, below and within the dust, the veins run deep in the reed of life."

Aaron begins to cry as he whispers, "My heart is not a dragon's heart any more, Trenton. Would you all like to hear a poem that addresses the reasons why?"

"Yes, please, Aaron," Bridgett says on behalf of all.

"I wrote this after Nicole's passing. It's called:

Sorrow

1

I am the Huŏlóng.

My heart is a dragon's heart.

At the highest peak, my brothers and I stand,

Gazing over the land.

2

We loved them,

And they loved us.

We gave them fire and rain.

We gave them life.

3

Wanting to please them more

We gave them the last flare we had.

Coughing out the fruit from within

We stood proud, as they ate the gift.

4

The villagers became intoxicated

With the fruit; they changed.

Wanting more, the swords flashed

As they cut my brothers down.

5

Flowing nets, arrows, and spears blackened

The sky. The wailing of my brothers engulfed

The winds. I looked upon the land,

Now covered in my brothers' blood.

6

Hunted, I am.

I find refuge in a cavern

Behind the fall, wondering why, yet knowing

We gave too much.

7

Darkness is now my home.

As I hide from my foes,

I creep slowly in the dark night sky, with fear,

Only to embrace loneliness.

8

In my heart, I know

I was loved once in my life,

And they loved me, too, at first,

Calling me lóng.

9

I offered love.

My brothers offered the same

But they wanted more;

They wanted our gift.

10

Now my brothers are dead

And I am alone,

Living in darkness,

The last of my kind.

11

I now fear the people I loved.

My heart is no longer a Dragon's heart.

Death calls my name, and I know,

I am the last to go.

Chapter Thirty-Seven
Loss of Sight

*T*renton replies, "Aaron, your heart softly glows in the night, feeling the darkness of day. I can see the sadness upon the shell that casts around the stones that lay upon the earth. I also see you have given up and your roots begin to lay barren."

"Trenton, you would understand why my heart fades if you knew how much I failed my wife, and my Father in Heaven. My eyes have seen much by the grace of God, and sometimes I wish I could un-see the unseen. But Trenton, Bridgett, and Johnathon, my Father in Heaven was not done showing me the world as it has come to pass with the evil whom walk the earth."

Bridgett replies, "Yes, Aaron, there is much evil in the world, but there is also good. Do not let the seed be crushed from the mill stone, but rather let it bear fruit in the wind."

"Bridgett, I am trying not to, but it is hard. Through the years, Nicole and I were getting tired. Her body was getting weaker and the medications had taken a toll on her, as well. I was exhausted and used all my faith to battle the Devil, as Nicole did when she learned faith. That is what 'Sorrow' was about – love, pain and suffering – and now that the love of my life is gone, I do hide in the shadows."

"Aaron, you said our Father was not done showing you the unseen. What did you mean?"

"As time went on, Trenton, I felt myself withdrawing inside from Nicole and what she and I had been through. She was still taking her medications and still addicted to her doctor-prescribed pills. My anger for the Devil had grown, and I hated the pills for what each one was doing to her body. Looking back, she was withdrawing, too, in subtle ways. She was very quiet when taking her pills and I was having a hard time accepting everything we were going through. After thirteen years of dealing with Heaven, Hell, the angels, the demons, the CPS and court systems, and the losses we suffered, to say we were both struggling would be an understatement. In fact, I remember Nicole telling me one night, as we laid together in bed, that life makes no sense anymore. I told her that she was right, and I missed walking and talking with the angels. She cried that night as we held each other, and she told me the Devil will never allow her and I to rest. It seemed impossible to deny, so I agreed with her…"

"I am going to take a break, if you all don't mind."

"We don't mind, Aaron."

As Aaron lights his cigarette, the others decide to get some fresh coffee for everyone. Aaron sits on the front porch, looking at the land before him, and wonders why this place has no name and very few people walking upon the breast of Mother Earth. The white marble angel statue stands tall and beautiful. The waters running behind the cabin are peaceful and the wildlife is abundant. Aaron thinks about Nicole and how her smile was like the breeze flowing on a mid-summer evening. Smiling once again, he rocks back and forth in his chair as he smokes his cigarette. The door opens and Johnathon, Bridgett and Trenton return with fresh-brewed coffee.

"Aaron, here is your cup of coffee. Will you tell us more?"

"Thank you for the coffee and, yes Trenton, I am ready to share more with you. I continued my studies at the community college and was learning as much as I could. I was riding my bicycle back and forth to save money. Nicole would help as much as she could around the house, but her body hurt every day and the medications had side effects that made her ache. On top of that, she had diabetes, which made her neuropathy kick in all the time."

"What is neuropathy," Johnathon inquired.

"Diabetic neuropathy is caused from high blood sugars. It is the firing of the nerves which causes pain in a person. Nicole's memory wasn't the best, and many times I had to take her to the hospital to get treated for high blood sugar levels. Sometimes her blood sugars would be five or six hundred and cause her to pass out. So we had the in-home healthcare worker coming over to help while I was at school. But the days were long, and Nicole and I didn't talk as much as we used to in the past."

"Did you and Nicole ever hear from the angels again?"

"Bridgett, we didn't, and on many occasions we agreed that we missed our friends in Heaven. I found myself meeting new people at the college and Nicole was still taking those highly addictive prescription pills. A year had passed and, although we loved each other, things were different between us. I was finding every excuse not to be home. I was setting up the medications, as I always did, and preparing pre-made meals for Nicole, but I also began seeing Pam, the psychologist, to try to get some direction in life. I needed help sorting out the issues I was having within myself. I was angry, for what happened to both my sons, to Nicole, with Dick and his daughters, and the CPS workers and corrupt lawyers. I was angry at myself the most for not being able to help my sons and, even though I loved my wife, it had become a different kind of love than before."

"Aaron, you and Nicole went through so much together…"

"Johnathon, I know we did, but…I started seeing other women and cheating on Nicole. I had just become numb to my life and learned to block out my feelings. I was running away from everything. Pam told me that, given what Nicole and I had gone through, with so much loss of family and friends, the feelings I had were intense and didn't have an outlet that was positive. Once I remember Pam asking me when I would take the armor off that I had worn for years. I told her that I couldn't take off my armor because I didn't want to feel any more. She replied, 'Aaron, you have helped so many people in your life and, at some point, you will have to rest.' Then she added, 'I have heard from a multitude of people that you have helped them, in one way or another, and that is why I call you the street psychologist. It's because you are not afraid to stop and listen to people on the streets and help them in any way you can.' I told Pam I appreciated her comments, but I couldn't rest because I always get hurt and can't allow that to happen, nor can I allow the Devil to continue his works against Nicole and me. She told me, in one of my visits, that cheating on Nicole and running away is not the answer, and my actions did not reflect me fighting the Devil. I knew she was right, but told her I needed some sort of normalcy in my life, to which she asked, 'What is normalcy, Aaron?'

I replied that normalcy, to most, is not dealing with Heaven, Hell, the angels, the demons, and remembering the evil I had seen and the horrific stories Nicole had told me. It wasn't Nicole's fault that I started cheating, or why things were the way they were in our life. It was all my fault and I know that."

"Aaron, that is a heavy burden to put on yourself," Johnathon stated sympathetically.

"It's true, though, Johnathon. It was all my fault, not Nicole's."

"But no man can control the works of the Devil."

"Maybe not, Johnathon, but I could have fought harder against him. I could have tried…"

"Aaron, you told me once that the Devil is subtle in his ways of enticements. That subtlety is like a fisherman fishing. The reel is cast, with something desirable being offered, and then he or she waits patiently. When the time is right, and the bait is taken, the fisherman sets the hook. That is when the deceit, masked as joy, sets within the soul."

Bridgett jumped in, "The Devil works in the same manner."

"Looking back, I can see that now. I remember Nicole would ask me if I was seeing someone else, and I would lie to her and tell her I wasn't. One of my excuses for staying away from home was that I needed to finish assignments for college. It was like I could breathe outside of the home. I didn't have to remember or fight the unseen. It was the illusory perceptions that can make a man or woman fall when the Devil casts unto him or her a fragment of what he or she desires. Finally, the things around Nicole and I started crumbling."

"What do you mean, Aaron?"

"We talked, Bridgett, and decided to move her to the tower apartments where she could be around other people."

"So, was that her decision, your decision, or did you both make that call?"

"Trenton, I was blocking out so many feelings during that time. We were arguing a lot, and, for the first time in over a decade, I just gave up. We separated, but we were still married. In answer to your question, it was all my doing to send Nicole to the towers. For a while I was there every day. I still meal-prepped, set her medications up, helped her bathe herself, and took her everywhere she needed to go in town. I gave her everything in the house and made sure things were taken care of for her."

"Aaron, if I may say so, I see why Nicole went to the towers. By having her there, it allowed you to play in the shadows and commit adultery. You suppressed your emotional side and began being deceitful to your wife. Is that an accurate assessment?"

"You are right, Trenton."

"That is a little harsh, don't you think?!" Bridgett piped up in defense of Aaron. "They went through Hell together, Trenton. They lost their children, fought the Devil, and were hurt in so many ways. It's not fair for you to judge…"

"Bridgett, Trenton is right. I was a liar and an adulterer. And to this day, I carry that burden with me."

"Aaron, I am not excusing what you did, but I am saying you were tired after fighting every day for thirteen years."

Johnathon replies, "We don't need to fight."

"Aaron, I meant no harm," Trenton admitted honestly. "I was just expressing what I felt."

"It's okay, Trenton, and again, you were right."

"Aaron, you became lost, and it is true that the Devil has many enticements, and the flesh is one of them," Bridgett added.

"That is true, and the Bible says in the book of James, chapter three, verse sixteen, 'For where envying and contention is, there is inconsistency and every evil work.'"

"If you all don't mind, I am going to smoke a cigarette."

"Aaron, it's okay with us. We understand."

Aaron's mind and body feels the burden of failure as he lights the cigarette. Taking the first drag, he inhales and images of his wife flash before him. He stands and walks down the cabin stairs, making his way to the cliff beyond the angel water fountain. He moves slowly and, with each step, gets closer to the cliff that overlooks the valley below. He tells himself over and over that he failed as he walks by the angel water fountain. One hand holds the cigarette and the other hand touches the marble angel. Tears stream down his clenched face as he stands on the edge of the valley, looking out at the beauty of Mother Nature…

"Aaron, what are you doing?! Bridgett yelled.

With no response from him, again Bridgett yells out, "Come back to us!" but he still does not say a word.

He watches the night set in and feels the cool, soft breeze brush against him. Looking out, he remembers how he let the lady down who loved him the most in the world. He falls to his knees, crying out into the wilderness, "I miss you my love and I am so sorry I let you down. My heart hurts every day and I am so sorry…"

Johnathon, Bridgett and Trenton run down off the porch and get Aaron up and back to the cabin. Bridgett tells him, "It's been a long day and the night is upon us. Let us all get some rest."

With the bedding out and the oil lamps and the fire burning, Trenton sits with Aaron on the couch in the living room and whispers, "I am sorry if my words hurt you."

"It's not your words that hurt me. It is the sinful works I committed before my Father's eyes, and before my wife, that plague my heart. It is the burden that weighs heavy on the temple stones of my soul. There is much you do not know about what went on in Nicole's life and mine. I always loved her, Trenton. I wasn't always the best husband and I know that, but I tried."

As the night moves on, Aaron is sound asleep, but Trenton, Bridgett and Johnathon are unsettled. Bridgett quietly gets up and whispers to Johnathon and Trenton, "Are you two up?"

They both respond softly, "We are, Bridgett. What is it?"

"I want to speak to you both outside."

Johnathon whispers, "This doesn't sound good."

The three of them quietly go outside and walk down by the cliff-side so Aaron cannot hear what is said.

"I called you both out here because I am worried about Aaron. I understand that Aaron cheating on his wife was wrong, but this man, *our father*, has a heavy burden on his shoulders. The stories of what he and Nicole went through were horrendous and I think a little bitterness is in your heart, as well, Trenton."

"Bridgett, you are right. I wish things would have been different and I would have loved to have known him."

"Well, all of us were robbed of knowing our mother and, in your case, your father, but we are all family and the time we have with him is short. You know what he and Nicole went through, so I am just asking you, Trenton, to embrace your father now."

"Okay, but I don't know how to act or even what to say to him..."

Chapter Thirty-Eight
Temptation and Lies

"Just be yourself, Trenton," Bridgett says calmly.

"I will try my best," Trenton whispers as they all return to the cabin to get some rest.

They enter the cabin soundlessly and, once they lay back down and are covered up under the bedding, their eyes grow heavy and they soon fall asleep. The cool, moonlit night is placid, and the only sound that can be heard is the soft crackling of embers in the fireplace and the gentle breeze blowing outside.

The rising sun announces morning through the cabin window, waking only Aaron. Rising out of bed, he looks at Johnathon, Bridgett and Trenton and thinks to himself, *I love you all.* He moves to the kitchen and begins making coffee. Cracking the window by the table, he feels the wind flowing into the cabin. The wood stove heats up and the coffee begins to brew. He sits for a few moments looking at the picture Mother Nature and God have painted outside. He thinks to himself that this wilderness is gorgeous, but fear surfaces within him, too, as he feels his time here in the place that has no name is coming to an end.

Breathing deeply, he re-establishes calmness and pours himself a cup of coffee. Walking out from the kitchen, he leaves a note on the china hutch buffet telling his friends that he will be on the bench down by the river. He grabs his coat and puts his boots on. Opening the cabin door, he quietly shuts it behind him and grabs the lighter and the cigarettes off the front porch. The morning is cool, and the wildlife roaming around brings a smile to his face as he sits and listens to the water rushing from the caps above. A few Mute Swans can be seen swimming in the river, and he remembers back to when he first came to this place that has no name. His mind, body and soul feels peacefulness, but he wonders why the light that led him here has not shined since he arrived.

Lighting a cigarette, he listens to Mother Nature and embraces her beauty. A voice echoes in his head, "Aaron, I love you and thank you, for I am proud of you and I am with the angels. I know your heart aches every day, and half of your soul is gone, but remember, my love, your heart is my heart, and my heart is your heart." He smiles and his eyes moisten as he whispers in the wind, "I love you, Nicole." Finishing his cigarette, he hears the crunching of the leaves on the pathway to the cabin behind him. He turns to see Johnathon, Bridgett and Trenton walking towards him.

"Good morning, Aaron. I brought you out a fresh cup of coffee," said Bridgett. "I was hoping you needed one."

"Well, thank you, Bridgett, and good morning to all of you."

Trenton is the first to respond and, after his talk with Bridgett the night before, he asks, "Aaron, will you tell us more about Nicole?"

"I would like that, Trenton. During the time that Nicole was at the towers, I would sometimes sleep in my car, and at other times I would stay with her in her apartment. I needed clarity, as I was struggling with everything. We had been through so much loss and heartache while fighting the Devil in a war between Heaven and Hell, as well as on Earth, that it took its toll on me. I was running away from everything, including Nicole. I was going on social media and dating sites to meet other women. I thought that, by seeking other women to date, I might find the normalcy I was looking for in my life. In my state of mind, which, looking back, was delusional, I thought that the further I ran away from everything that happened, the better chance I might have of finding peace. But, oh, was I wrong, as the many hard lessons I have learned since then have shown me.

Nicole was patient with me, and most of the time she didn't question what I was doing. And when she did, I would lie to her and make up some excuse. I ignored all my feelings and completely suppressed the voice inside of me. I started dating another woman and lied to her about being divorced when I was actually married. I moved in with her and led two different lives – one with my mistress and the other with Nicole. And then the day came when my mother passed away."

"Aaron, that sounds very complex, and I know you feel guilty about what happened. Then, to have your mother pass on top of everything else. I am so sorry. What was your mom's name?"

"Bridgett, her name was Donna and I was her baby. I remember I was with my mistress when my cousin came to the door and told me my mother was dying."

Trenton asks, "What was wrong with your mother, Aaron?"

"Mom was diagnosed with cancer. It took her life in twelve months. The first three months she could walk, but the following four months she was in a wheelchair and getting blood transfusions once every week. In her final months, she was having blood injections twice a week, receiving three pints of blood each time. I remember when I went to see her before she died. She was sitting on the couch and she asked me, 'Aaron, how come you wanted me to make you something instead of giving you a Christmas gift during the holiday season?' You see, I would ask my mother to make me one thing every Christmas. It could be apple salad, coleslaw, or old fashioned ham spread that I would ask her to make me. So, I replied to mom, 'Don't you know why?' and she said, 'I do not know, Aaron.' I looked at mom and told her that a store-bought gift is okay, but will only last for a while and then it's gone. But a gift such as coleslaw, apple salad, or old fashioned ham spread will last forever because it was made from your hands, with love. It was the memories of how you loved so much that you would take the time to make me something like you did so many years ago when I was a child. Mom started crying and I rose up off the couch and turned towards her. I knelt and whispered in mom's ear as I hugged her and said, 'Momma you don't have to worry about your baby any more. I will be okay.' We both started crying and mom whispered back in my ear, 'I love you, Aaron, and I will always be with you.' When my cousin came to tell me my mother was in her final hours. I became numb with the news. She passed away at eight a.m.

that next morning at home in her bed, as she wished."

Tears flow from Aaron, Bridgett, Johnathon and Trenton with sadness. No one knows what to say.

Bridgett, breaking the uncomfortable silence, tenderly says, "Aaron, your mother sounds like a very loving lady and, with her short, red hair, she looks beautiful."

"Bridgett, how did you know my mother had red hair?"

"Oh, I just assumed she had red hair because your hair has a red tint, as well."

"That was a good guess on your part, then," Aaron responded, as if he knew Bridgett wasn't telling him everything. "Even then, I lied to Nicole and kept up my sinful ways. I went to the funeral with my mistress and lied to Nicole by saying I wasn't going. I know that broke Nicole's heart because she loved my mother and would have wanted to see her one last time. I remember one time when she told me why she loved my mother so much. She said that my mother was the mother she should have had, and she knew my mom always accepted her as her own. When I did go to my mother's funeral, looking back, I was a fool that only cared about myself."

Bridgett replies, "Aaron, you were lost, and I know that doesn't take away from how you are feeling, but you fought hard and lost so much in your life."

"But I should have been stronger Bridgett."

"I have said it before and I will say it again; you can't control the Devil, and you can't control what happens in life. We can only control ourselves and sometimes, as you know, Aaron, when we become lost our direction fades."

"I know, Bridgett, but Nicole always told me I was the strongest man she ever knew and loved. But, despite how much I loved her, ultimately I let her down. I always said I was a traveler and I wrote many poems about the lonely road, which she loved, but now I live with deep regret for my wayward ways."

Bridgett gives Aaron a hug and says, "I love you, dad."

"You did it again, Bridgett."

"What did I do?"

"You called me 'dad.'"

"Oh, Aaron, can we please talk about it later?"

"Sure thing, Bridgett, but let's make sure we do. Right now, I was going to see if you all wanted to hear a poem."

Johnathon, Bridgett, and Trenton all shake their heads in agreement.

"It's titled:

Regret

The traveler sits alongside the dusty road, on the silver stone

as he gazes upon his rucksack he carries. He goes deep within to understand

why he failed her wants and needs. He slams the door

within the walls of his mind and looks upon the distance.

Pressed against the morning sky, he wonders with sadness

where life will take him now. Unaided, he picks up all he owns

and steps upon the lonely road that calls his name.

He strides, one foot in front of the other, as he feels only loneliness.

With each step, he walks further away from the silver rock.

The wind carries him upon the open road now

as the sun begins to rise high into the Heavens.

The birds sing and the warmth surrounds him

as if he was the only one left in the world.

The old boots that he wears cling to his feet

and the breeze brushes against his flesh, as he walks

into an uncertain abyss. He reaches into his back pocket

for his threadbare rag to wipe the tear that gracefully falls

from his eyes. He moves on and thinks back to the lady he once knew.

He remembers how they laughed; how, together, they were one.

She shined like a diamond freshly cut by the maker.

But, to his own accord, the traveler, who now walks upon the dust

somehow lost the diamond he cherished. With every passing second,

he wonders how she is in Heaven above. His mind slowly shifts gears,

not wanting to think about the mistakes he made and the fool he was in life

when he left her. The traveler now moves on, into the world,

with only a remembrance of a life with her and now without her.

He calls her name as the wind echoes the sad, but beautiful song of a love lost.

"Aaron, I don't know what to say."

"There is nothing to say, Johnathon."

Bridgett replies, "Aaron, are you going to tell about Nicole's final days and why you feel like her passing was your fault?"

"I am not quite ready, but I promise I will tell you. But I would like to share something profound that happened after my mom died. I crashed hard. I broke in mind, body and soul. I bought a bottle of whiskey, found some pills, and drove to a place in the woods by the river. I parked my car, got out, and started walking in to the woods. I had been there many times with Nicole, and sometimes by myself. But, as I entered the woods, I began to cry. I couldn't find my way to our spot on the old river bed. It was like I was trapped within the woods. I began to say, 'Momma, I can't feel the angels any more. Momma, I can't feel the angels.' Every way I turned, the clearing of the woods was not there for me to walk through. Finally, the trees cleared, and I found the spot. It seemed like days had passed while I was in the woods."

"Aaron, how did you find your way through the woods?"

"Bridgett, I looked, with tears running down my cheeks, and there was this light that shined bright and I went towards the light. When I found the spot, I cried for what seemed like hours and bellowed into the wind, 'Momma, help me. The angels are gone, and I am alone.' About the time I picked up the bottle and the pills, a cool breeze blew with great force against me. I suddenly felt at peace. I set the bottle and pills down, turned, and fell on my knees. I heard a voice from within say, 'My baby, I love you, and it's okay.' At that point, it was like I could see my mother, as she wrapped her arms around me and held me tight. I felt her kiss my forehead and she whispered in my ear, 'I love you, Aaron,' and then she was gone. When my mother left, my Lord in Heaven appeared before me and stood on the sands of time where the water flowed. I asked him to release me from my oath."

"What was your oath you made to Father in Heaven, Trenton asked?"

"When I first met Nicole and talked with John, he asked me to go to our Father in Heaven. I went, and when Father and I talked, I gave him my word and my oath that I would fight this battle against the Devil. I thought that, because everything was closed, and Nicole was safe, I would be released from my oath."

"Aaron, when John talked with you about God and the Devil, when did he ask you to go to Father?

"Bridgett, some things are personal and I tell you this now because, for some reason, through our journey together, I believe in my heart you know what it is like to stand before our Lord Jesus in the time of disparity and hurt."

Johnathon speaks up, "Aaron, all of us understand."

"I love my Father in Heaven and I love my wife. And when I asked Him to release me, I felt his thoughts inside of my mind."

"What were his thoughts, Aaron?"

"Bridgett, I could hear him say, 'My son, I love you, and every man, woman and child must choose a path in life, and if this you must do I shall think no less of you, for I understand and have compassion upon my children. No matter what path you take, I shall always be with you and I know, my son, for a day will come if you leave, I shall call upon you. And I know you will be there, for your heart is a good heart.' My Lord kissed me and said, 'Blessing be upon the house of the servant.' After I prayed, I left the bottle of whiskey and the bottle of pills and went on my way.

After that night, I left my mistress and stayed at the towers for a while, but I was still on the dating sites looking for something, anything. Nicole and I weren't talking much, and most days she was just coloring while on the pills. It had been years since we had made love. I had to play so many roles in our marriage that it was hard for me to feel intimacy with her."

Johnathon replied, "Aaron, you were the doctor, pharmacist, husband, psychologist, the fighter, the father, the caregiver, the watcher, and the teacher. I understand why things went the way they were going, but I also know the Devil wanted you away from Nicole, even after the war was over…"

"May I tell you all something?"

"Please do, Aaron," Bridgett said encouragingly.

"Through the years, our Lord in Heaven always said the chapters of the book are being written by the scribes in Heaven. I never understood what our Lord meant, but I do now, to a certain extent. Looking back, I see that now, in the end, everyone will know why I failed and why Nicole's death was my fault."

"So what happened next, Aaron?"

"Bridgett, I started talking to a lady in South Dakota. She was captivating in every way. We messaged each other and began talking on the phone, and after a while I decided to drive up to South Dakota for the weekend. I checked into a hotel just off Interstate 29. We met that night at the motel where I was staying and had a good night together. We went to dinner and then she stayed the night with me. I didn't have to think about anything while I was up there. I felt freedom for the first time since I could remember."

"Aaron, you now know that wasn't freedom. That was the Devil and his deception."

"Yes, Johnathon, hindsight is 20-20 vision, and I understand that time in my life more clearly now."

"Please go on, Aaron," Bridgett interjected.

"The next day my new mistress took me around to see the sights in Sioux Falls. It was amazing, and I was like a kid in a candy store, standing in awe. The city was huge, and I had never seen so many enticements. The lady and I enjoyed our time together and then I had to leave for Iowa again. I felt this calling back to Nicole, but I was also doing everything I could to block it out. However, I did return to Iowa, but after a few more trips to South Dakota to see my new girlfriend, she asked me to move in with her. I had to make a choice: leave Nicole and move, or stay with Nicole and leave my mistress…"

Chapter Thirty-Nine
Fallen

"What did you do, Aaron?"

"I'm sorry to say, Johnathon, I left Nicole and moved in with my mistress. I lied to her and told her I was transferring colleges from Iowa to South Dakota. I had to lie to her because I didn't want to hurt her by having her know I was with someone else."

"But, Aaron, you were lying to your mistress about being married, weren't you?"

"I was, Trenton. I was living a lie all the way around. But I kept going on with my selfish ways and was trying to have my cake and eat it, too."

"Aaron, you were lost and fell from grace," said Bridgett.

Johnathon added, "You were running away from what you were meant to do, but I also understand that the human mind, body and spirit can only handle so much."

"You were right, Bridgett. I did fall from grace and landed in the works of the Devil. It's hard to explain how I was feeling. A part of me loved Nicole and wanted to be with her, and then there was this driving force deep within me that said to keep running. My mind was confused, my soul felt empty and the voice inside of my head kept telling me to go back. But my stubbornness blocked out that voice that was within. So, when I was in South Dakota, I made sure to call Nicole every day to check on her. Many times, she wrote me letters asking me to come home and I would tell her I couldn't. Sometimes, she would cry on the phone when I called her, or she would call me. She would often ask me to come back, but I wouldn't. I remember she called me one evening and told me if I didn't come home, she wanted a divorce. She pleaded with me to come home, but I didn't move back to be with her. I did come back, however, to file for divorce. I knew that was something Nicole didn't want, but she let me go."

Bridgett, speaking from the heart said, "Sometimes, when people love each other the way Nicole loved you, their love is strong enough to let go and they hope that, one day, the one who has let go will return."

"Well, Johnathon, Bridgett and Trenton, I left that day from the attorney's office feeling free in my mind, but my heart told me I was a fool. Even after the divorce, I called Nicole every morning and night when I was living with my mistress, whom I lived with for about six months until our relationship failed. She found out I was calling Nicole and wondered why. I told her it was none of her business and if she didn't like it, she could get down the road. So she told me to get out of her house. After that, I went back to Iowa, but I didn't want to be there. I hated the memories our town held and felt this anger toward some of the people who tried to destroy Nicole and me. I stopped in and checked on Nicole while I was in town. After a few days of camping out in the park, I decided to go back to South Dakota and try to make it on my own."

"Aaron, was the in-home health aide still helping Nicole?"

"Yes, Johnathon. Before I left the first time, I made sure everything was taken care of for Nicole. The pharmacy was making the medication packs, she was her own payee, and the nurse was overseeing her health care. I also told Nicole that if she ever got in a jam and she absolutely needed me, I would come and be there for her."

Puzzled, Johnathon asked, "Aaron, if you were willing to come back when Nicole really needed you, why wouldn't you just stay? I mean, she needed and loved you with all her heart."

"You're absolutely right. My thought process was skewed, and now that Nicole is gone, I have to live with the guilt of knowing I let her down. Every night when I lay my head down on the pillow, images flash through my head of how she would stand at the window of her apartment and wave goodbye to me as I drove away. I can still hear her crying as she would ask me to come home. Every single day I live with the pain of knowing I failed her, and sometimes the pain I feel is too much."

"Aaron, we all make mistakes," Bridgett said in a soothing tone. "How did it happen that you finally went back to Iowa for good?"

"After I went back to South Dakota for the second time, to try and make it on my own, I remember I was driving and thought to myself, 'this is stupid. I have no job and nowhere to live.' But, as I was coming into Sioux Falls, I looked through the windshield of my car and there was a concrete plant that needed drivers. I pulled in and asked the manager if they were hiring. He replied, 'we are and when can you start?' I told him immediately. After I completed the paperwork, I asked Jim, the manager, if he knew of a place that was for rent. Jim told me one of his drivers had a fully furnished basement for rent. He walked me out to the guy who had the place for rent and introduced us. That night, I had a place to sleep and the start of a new life."

Trenton began, "Aaron, I respect you, but starting a new life is not built on deception, nor is running away from the past a healthy way to live."

"I know that now, and I also know that my Father in Heaven was displeased with me and my works. But He still watched out for me."

Bridgett replied, "Aaron, our Father in Heaven always watches out for his children." About that time Aaron looks over and sees Trenton whispering to Johnathon.

"Trenton, is something wrong?"

"Aaron, I must go for now."

"Why so abruptly?"

"I must leave for now, Aaron, but you will see me again."

They all stand from the bench by the river, give Trenton a

hug and say good bye, and walk to the cabin. As Trenton walks into the canyon, Aaron looks up and sees an eagle flying high in the sky. Smiling, Aaron makes his way into the cabin with Johnathon and Bridgett. They brew a new pot of coffee, start a fire in the fireplace, and head toward the living room. However, as Aaron moves into the sitting room, he notices pictures of himself and Nicole on the mantle. Bridgett enters the sitting room and Aaron, with amazement, turns and looks at her.

"Do you know how these pictures came to be here on the mantle?"

"I do not, Aaron."

"Bridgett, what is going on?"

"Soon you will understand, and your heart will be filled. But for now, let us sit and enjoy the time we have together."

Johnathon brings in the coffee and finds his seat. The afternoon is upon them and the coolness of Mother Nature can be felt throughout the cabin.

With a look of curiosity, Bridgett asks, "Aaron, if you and Nicole were divorced, why do you still call her your wife?"

"May I come back to that question? I will answer all you have for me."

"Okay, Aaron, but can you tell us what you accomplished by divorcing Nicole and moving away?"

"I was in South Dakota for almost two years. When I was there, I was looking for normalcy, but I was also looking for a new start."

"With another lady, as well…" Johnathon added. "Didn't you understand your heart was with Nicole?"

"Looking back, Johnathon, my heart was with Nicole, but again, I didn't want to feel. While I was in South Dakota, I met this man who became my friend. He owned a scuba diving shop and was very kind. He took me in, and we talked all the time."

"What was his name, Aaron?"

"His name was Colonel, Johnathon. He knew I was hurting

inside, and could also tell I was lost. I remember Colonel and I had only known each other for about three months and one day he looked at me and said, 'Aaron, I can see your heart and how much it hurts. If you will put your trust in me, in my hands, I will give you rest, shelter, and time to heal.' From that day on, he helped me to regain strength and rebuild the faith within me. He taught me to scuba dive and the divers took me in as part of their family. I was dating as many women as I could, and some of the men and women we dove with made a joke about me being a prostitute."

"Why is that, Aaron?"

"Bridgett, they called me that because I was sleeping with as many women as I could. Then, one day, Colonel said, 'Aaron, there is a difference between sleeping with a lady and loving a lady. Which is right and which is wrong? You, Aaron, must decide.' I asked Colonel, 'What do you mean?' and he replied, 'I want you to listen to these things I say, for the words spoken may lead you to the faith that is blinded by the desires of your flesh. It's called:

A Lady's Heart

"Sir Walter Scott was a Scottish author of poetry. He wrote 'Lady of the Lake' and in the poem there is a part where Scott says: *The rose is fairest when 'tis budding new, and hope is brightest when it dawns from fears. The rose is sweetest with morning dew, and love is loveliest when embalmed in tears.'* Colonel said, 'I tell you that poem, Aaron, because a lady's heart is like a rose bush. A man can ignore the rose bush altogether and watch his love, his lady, wither and die. A man can tend to the rose bush too much and watch it, his lady, wither and die. But, Aaron, if a man waters the rose bush and tends to every need with kindness and tenderness, that man can watch his lady, the one he loves, flourish for the rest of his life.' Then Colonel said, 'which man are you, Aaron, and what do you decide?' It was at that point Colonel and I sat down, drank a beer together, and I began telling him everything Nicole and I went through. He listened to me without interruption."

"Aaron, was Colonel a spiritual man?"

"Yes, Bridgett, he was. I hope it makes sense that, even though

I had a place of my own, he gave me shelter, food and an ear. I told Colonel I was tired, and I had exhausted all my faith in the thirteen years I was with Nicole, so he told me I needed to rest. It was hard telling him about the loss, the evil, and what Nicole and I went through. But, as our friendship grew and the more we hung out, we became like brothers. He always made me think, and the more I told him about Nicole and me, the more he listened.

After numerous conversations, he told me, 'Aaron, I believe you, and I also believe you are a spiritual warrior. You have seen much and lived a life that many have not. You are in your forties and look like a fifty-five-year-old man. I have no doubt that the Devil was among you and Nicole for years, but I have one question for you.' When I asked Colonel, 'What is your question?' he responded by asking, 'Why do you hate yourself?' I asked him why he would think such a thing, and he told me he could see beyond my flesh and what he saw was a man who doesn't like himself. I told him that I hate what I am, to which he inquired, 'What are you, Aaron?' I answered by saying, 'All my life I have tried to do as my Father in Heaven has wanted me to do and many times I have failed.' Colonel then said, 'Aaron, we all have failed one time or another, but I want to know what you are.' My response was, 'I am just a servant who fell from grace.'

'Aaron, you make yourself out to be the dust molded in the soiled land when you describe yourself as a servant, and that's not right.' I told Colonel, 'Here is a story. A friend of mine walked up to me one time and asked, 'Aaron, why do you continue to help Nicole? I told my friend that I made an oath to God my Father that I would fight and help her.' Colonel responded and asked, 'Was this when you were with Nicole, Aaron?' I told him that it was, and that my friend told me God would not think less of me if I walked away. I told my friend he was right – Father in Heaven wouldn't think less of me, but I would. I told Colonel that story because I felt lost for many years, and he thoughtfully responded by saying, 'Aaron, hating yourself because you chose to help another is like the river flowing backwards.' I told him that day, 'My heart hurts and my soul cries,' and he told me to remember what I always said. I wondered what he was referring to, and he reminded me that I once said 'It is the unspoken words of the soul that speak the loudest, but if no one can hear those words spoken, then the world is not seen of a man or woman.'"

After listening intently, Bridgett stated, "Aaron, it sounds like you were screaming out from within your soul trying to find a reason for your existence."

"I was, and Colonel helped me through that rough time in my life. We began going to church, praying at the table before we ate, and reading the Bible together."

"Did you visit Nicole any more?" Bridgett asked.

"I did visit her more, and I would take her birthday and Christmas presents. I wouldn't stay long, but I always tried to make sure she knew a part of me was still with her. I remember that, when I would visit Nicole in the towers, she would ask me for a kiss. Sometimes I would kiss her and sometimes I wouldn't, due to the guilt I felt. If you don't mind, I'd benefit from taking a break and getting some fresh coffee."

"Not at all, Aaron, and if you want to smoke a cigarette on the front porch, Johnathon and I will get the coffee."

"Thank you, Bridgett and Johnathon. I will meet you back here when I'm finished."

Aaron throws his coat and boots on and proceeds to walk outside. The wind is moderate, and the smell of the lilies and roses, mixed with the scent of Mother Nature's other gifts, is miraculous. Aaron sits in the rocking chair and lights the cigarette. Looking out upon the view he has grown to love, a strong feeling overcomes his body, as he thinks to himself his time is drawing near to leave this place that has no name. He wonders when that day will come, about the light that led him to the cabin, and why the wooden box in the loft had a picture and letter hidden under the covers. There are so many questions and very few answers, he muses, before rising and walking down to the angel statue. Extending his hand to the statue and feeling how perfectly it was made, he hears an eagle high above the plains. Smiling, he wonders if he will ever hold Nicole again. He finishes his cigarette and heads back into the cabin. Inside, Johnathon and Bridgett are rocking back and forth in their rockers. Aaron sits and grabs his cup of coffee.

"Would you like me to continue?"

"We would like that, Aaron" Bridgett said excitedly.

"For the first time in a while, my faith was getting stronger because I became aware of something inside of me feeling off."

"What do you mean?" Bridgett inquired.

"I felt this odd feeling and I kept hearing this voice speaking in a loud voice, calling my name. Then, one night, I went to bed early at my apartment. It was about three o'clock in the morning and I was awakened by the presence of two figures standing in the northeast corner of the room. I sat up and, positioned on the side of the bed, I spoke out and said, 'I know you are there, my Father in Heaven and St. Michael.' In a soft voice I heard my Father speak and say, 'Aaron, your time here is at an end and soon you will leave.' I asked my Father where I was needed and he said, 'Aaron, it is time you go home. And when you return it will be harder than the thirteen years you and Nicole went through.'

I told my Father and St. Michael that 'Nothing could be harder than those years.' Father again said, 'Aaron, trust in my words and cling to your faith, for you will surely find the words I have spoken will fill the heart. And when your heart is filled, your cup will find emptiness forever.' My Father and St. Michael blessed me and then left. I didn't sleep the rest of the night and wondered what was about the happen. The next morning, I went to Colonel and told him my time was coming to an end and I explained what happened. Colonel told me, 'Whatever path is laid upon you, Aaron, you must go and you must listen to your heart.' It was about a week later I was informed I must move out of my apartment."

"What happened, Aaron?" Johnathon asked.

"I was told by my landlord that his mother was moving in because she had cancer. So, about a week later, I moved in with Colonel. Then I got a call from a doctor in Iowa City."

"That doesn't sound good," Bridgett said worriedly.

"Your intuition is accurate. The doctor told me that Nicole was sick with cancer. I asked how bad the cancer was, and he explained that it was in stage one, but the grade was severe."

"What does that mean, Aaron?"

"Bridgett, I was informed that the higher the grade, the more aggressive the cancer is. The doctor strongly suggested that I come back because Nicole needed me there for her. I remember, when I heard the news, it was like someone punched me in the gut. I started crying and I felt this pain deep inside of me. My wife was diagnosed with an aggressive form of cancer, and the doctor told me that she only had six months to a year to live and chemotherapy would not be a life-saving measure. I asked him if Nicole was there with him in the room, and he said that she was, and the doctor asked if I wanted to speak to her. Naturally, I wanted to, and when I spoke to Nicole, I told her I would be down as soon as possible. She told me her surgery was in a week to remove the tumor and I promised her I would be there. I drove down a week later and was there for her surgery, and afterwards I returned to South Dakota."

"Aaron, why didn't you stay?" Bridgett wondered with a pained look on her face.

"I had to return to sell some of my things and let my employers know I was quitting. So, I left my jobs, my place at Colonel's, and some of my belongings. I rented a U-Haul, loaded up what I could, and drove back to Iowa to be with Nicole."

Chapter Forty
Home at Last

"*I* called Nicole after I loaded up the truck and was on the road. It's about five and a half hours from Sioux Falls to where she was in Iowa. I remember her calling me about three hours later and asking me how close I was to her. I could hear the excitement in her voice when I told her I was about two and a half hours out. She sighed and said she would be waiting for me. I told her I loved her, and she said, 'I love you, too.'"

"What were you thinking on your way home?"

"Bridgett, I was scared, and hurt, but there was also that part of me that thought it would be okay. I also felt the hurt of leaving my friends, but I knew if I didn't come back to Nicole, nobody else would be there for her. I still loved her with all my heart, but it was also hard to show my love."

"Why was that, Aaron?"

"I was afraid, Bridgett, because of the unknown and of what I might encounter throughout this situation because, in the back of my mind, I kept hearing my Father's voice saying this will be harder than the thirteen years we endured. Nicole's girls didn't care, and I knew her daughters wouldn't lift a finger."

"That is incredibly sad, Aaron," Bridgett said, somberly.

"Yes, it is sad, and I will tell you both how insensitive her girls were throughout her being sick."

"I am not going to like this, am I?"

"Probably not, Bridgett. There were many fights I had to battle, but some I didn't think in a million years I would have to deal with."

"Between you and Nicole?"

"No, Bridgett. There were others who were doing the Devil's work that I would soon encounter. I remember I was back in my hometown and it was about nine o'clock at night. I had to stop at my dad's house to drop off my car and dolly. Nicole called me and asked where I was. I told her what I was doing and that I would be over there soon. She asked me, 'How long is soon,' and I smiled and said I would be there in thirty minutes. I could hear her voice change and say, 'Hurry, hunny, hurry.' I told her I would, and it didn't take the full thirty minutes for me to get over to her apartment."

"Aaron, I bet Nicole was elated that you were finally home."

"She was, Bridgett, but what I witnessed at her apartment when I got there was frustrating."

"Aaron, I really want to hear more, but I am getting tired. Do you mind if we get some sleep?"

"Of course not, Johnathon. I understand and agree that we could all use some rest."

Aaron gets up and walks into the kitchen to empty the percolator and make sure the wood stove is out. Johnathon and Bridgett gather the bedding, throw a log on the fire, and make the beds. With the oil lamps out, they all lay down for the night, nestled comfortably under the covers. The only light that can be seen is the flickering of the waning flames in the fireplace. The night air is cool outside and the cabin has a peaceful air about it. Yet, while Johnathon and Bridgett sleep, Aaron is restless. His mind wonders why there is a letter addressed to him with the picture of him and Nicole in the wooden box. Pressed by his thoughts, he slowly gets up and makes his way to the front porch. He thinks that having a cigarette might relax him enough to sleep, so he steps outside and finds his rocking chair. The moon is gorgeous, and the crisp silence of the mountain environment is remarkable. The white marble angel statue shines bright from the sphere above. Aaron lights his cigarette and thinks to himself how Nicole would love this picture before him.

His thoughts of his wife, as well as the perfect silence, is broken by a flock of mute swans flying overhead, breaking through the moonlight and casting shadows across the earth. He smiles and looks to the heavens, and then softly hears this voice in his mind: Aaron, soon you will have to leave, but I will be with you always. He whispers back, 'And I will always be with you, my love. But why do I have to go? I want to stay in this place that has no name.' Rocking in his chair, he finishes the cigarette and puts it out in the old tin can. He stands and quietly moves back into the cabin, finds his bed, and covers up with his blanket. His mind is slow, and his thoughts are filled with the love he has for Nicole, which allow him to finally fall asleep along with the others.

In what seems like seconds later, the light crests in the east and enters without permission through the cabin windows. Bridgett opens her eyes and looks around, then smiles at Johnathon and rises from the couch. Walking into the kitchen to start the wood stove and brew some fresh coffee, she thinks to herself that it's a beautiful morning. She throws a log in the oven to get the coffee ready, then quietly walks up the stairs to the loft and looks around. She moves over to the bed and pulls the wooden box out from underneath the covers, opens it, and smiles. She thinks to herself, "I love you, dad, and I hope this gift from mom is something that you will always treasure." With a tear running down her cheek, she puts the pine wooden box back where Aaron found it, and then opens the drawer in the nightstand and begins writing a letter of her own to him, her father.

With the pen in her hand and the canvas of white, Bridgett's letter takes form as the tears come from deep within. Her heart feels sadness, but also happiness, as she writes for herself and for Johnathon. Time passes and her letter is fully composed, so she rises from the chair and puts the letter in the drawer. Back downstairs, Bridgett enters the kitchen to dry her eyes. Johnathon and Aaron are still sound asleep in the living room as she pours three cups of hot coffee. Grabbing a tray from the countertop, she sets the coffee cups on it and the fresh coffee to her father and brother. She speaks in a loud voice, 'Get up, sleepy heads. Your coffee is done."

Both Johnathon and Aaron slowly open their eyes and see Bridgett standing over them. Aaron takes his coffee and, enjoying the first sip, smiles at Bridgett.

"Thank you." Bridgett.

"You are welcome, Aaron. Are you going out to smoke?"

"I usually start my morning that way, yes."

"Bridgett and I will be waiting in here for you," said a waking Johnathon.

Aaron steps outside to smoke his cigarette and, once again, Johnathon and Bridgett begin to talk.

"Bridgett, did you finish the letter?"

"I did, and it's in place. I am so sad, though."

"I am, too, Bridgett."

"Aaron means a lot to us and I will miss him."

Johnathon replies, "We will both miss him."

Aaron finishes smoking his cigarette and walks back into the cabin. The three meet back in the sitting room and Bridgett speaks up, "Aaron, will you play us a song on the piano?"

"I sure can. It would be my pleasure."

Setting his coffee cup down, Aaron stands and moves to the bench. He sits, stretches his hands and then closes his eyes as he thinks about Nicole. There is silence in the room for a moment.

"What are you going to play for Johnathon and me?"

"Bridgett, this song was very dear to Nicole's heart and it's called, '*In the Arms of an Angel*' by Sarah McLachlan."

Joining the serene morning sounds outside the cabin, Aaron begins to play. Johnathon and Bridgett listen intently to each chord, the music filling their hearts and souls. Aaron looks over and sees the moisture coming from their eyes and, as the last key is struck, he closes the fallboard and moves back to his chair.

"Aaron, that song has a lot of meaning, and I see why Nicole loved it," Johnathon said appreciatively.

"Who do you think Nicole's angel was in life, Aaron?"

"Bridgett, she always said I was her angel, but I never thought of myself in that way."

"Maybe you *should* believe that you were her angel."

"I will give it some more thought. But, would you both like to hear more about Nicole?"

"We would love that," said Johnathon.

"When I made it into town and got to her apartment, we both embraced, and we gave each other a kiss. She was happy and my emotions were up in the air. I just didn't know how to feel. But, as I looked around the apartment, I was disgusted."

"What was wrong?"

"Johnathon, the worker I had put in place before I left was not doing her job. There was trash everywhere and all of the furniture was dirty. I was very upset, and that night I told Nicole I would get her place cleaned up after she went to bed. We talked for quite some time, and then I got her to lay down and go to sleep. I stayed up and cleaned quietly, taking out eight bags of garbage that night. I did all of her dishes, swept, mopped and cleaned."

"Weren't you tired from the long drive and your conflicting emotions?"

"I was, Johnathon, but I didn't care. I had been up since four that mourning, but I was not going to have her living in filth. I think it was about three a.m. when I got to sleep. The next morning, I woke up and went to cook Nicole something to eat. When I looked in the refrigerator, there was not a speck of food in her apartment. I sat her down and asked why she didn't tell me what was going on while I was away."

"What did she say, Aaron?" Bridgett asked, concerned.

"Nicole told me she didn't want to bother me with little things like her apartment and food. I told her she should have told me what was going on. I was frustrated, not with Nicole, but with the worker who was getting paid to help her and keep her place clean.

"But why didn't she have any food? Surely, she was getting food assistance."

"She was, Johnathon, but this one lady who called Nicole her friend was always taking her food. I also found out her home health aide worker was taking her money and ordering stuff on her debit card. I gave Nicole a hug, told her all of this was going to stop, and called Heather at CPS and explained what was going on with the home health aide. I also explained that I took photographs of her apartment. Heather told me I could let her worker go if I was going to be there for Nicole, and I told her that I wasn't going anywhere.

After I got off the phone with Heather, I called Nicole's worker and explained her services were not needed any more. Then I went to the lady who lived on the seventh floor of the towers, that was taking her food, and told her she was not going to take anything away from Nicole again. The lady who claimed to be her friend said, with a few choice words, that I could go to Hell. I told her that was exactly what I was hoping for…"

"Aaron, that lady who was taking Nicole's food was just upset that she got caught," Johnathon pointed out.

"Yes, she was, but I sent a clear and precise message to everyone: I was back, the bullshit stops, and no more would I tolerate anyone taking advantage of my wife."

With a smile on her face, Bridgett said, "The way you said that had great force through your tone."

"Well, I had to have that stern tone because I did not like what I had seen."

"I would hate to get on your bad side, Aaron, when you are protecting someone."

Smiling, Aaron humbly added, "I just wish Nicole would have told me everything that was going on with her."

"So what happened next?"

"Bridgett, after I handled those unpleasant situations, Nicole and I went to breakfast and then I took her shopping."

"If I may ask, how did she look, at that point?"

"Nicole looked sick, and tired, and I could tell she was hurting inside, but she smiled and kept fighting for every day she could. I remember that, when I took her shopping, she was happy. After we were done shopping, we went back to the towers and got everything up to the sixth floor where her apartment was. When everything was put away, I looked at her and told her I would be back in a few hours."

"Where did you go, Aaron?"

"No worries, Bridgett. I had to go and unload the U-Haul truck into the storage unit and return it by that night. After that, I went back to the storage unit and got my motorcycle out and rode it to a shop to sell. You see, Nicole always loved surprises, and a surprise was what I was going to give her. I sold my motorcycle for less than it was worth, but I didn't care. It was all for her. After I sold the bike, I went to a furniture store and bought her a new recliner, a bedroom outfit with a new mattress and box spring, a new microwave, a fifty-inch flat screen TV, new carpets for the floor, a fireplace, bedding, a blender for smoothies, a countertop oven and a new stereo with tower speakers. I had everything delivered that day to the apartment."

"Oh, my dear heavens, Aaron, that is a lot!" Bridgett gasped.

Johnathon added, "Aaron, you told Bridgett and me that you had a hard time showing love, but your actions showed Nicole something different."

"And what is that?"

"You showed her the undying love you had for her."

"I don't know about that, Johnathon."

"I do, Aaron, because even when you told us about the times when you were unfaithful, your words were full of love and the actions you displayed toward Nicole are those of a protector who loves immensely."

"I did always love her, and I always will. But her death will forever be on my shoulders."

Chapter Forty-One
Preparing for Battle

"Before everything was delivered to the apartment, I told Nicole I had a surprise for her. She smiled and asked me what the surprise was that I had gotten her. I told her she would just have to wait and see. She smiled, and about an hour later I received a call from the delivery driver. It was time to bring up the gifts I had purchased. I asked Nicole to wait in the apartment and I would be right back. She was excited and anxiously awaited her surprise. When everything was unloaded from the delivery truck, the drivers and I packed the elevator and went to the sixth floor. When we got to Nicole's door, I entered and told her to close her eyes. After I knew her eyes were closed, I brought in the new recliner. She opened her eyes, covered her mouth and immediately started crying. She ran up and gave me a hug and said, 'I love you, Aaron. It is beautiful.' I smiled and told her that there was more coming. I hurried up and put the back of the chair on the base and let the delivery men bring in the rest. Nicole cried almost all day and couldn't believe she had entirely new furniture. I told her she deserved everything I bought for her and told her I loved her. It took a few days for me to get everything rearranged in the apartment but, with her help in telling me where to put everything, I was successful. She must have been overwhelmed with joy, because I remember that she asked me if we could get married again."

"Aaron, what did you say?"

"I had to tell her 'no,' Bridgett, and she said she understood. But, I looked at her and said, 'Honey, marriage is a piece of paper and we are already married again in the eyes of God the Father.' Nicole asked me how I knew that, and I explained that, 'Love is a powerful entity and my heart, our hearts, are once again whole, and I love you. In the eyes of God, I returned, and your love brought me home.' I also told her, 'It is not man or woman that judges who shall be married, but God, and with faith and God's blessing in our hearts, that makes us husband and wife. Nicole smiled, and we embraced. Now, I was still having a hard time finding that love I once had for her, but I did consider us married again.

Her heart warmed, Bridgett comments, "Aaron, it would be hard, but that was the first step to finding that love you have for Nicole and, as Johnathon said, your actions tell a different story."

"I agree, but sorting out the confusion in my mind was extremely hard."

"Returning home meant cleansing your soul and it was our Father in Heaven that led your heart and will," Johnathon added

"Please continue, Aaron," said Bridgett.

"Nicole and I discussed what we needed to do in terms of making sure I could take care of her. So, we went to a notary and had a living will drafted and signed so that I had the authority to oversee her medical decisions in the event she was not capable of making them herself. I stayed at the apartment with her and decided to go through her medical records."

"Aaron, if I may ask, what type of cancer did she have?"

"Bridgett, the doctors called the cancer 'adenocarcinoma' with large, poorly differentiated cancer cells of the cervix, stage one. Two pathologists explained to Nicole and me that this type of cancer only effects one out of every two hundred women. I was hopeful, though, and looked to the doctor for confirmation that stage one cancer is positive, in a way, because it means that they caught it in time. The doctor explained that, yes, stage one is the best time for finding cancer but, with her type of cells, it would be an aggressive cancer. I promised

Nicole I would be there for her and not to worry. After I read through her medical records, we went to sleep around nine o'clock because we had a doctor's appointment the next morning at the university hospital.

Before I finish telling you about what went on with Nicole and me after she developed cancer, I'm going to take a break to have a smoke."

"Ok, Aaron, we will wait for you in here," Bridgett said acceptingly.

Aaron rises and walks to the front door of the cabin and reaches for the handle. Opening the door, he feels the light breeze and smells the fragrances of Mother Nature. Lighting the cigarette, he smells a familiar scent and thinks to himself that it smells just like the perfume Nicole always wore. Smiling, he sits in the rocker on the porch and remembers how she would dress up for dinner and spray on her perfume. He feels the relaxation he needed and finishes his cigarette. Rising out of the chair, he stands for a moment before returning inside the cabin and breathes in deeply, smelling Nicole's fragrance in the air. Walking back into the cabin, he rejoins Johnathon and Bridgett in the sitting room.

"Welcome back, Aaron. How was your time outside?"

"Bridgett, it was good for a few moments, but I could have sworn that I smelled Nicole's perfume in the air."

Johnathon and Bridgett both smile and Bridgett tells Aaron, "Nicole is with you."

"Will you tell Bridgett and me more about what happened with you and Nicole?"

"Yes, Johnathon, we have come this far in our story. That next morning, we got ready for the trip and left for the University Hospital around seven in the morning. Nicole's appointment was at nine-thirty a.m. When we arrived at the hospital, we found the doctor's office, and waited for about ten minutes before the nurse came and got us. The nurse took Nicole's vitals and then the doctor came in to talk with her and me. I remember that Dr. Sorenson brought another doctor into the room to consult with us.

Everyone was sitting down when we were told chemotherapy and radiation were not life-saving measures. Dr. Sorenson and his colleague said their pathology department tested everything and, even if Nicole decided to try the chemotherapy and radiation, they couldn't guarantee it would extend her life. We were both completely devastated. Dr. Sorenson looked at me and asked to talk with me outside the room while his colleague talked with Nicole. When we stepped outside the room, he told me. 'Aaron, I want you to listen to me. This situation Nicole is in will be a damned if you do and damned if you don't scenario. Because she has large, poorly differentiated cancer cells, she will need you more than ever.' Then he told me this will be the hardest situation to watch and go through, as the rarity of Nicole's cancer, plus the fact that it is an aggressive cancer, means she will endure great pain. The last thing he said to me was to watch over her and protect her with all your soul. He said he was sorry that he couldn't do more for us and suggested palliative care for Nicole. We were hurt and sad, to say the least, but as we were leaving the office both doctors shook my hand and gave Nicole a hug while telling her and me, 'May God bless you both.'"

Bridgett can see Aaron's eyes tearing up and how hard it is for him to tell her and Johnathon about Nicole's diagnosis. She rises and gives Aaron a hug and whispers in his ear, "We love you so much and it will be okay."

Aaron looks at Bridgett and says, "I miss her with all my heart."

Johnathon suggests to Aaron, "Take a sip of coffee. As Bridgett says, it will make you feel better."

Aaron replies, "There are so many emotions inside, but I will be okay. We left the hospital and, on the drive home, there was this silence that I cannot explain."

Thoughtfully, Johnathon responds by saying, "Aaron, if I may say, what Dr. Sorenson told you in the hallway sounds a lot like what Father and St. Michael said that night in your apartment."

"Yes, when he said those things to me, that is the first thought that ran through my head. It was like I was being reminded to be strong for Nicole. The one thing she asked of me on the way home was this, 'Aaron, all these years you have been my watcher and protector. I need you to be strong so I can be strong and so I can feel safe, honey. Your strength gives me strength, and even if I suffer or am in pain, I know your being there like a lion will give me peace'. Then she asked me to promise to be strong. I promised her I would be like a dragon sitting on the mountainside, without fear. She smiled and said that soon she would be home, but she must go through this situation, and in the end she will forever walk with Jesus in Heaven."

"Aaron, remember the poem 'Emotions' where you talked about being strong?"

"Yes, Bridgett, I remember. 'Sometimes, a man or woman's armor can hold until the feather weighs as much as the sun glistening in the wind before the man or woman's armor cracks.' I felt my armor on that day crack, but I mended it because Nicole had me promise to be strong. Before we went back to the apartment, she and I went to the local pharmacy that sold medical equipment and we picked up some supplies."

"Why did you need medical supplies, Aaron?"

"Johnathon, I needed diabetic supplies, an oxygen meter, stethoscope, a thermometer and other stuff like gauze, medical tape and medical scissors. I had to be prepared for anything we needed for treatment. I also decided to drop out of the Master's Program I was enrolled in so I could focus solely on Nicole."

"How close were you to completing the Master's Program, Aaron?"

"Bridgett, I was three terms away from graduating. I still had my Minor degrees in Criminology and Criminal Justice, and my Major in Psychology. But, if you are both wondering, I didn't care about the degree. All I cared about was taking care of my wife. Once, a friend asked me if I regret doing the things I did for Nicole, and I told him, absolutely not, and I would do it a million times over for her. I set up my laptop and documented her blood sugar levels, blood pressures, medication distribution, any signs of diabetic ulcers, her temperature, and what she was eating. I remember when the housing authority found out Nicole had cancer, there was a lady named Beth who found a one-bedroom apartment open and told us to take it. We were shocked, but we moved into the apartment with joy, as Nicole lived in an efficiency apartment and moving into the larger place meant I could better take care of her. Beth was compassionate and she always treated Nicole with kindness. Nicole asked me how we would get moved from one place to another. I told her I would move everything in one day and I did, from the sixth floor to the third floor, little by little, piece by piece."

"When did you come back from South Dakota?"

"I came back in August of 2017, Bridgett. Why do you ask?"

"I was just curious as to the timeline of events."

"Once everything was moved and organized, I reset all the medical equipment and my charting. We had the county nurse coming once a week to look over my charting and to see how Nicole was doing. Bridgett, do you remember when I talked about how her daughters didn't care about their mother?"

"Oh, yes. I remember. I recall being particularly angry upon hearing about their treatment of Nicole."

"Well, after the move into the one-bedroom apartment, I called her daughters and explained to them that their mother was dying from cancer. I suggested that they try to spend as much time with Nicole as they could. The first daughter to come down was the oldest daughter, and she stayed for a total of about three hours while visiting. Right before she left, she looked at her mother and said, 'When you die, I want your rings, pictures and all your shot glasses.' Nicole looked at her daughter and replied, 'I am not even dead yet and all you are concerned about is what you are going to get!?' Her daughter came back with, 'Mom, I deserve those rings and you shouldn't be selfish and want to keep them.' Nicole, rightfully upset, told her to get out. She couldn't believe that was all her daughter wanted. As she left, she laughed at Nicole. That is when I stepped in and told her to listen to her mother and go.

When I talked with the middle daughter, I had to pay for her fuel just so she would come down and see her mother. She came down and visited with her mother one time. Nicole asked her if she loved her, and she replied yes, but then proceeded to ask for her rings just as the oldest child did. Nicole explained that her older sister asked for the same things, and the middle daughter responded by saying, 'That bitch doesn't deserve anything, nor does my younger sister.' It was a constant fight with the girls and what they wanted to take from their mother. The middle daughter left and called me about an hour later, telling me that she talked with her sisters and they weren't going to help their mother at all if they didn't get what they wanted. Then she went as far as to say that she and her sisters had their own lives to live, and they wouldn't put their lives on hold just because their mother was sick.

I explained to Nicole the situation and she told me to call them back and explain, with her, that if the girls come back, they will be escorted off the property. Furthermore, she wanted them to know that life isn't about what they can get from others. It's about making memories and loving one another. But her daughters didn't care and, even though she loved them, she felt liked she had failed. I told her that it was not her that failed; it was her greedy girls that did, because they only cared about themselves and are heartless and filled with evil. It was hard for Nicole, and I comforted her as much as I could. The girls held true to their word and never lifted a hand to help."

Johnathon looks at Bridgett and says, "Calm down. I can see the anger about to boil over inside you."

"Aaron and Johnathon, I tell you what…oh, I could just… ugh!"

"Bridgett, some people in this world don't understand and never will. Then came the day when Nicole and I were in the car. I looked over and she looked flushed, her eyes were different, and she was slurring her speech. I rushed through town and took her straight to the emergency room. They admitted her to be evaluated and ran a battery of tests. The doctor discovered that her body was riddled with blood clots in her femoral and popliteal veins in her left leg. The clots ran from her hip down to her knee and, on top of that, she had a major pulmonary embolism in her right lung. As Nicole laid in the hospital bed in the emergency room, she became tired and started to rest. The emergency room doctor pulled me into the hallway and told me everything they found. To make matters worse, her blood sugar numbers were through the roof. Her temperature started rising and the emergency room doctor told me I had a choice to make: the hospital can rush her to the University Hospital and the doctors up there can start a blood thinner and try to control what is happening, or the hospital can take her by ambulance back to the apartment where she can pass away in her sleep.

At that moment, I remembered that Nicole said when I got back from South Dakota to make sure she and I could have as much time together as we could. So, I told the doctor transport her to the University Hospital. Immediately, he called for the ambulance driver and they transported her there with the emergency lights on. Before I left the hospital to get some of my things, the emergency room doctor stopped me in the hallway. He told me he was sorry he couldn't do more, but he was happy Nicole had me there, and even though the situation wasn't good, he said that God was with us."

Chapter Forty-Two
The Devil in Dove Form

"I gave Nicole a kiss before the hospital staff loaded her into the ambulance and told her I would be at the University Hospital as soon as I got some clothes and necessities. She smiled and said, 'Hurry, honey.' I smiled back and left to gather my things. I was only an hour behind her from the time she arrived in at the hospital. When I got there the doctors had started her on blood thinners in an attempt to get her blood sugars down. We spent Christmas in the hospital and our stay went through the first of the year. I stayed by her side the whole time, except when I went outside to smoke. I remember, on the third day at the hospital, in the morning, Nicole had woken up and she looked at me with this look of peace on her face. She smiled and said, 'I saw your dad's sister.' I asked her, 'You saw Charlotte?' and she said, 'No, I was with Marsha, your dad's sister.' When I followed up with, 'Where did you see Marsha?' Nicole smiled and said, 'Marsha was in the field in Heaven. She wrapped her arms around me, gave me a kiss on the forehead, and told me it would be okay, and that I would be coming home soon.' I asked her if my aunt Marsha said anything else and she replied, 'Yes, honey, she did. She told me I was beautiful and that Father in Heaven loves me.'"

"Aaron, how long had your aunt been gone?"

"Johnathon, Marsha had been gone for many years, but she was with Nicole that day."

"How did you know that?"

"Bridgett, I know because of my faith and I believe Nicole. She also said Marsha told her, as they stood in the field, that she would be young again – without pain and suffering – and she would no longer be tormented by the Devil. And, keep in mind, Marsha knew nothing about what we had gone through, yet she knew Nicole was plagued by the Devil."

"I bet you were shocked."

"I was, Johnathon, and I didn't know what to say. But I remember it was January 2, 2018, and Nicole and I could finally go home. But, before we left, the doctors gave Nicole a prescription for blood thinners. I was trained by the staff at the university hospital in wound care if they should arise on her body. I learned everything I could from the doctors about the signs and symptoms of any other physiological issues that may arise. Once, during our stay, the doctor pulled me aside and told me this would be the last time they would see Nicole. I asked him why he said that, and he replied kindly, 'Aaron, between the blood clots and the cancer, she will be in Heaven soon.' Nicole and I left that day headed for home. When we got back to the apartment she was glad to see her cockatiels again. There was Molly, Rocky, and their three babies, George, Marcus, and Rita. Rocky didn't care for me a whole lot."

"How do you know, Aaron?"

"Well, Johnathon, when I cleaned their flight cage there was one time that Rocky came at me. On another occasion, when I reached into the cage, he pooped on my head. The flight cage was huge and, if I didn't put my head in, I couldn't reach their food and water bowls."

Bridgett and Johnathon laugh heartily as they look at Aaron. The momentary release from the intensity of his recalling of this time period is welcomed by everyone.

"So, were you and Nicole back from the hospital for good?"

"Yes, Bridgett, and she was now on blood thinners, on top of all her other medications, and it was at this point when I noticed her losing some of her motor functions. Her cancer was very aggressive, just as my mother's cancer was, and it was taking its toll on her. Because the chemotherapy and radiation would not prolong her life, nor was it a life-saving measure, we were referred to hospice care. This hospice agency was stationed in another town thirty minutes west of where we lived. The first lady that came to the apartment from hospice was very rude. In our meeting, Nicole and I were told that we needed to sign up with hospice and, if we didn't, we could not get an oxygen machine, nor could we get a hospital bed. I asked the lady, Hilda, why I couldn't get the medical equipment to help Nicole without needing theirs. She responded that it was an insurance thing. Then she said, 'If Nicole needs any morphine, it will have to go through us. I told Hilda I didn't like being bullied and that her attitude was of one of arrogance, and then I asked her to leave. I called Heather and talked with her, and we both talked with the county nurse and found out insurance companies do dictate what patients can and can't have for hospice treatment.

So, I called and spoke with the director of hospice and explained how demanding and rude Hilda was to Nicole and me. The director of this hospice, Lilith, came down and we talked with her and signed papers. Lilith apologized for her staff member and assured us that everything would be okay. But, I had no idea of the lessons we would learn from this experience. I thought my Father in Heaven had showed me a lot, up to that point, but he opened my eyes even more to the deception hospice hides behind."

"What do you mean, Aaron? Aren't hospices intended to help people be comfortable?"

"Jonathon, one of the first things I realized was that hospice has unlimited access to morphine and their staff hands it out like candy. Nicole began having some mild to moderate pain, and Lilith told me that she needed twenty milligrams every four hours. I asked her why we needed to start Nicole out on a pain medication that was so potent, instead of starting her of on something milder. Lilith responded by saying that morphine was 'not that bad,' and added that, to stay ahead of the pain by giving it every four hours, it would ensure that she was comfortable. Of course I wanted my dying wife to be pain-free, but that is a lot of morphine to give a person. Nicole even spoke up and told Lilith she didn't need that much morphine, and Lilith responded, 'Too much won't hurt you.' I asked Lilith why she was so willing to give out governed narcotics to patients, a bottle at a time, and told her that my wife didn't need an entire bottle every four days. Nor did she need twenty milligrams every four hours."

"What did she have to say about your concern?"

"She just avoided the question, Johnathon, and told Nicole she would get less hungry and need less water, and not to eat or drink because she would only be feeding the cancer. I told Lilith that sounded insane, because Nicole could still eat, drink and go to the bathroom. This was the first time I actually heard the following come from Lilith's mouth, 'Aaron, if you have to morphine Nicole out, it is okay. At least she will not be in any pain.' Heather couldn't believe what she was hearing, and neither could I. At this point, I told Lilith I was Nicole's primary care giver, and nothing will be done without my consent or hers.

Hospice was supposed to be there to help, not to speed up the process. However, Nicole and I decided to administer the morphine, but we started out with just one milligram, as needed. I also discussed this with Heather, and we all felt this was a proper dose to start out with for pain management. Lilith left frustrated and we thanked our Lord in Heaven that we were at home. As time went on, though, Nicole started losing her ability to use her hands, and my nights were long and the days were even longer. Our apartment at the towers was turning into a hospital room. In the living room we had a hospital bed, oxygen machine, all my medical supplies, the computer to document every dose of medication given, and the medical history reports in the event of a doctor or hospital needing the documentation. Lilith was sending down an aide to help me thirty minutes every other day and also to look over my charting.

I could tell that the hospice staff was frustrated with me because I wouldn't 'morphine out' Nicole and I was still feeding her. Some of the staff would make comments like, 'It is a proven fact that when people get cancer, they do not want to eat or drink' and that 'I was hurting Nicole' because I wouldn't debilitate her with morphine. I tolerated those comments for a brief time before I spoke up and said, 'You are in the wrong house to be running your mouth. Either keep those horrific comments to yourself, or piss off.' When the hospice nurses were not at the apartment, it was just the two of us. I was taking Nicole's blood sugar readouts three times a day, monitoring her blood pressure twice a day, logging everything I could, and every week I let Heather and the nurses evaluate all the documentation. I remember one night Nicole and I were sleeping and were awoken by this hissing noise. A steam pipe had broken and it was flooding our apartment. It looked like there was a fire because the steam clouded the entire floor. It triggered the fire alarm and when the fire department arrived, they called for an ambulance to get Nicole out of the apartment. From the third floor down, on the west side, it was flooded."

"Aaron, did it feel like there were forces at work?"

"It did, Bridgett, and I was seeing more of the Devil and his handy work again, and it came from hospice and their desire to push me to use more pain medications on Nicole than needed. I always told the hospice workers that there is a natural order set forth by our God in Heaven, and it must be followed, for our Lord God will call her home when He feels it is time. The rupturing pipe in the apartment was odd, and the magnitude of the flooding was unreal. But don't mistake it, our Lord God was right there."

"Aaron and Bridgett, would you both like some more coffee?"

"We would, Johnathon, and thank you."

Bridgett and Johnathon walk into the kitchen and grab some fresh coffee for everyone before returning to the sitting room.

"So, Aaron, the apartment flooded, and Nicole went to the hospital. Is that where we left off?"

"That is correct, Bridgett. When the ambulance crew showed up, I remember the paramedics walked in and I had Nicole in the recliner with her feet up off of the floor. I didn't want her feet to burn from the steaming hot water. I asked for help from the paramedics to move her out of the apartment. Her oxygen machine was off because I didn't want her getting electrocuted, but she needed oxygen. The paramedics just stood there and that is when I raised my voice and said, 'Get your asses in gear and help me lift my wife.' The one paramedic said, 'Do not speak to us in that tone of voice,' to which I replied, 'If you did your job, I wouldn't have to raise my voice. That is when one of the firefighters said he would help me move Nicole. With the help of the firefighter and the other paramedics, we got her on the gurney and on her way to the hospital. The housing authority came and turned off the steam pipes and I followed the ambulance to the hospital. When I arrived, I told the receptionist who I was and that I wanted to see my wife.

The lady told me I had to wait and, out of patience at this point, I told her she was full of shit and to let me back there where my wife was. She called security and the guard came down and asked me what the issue was. I plainly said, 'The issue is stupidity and, unless he was going to let me in to see my wife, we had nothing to talk about.' The guard told me I was rude, and that he had the authority in this situation. I asked the guard his age, and he told me he was twenty-seven years old. I told him to respect his elders and, furthermore, to get the doctor out here now. The guard called the doctor in the emergency room and then he came out to see me in the waiting room. I remember that he looked at me, and then at the receptionist and guard, and asked them what their problem was with me seeing my wife. The guard was stunned and so was the receptionist, as I walked back with the doctor to Nicole's room. The diabetic ulcer on her leg needed changed, so I changed it and made sure it was properly dressed. I called the nurse on call for hospice and let her know what was going on with the apartment. I planned for Nicole to go to stay in their facility until I could get the apartment clean and organized.

The nurse called the hospice doctor and the hospital transported Nicole to the facility. But, before she left, I told her I would get her home as soon as possible. I also told her I loved her and, if she needed me, I would be up there in a minute. I didn't trust Lilith, but I had no choice but to let Nicole go because I had to clean up the mess. We gave each other a kiss and a long hug. When she left, I called the hospice nurse back and politely explained that if she changed any medications, did not feed Nicole, or did anything without my consent, that I would sue their asses for everything they had. I asked if I had made myself clear and she responded by saying she understood. I waited to leave until the transport took her, and then I went back to the apartment and looked at the aftermath. There was water everywhere and everything was wet."

"Aaron, I have to say, you didn't take any poop from anyone when it came to protecting Nicole, did you?"

"No, I didn't, Bridgett."

"So, what happened next?"

"It was four o'clock in the morning and I started getting everything out of the apartment into the hallway so I could scrub the walls and dry out our place. I worked hard all morning and I called the facility where Nicole was at to make sure all was good with her.

Once I knew she was settled, I went back to cleaning. I remember it was about eleven in the morning when this gentleman walked up to the apartment door and knocked on the frame because the door was open. I told him to come in and he shook my hand and said, 'My name is Ray.' I told him my name was Aaron and it was a pleasure to meet him. Ray asked me if there was anything he could do for me, and I told him I was okay, and he smiled and said, 'You have a lot going on, let me help you.' I asked Ray if he had something to drink and he had this sack with him filled with water. He reached in his bag and handed me several bottles of water and said, 'What else can I help you with?' I told him that all of our clothes were wet and needed dried and that I just needed help in general. He smiled and said he would be right back. Ray was gone for maybe twenty minutes and then came back with some other people. There was Jaimee, Justin, Janice and Tru, and everyone pitched in to help me for as long as they could. Janice did our laundry. Ray paid for all the laundry expenses at his request. Jaimee and Justin helped me clean the apartment, and Tru cleaned our furniture in the hallway.

We all worked to get the apartment back in order and by nine o'clock that night it was almost done. Everyone that night was tired, but Ray stayed behind for a few minutes and told me that if Nicole and I needed anything else, to just let him know and he would be there. I believe the Lord my Father sent angels that day to correct the evil that was done, and I was thankful. I stayed up till about one in the morning before going to sleep. I missed Nicole and was worried about her the whole time. I knew she wanted to come home as soon as possible. When I woke up around eight in the morning, I called the facility where she was at and told the doctor I was ready for her to come home. The doctor asked me if the apartment was habitable and I said it was. The housing authority cleared the apartment after the inspection, and Nicole was coming home. It was about one in the afternoon when she arrived by ambulance. I greeted her outside and Ray came with me to meet her. I was happy and she was, too. The paramedics that brought Nicole from the facility in the other town were pleasant and aided me in getting her comfortable. It's amazing how Father in Heaven works. If it weren't for Him sending his angels, Nicole would have been up there for a few days. After everyone left, I hugged her and gave her a kiss. I even made her favorite strawberry smoothie to drink."

Chapter Forty-Three
The Angels, Demons and Lucifer

"As the day passed and evening settled in, I got Nicole into bed so she could relax. We talked for a while and I took her vitals, administered her medications, her one milligram dose of morphine and her blood thinner shots. Heather was visiting every day after work and Nicole would smile when she came. They were best friends and Nicole knew that, no matter what, Heather would always be there for her, just as I was, until the end. I remember one time I needed a car battery because mine wouldn't hold a charge. So, Heather called the organization, *However We May Help*, which is run by a lady named Ann, who was also the founder. It was about four-thirty in the afternoon when Ann called my cell phone and explained that Heather had told her about a man who left his home and jobs in another state to come back and take care of his ex-wife. Ann was very kind and said her organization would love to help us in our situation. The next day I had a battery for my car, and she didn't stop there in making us feel loved. Ann posted the story about Nicole and me and what we were going through on their social media page. It didn't take long, and people were asking what they could do to help.

That's when I received another call from *However We May Help*. Ann asked me, 'What are some things Nicole would love to have done for her?' and I told her I was painting Nicole's fingernails, toenails, and doing her hair, but it would be nice if she could get her hair done professionally and have pictures taken of her and me together. A few days later, Ann called and told me a licensed beautician wanted to give Nicole a full makeover, a professional photographer would take our picture, and I was put on a meal list – which meant every day someone would bring me a home-cooked dinner. If that wasn't enough, she said she had another surprise for us, but she couldn't tell me yet. After I got off the phone with Ann, I told Nicole everything, and let me just say that she lit up with sheer joy. I kissed her and told her she was loved by many.

It was the following Monday, and everything was set in place for everyone to come over and Nicole was happy, even though she was getting sicker. At five-thirty in the evening she was getting her hair done. We were both smiling at such a kind and thoughtful gesture, and Nicole surprised me by telling the stylist that she wanted eight inches of her hair cut off. Her hair had always been long, and I loved it that way, but the cut was beautiful and he did her makeup and fingernails, as well. She looked absolutely gorgeous! The apartment was filled with people and Ann brought over bedding, towels and necessities for us to use. Then the photographer showed up and took pictures of us. Nicole received flowers and hugs from everyone and finally, her big surprise showed up at the apartment. Ann had asked the high school choir to sing to us. When the choir group showed up, they all brought her flowers and sang "You Are My Sunshine." Tears of joy streamed from both of us and we thanked everyone for their amazing generosity. It was truly a blessing from our Father in Heaven."

"Aaron, all who were involved were angels, and what the world needs is more people like Ann to touch their hearts and minds."

"We were very fortunate, Bridgett, to have Ann facilitate that wonderful night, and I know in my heart this world is blessed to have her and all of the people who came together to make Nicole's life better in her time of sickness. Heather was a miracle from God, and Ray, Jaimee, Justin and Janice were beacons of light. That evening was the high point of our final days together, as times became harder for us. Nicole began slipping in and out of consciousness and eventually became unresponsive. I sat with her twenty-four hours a day, swabbing her mouth, bathing her, and taking her vitals. Ray was there to relieve me so I could sleep an hour here and there. My blood pressure was at stage two hypertension. I was living off three packs of cigarettes a day and a twenty-four pack of diet soda to keep me awake. It was unimaginably hard…"

"Oh, don't cry, Aaron. It's all okay now," Bridgett said in a comforting voice.

"I'm sorry for crying, you two. Each time I relive those moments I am surprised at how emotional it still is for me."

"Don't apologize," said Johnathon. "Crying cleanses the soul."

"I can't say I know how you feel, but I understand how it would be hard for you, Aaron."

"That's an understatement, Bridgett, but I appreciate your sympathy. I'd like to get some sleep now. How does that sound to you two?

"Absolutely," Bridgett replied.

Aaron rises out of his chair and makes his way to the living room to lay down. Johnathon and Bridgett make the beds, throw a log on the fire, put the wood stove out, and silently pray for Aaron, who they can hear crying softly. The night is still and the moon is suspended beautifully in the black matte of stars below the heavens.

Morning arrives and Bridgett is the first one to rise out of bed. She tends to the fireplace, the coffee and wood stove. The rushing water behind the cabin gives her peace, but her heart feels for Aaron. She thinks to herself that he will be gone soon, and she and Johnathon will miss their dad. Tears fall from her face as she gets the coffee ready for everyone. Walking back into the living room, she wakes Johnathon and Aaron. After rising, everyone goes out to the front porch to sit and sip their coffee while Aaron lights his morning cigarette.

"Are you up for telling us more about what happened to Nicole?"

"Yes, Bridgett, I am doing much better after a good night's sleep. It was the seventh day of her being unresponsive and Jaimee, Justin, Janice and Ray were sitting around the bed with me at three in the morning, watching over her. I had been playing the St. Michael Rosary prayer to comfort her. After the rosary was done playing, Nicole woke and sat up in total fear. She wrapped her arms around me, saying 'Don't let go.' I had never seen her that scared before, and you know the types of experiences we had been through together. The bedroom door started slamming, the room got cold, and Nicole just kept begging, 'Help me, Aaron!' It was at that moment when the St. Michael Rosary turned on by itself in front of all of us in the room. I started reciting prayer, as did Jaimee, Justin, Janice, and Ray. Nicole spoke in a loud voice, 'Aaron, he is here with us!' I asked her who was here and, after a long pause of her gasping to speak, Nicole was able to utter, 'It is Him. It's Lucifer.' Her voice had changed, and she spoke again to me, 'Aaron, I will see you in Hell for this and all you have done to help her through the years.' I told the Devil, 'You are damn right you will, and I will come with my sword drawn and with one purpose, mother fucker! You should have kept your deal and left her alone!' After about thirty minutes, the door stopped slamming and Nicole was calm.

The praying continued and, as I looked at everyone in the room, I could see that Jaimee, Justin, Janice and Ray wanted to leave. They had no idea what to think about what they had just witnessed. I talked with Ray before he and the others left and they all said they felt this cold, eerie and evil presence among us. I asked everyone in the room if they had turned on the St. Michael prayer and they said they hadn't. I had asked if one of the four witnesses had turned off the lights in the room during the encounter and, again, they all said no. As frightened as I had been, I thought to myself that others have now witnessed what we dealt with for so many years. Soon after that incident, everyone left, but they all seemed different in a way I cannot explain. I sat with Nicole until I knew everything was all right and then I slept on the floor by her bed.

Morning came and Nicole was awake, but she wasn't tracking all that well. She was confused and didn't know where she was. She kept asking me to take her away. The maintenance man came to check out the apartment and to see if we needed anything. He had heard from one of the four witnesses what had happened with the lighting, and wanted to check out the electrical box and outlets. After about an hour, he reported that he found nothing wrong with the wiring. Before he left, Nicole also asked him to take her away. He didn't know what to do or think. Finally, the hospice nurse showed up, and Nicole asked Brandi to take her away. That is when Brandi got on the phone and told her social worker that she needed backup. I looked at Brandi and told her, 'You want backup and you want to remove my wife?! Honey, I will show you backup. I called Heather immediately and explained that Nicole was not tracking, and that Brandi wanted to remove her.

Heather said, 'I will be right over,' and about five minutes later she arrived from work to find out what was going on. She evaluated Nicole and was in agreeance with me that she was not tracking right. Brandi and the social worker from hospice said they were removing her, until Heather stepped up and told them both, 'You will not take her out of his care, nor will you remove her from this apartment. I have been a state worker for forty years and you will not attempt anything, do I make myself clear?!' Brandi and the social worker left, but this was not their first attempt to try and separate us. Hospice was clashing with me something fierce. Brandi and her social worker left pissed off that day because Heather stood her ground and protected Nicole and me. I was finding out that Hospice was a joke and only cared about killing off those who could not contribute to society as they saw fit. Their workers would take forty-five minutes to an hour to show up when I needed them, and they were always trying to push more morphine onto Nicole than was needed. Moreover, their doctor wouldn't evaluate her on a regular basis, I suppose due to spite at my reluctance to let them have her so they could kill her.

It was one thing after another with the House with the Dove. Heather was still coming every day to visit, but Lilith wouldn't address the pills that Nicole needed to take – those that she had been on for seventeen years. Between Brandi, Lilith and Jozi at Hospice, it was a constant fight, tooth and nail. Brandi made it very clear that I shouldn't be swabbing Nicole's mouth, nor should I be feeding her. They just kept saying, 'Give her the morphine.' I told Lilith they wanted to kill her as fast as they could and mask her death behind the name of Hospice. I made it very clear to them that they were there to help people, or at least that was the deceptive veil that they hid behind, and not to commit murder or euthanize my wife. Then, one night, Nicole was bleeding from her nose and couldn't get comfortable. Her temperature was rising, and she was in and out of consciousness, so I called the Hospice nurse to come to the apartment and evaluate her.

Naturally, the nurse showed up with another nurse and a police officer. Ray, Jaimee, Janice, Justin and I were there at the apartment when they arrived. When the officer and the nurses came into the apartment, I shook his hand, but then he swiped my hand away. I dismissed his arrogance and proceeded to tell the nurses what was going on with Nicole. I printed all my records of charting and the Hospice nurses did absolutely nothing that night. But, when the nurses walked out of the apartment, the officer stopped and shut the door behind them. He turned around to face me and said, 'Aaron, I would like to shake the hand of the man who is taking care of this fine lady. In my profession, I have never seen someone give this much care and love to their ex-wife as you are doing now for her.' I told the officer that we may not have the piece of paper any more, showing we are married, but we are and I love her. The officer replied, 'From what I have seen tonight, I know you are giving the best care you can, and I know animosity is elevated between you and Hospice, but I am proud of you for what you are doing.'

Then the officer asked if he could meet Nicole. I told him she was fading in and out of consciousness, but if he would like to meet her, he could. Together we walked into the living room and the officer took her hand and held it for a few moments. I had never seen so much compassion from law enforcement than I had that night. The officer then left, and I felt relieved because the evil from Hospice tried making me look bad, once again, but ultimately the light was shown. That night, I was also told the doctor wanted Nicole to have less morphine. I explained that she was barely taking any now, but Lilith didn't care, which prompted me to express my discontentment with her yet again. I told her, 'You won't address her medications, you are now restricting her morphine when she finally needs more, you bring an officer with you to intimidate me and possibly stress Nicole out even more, and your arrogance and disregard for human life is sickening.' Lilith just laughed and said, Hospice can do many things that people don't know about because they don't care.'

The next morning, I called Heather and explained what happened. She couldn't believe the unprofessional manner in which Hospice was treating us, especially during the time when Nicole was dying. We talked and, with no other choice, decided to try and get her in with the Hospice house in town. I made the phone call and Heather called, too, on our behalf. The staff at Hospice house told us they had to wait for the doctor to approve the switch. I was exhausted and my blood pressure was still stage two, and I was having to fight way too many people. Then, about one o'clock in the afternoon, Heather showed up with another social worker, named Jeff. She told me that the Hospice nurse and director turned me in for adult dependent abuse on Nicole. Their claim was that I was giving her too much morphine.

Heather told me that she and Jeff questioned Lilith and Brandi about their accusation, but neither one could answer their questions. She stated that there were doctor's orders for the morphine and I was following the orders. In fact, she explained to them, 'Aaron does not have any extra morphine on hand. He keeps it locked up with the other medications and, furthermore, I am there every day visiting, and he keeps his charting current and accurate on a daily basis. So, how can you accuse him of wrongdoing?' Lastly, Heather even told Lilith and Brandi, 'On numerous occasions, Lilith, I have heard you tell Aaron to morphine Nicole out against his and her wishes,' and that she believed, 'They were the ones doing wrong because, as a state employee for forty years, I know when someone is full of shit.'

Lilith, of course, had no answer for Heather. Nonetheless, however, Jeff had to do his investigation, so he came in and luckily Nicole was awake and lucid. She and Jeff both talked while I was in the hallway. Then Jeff came out and brought me in and I showed him the medical supplies, the charting, and my daily routine. I had forty some pages of charting and he looked at me and asked if he could have them. I handed them all over to him and told him they were his to review and keep. It was at that moment that Jeff said he needed to step out into the hallway. I asked him if I did anything wrong and he said, 'No, I will be right back.' A few minutes later he returned and said, 'Aaron, I am a two-time cancer survivor and seeing what you are doing for Nicole is something that I have never seen before.' He added, 'There is so much love, tenderness and attention to her. I wish everyone loved like you love Nicole.'

About that time, she woke up in pain and Jeff was right there. I explained to him that Brandi and Lilith are restricting her morphine. He talked with Nicole and his face got red. He left the apartment, walked out into the hallway, and called Lilith and told her they had less than thirty minutes to get to the apartment. Everyone in the apartment could hear the anger in is voice as he talked with Lilith. He also told her the only people that are harming Nicole was them."

Chapter Forty-Four

When You Lose

*I*t took less than twenty minutes for my phone to ring. It was Lilith and Brandi downstairs in the lobby. But, just as I hung up with them, the other Hospice called and said they would take Nicole. I was happy and I hugged her, along with Heather and Jeff, because I didn't have to fight Lilith and her Hospice team. I remember looking at Heather and asking her what I should tell them. She smiled and said, 'Fire them.' With a smile on my face, I went downstairs and looked at Lilith and Brandi and told them, 'Nice try turning me in to CPS and, by the way, you're fired, so take your murdering asses out of this complex and go back to Hell.' About that time, Lilith reached for her phone and I saw her start to call 911. I told her, 'Jeff and Heather are upstairs and the other Hospice is on their way with the ambulance to get Nicole. But, by all means, call 911. You already have way too much attention on yourselves. So, either call or get the hell out, and do not come within thirty feet of Nicole or me ever again.'

When the paramedics came, Nicole was crying, and I explained with Heather what happened. The paramedics could not believe that a Hospice organization, or any of their employees, could be so cruel as to withhold pain medication and to create so much hostility for a lady who was dying from cancer. Yet, we were all happy that Nicole would not have to deal with Lilith. We walked downstairs to the ambulance and watched the paramedics load her into the back. But, before they did, I gave her a kiss and told her I would be right behind her. The Hospice director in town explained that I would need to bring her medications, oxygen machine, and my charting so they could get organized and know what she needed. I felt relieved that she was out of the hands of liars and murderers. The new Hospice seemed great – at first. The facility was beautiful, and everyone was friendly, which was a refreshing change. They got Nicole's pain under control and seemed to genuinely care about our welfare and comfort. But, as time passed, some of the staff became cold-hearted and I began to see the illusion that this House with the Dove portrayed.

It became apparent to me that one House was just the same as the other, full of all that is unclean, like the Devil himself. I remember hearing one of the daytime nurses whistling a pleasant tune as she walked down the hallway to a room with a heavy dose of morphine for a patient. It was as if she was getting pleasure from doping out the ones she took an oath to help. At other times, I witnessed nurses yelling at their patients who needed help, telling him or her, 'You're not getting anything to eat or drink because it will do you more harm than good.' Johnathon and Bridgett, one lady would cry out for company almost every night. She had no family and was incredibly lonely. After a few nights of not hearing this lady, who was right next to Nicole's room, I asked a nurse why she was so quiet. I hadn't heard a word out of her. The nurse replied, 'We morphined her out.' It took less than two weeks for the lady in the next room to pass away. The staff withheld food and water from her. Another man needed help and the new nurse that was hired walked in before her shift ended and told him, 'You want your pills this late, you can have them. When you shit yourself in bed you can just lay in it all night long.'"

"Oh, my dear heavens, Aaron, that is wrong on every level!"

"I was surprised, as well, Bridgett, to see that level of unprofessionalism and downright cruelty. It was that same nurse that knew Nicole's medications needed to be crushed and she didn't crush them. I didn't check the pills before she gave them to Nicole, who started choking when she tried to take them. I told the nurse she needed to do something, and her response was, 'That's just a part of dying.' I looked at the nurse with rage and told her if she didn't get Nicole's throat vacuumed out, my next call would be to the police for negligent homicide. The director was there in two minutes, clearing

Nicole's throat. The Hospice House had a kitchen in their facility, but we were repeatedly told that it was closed. I always spoke up to the nurses and told them it's their job to make her comfortable, so do it, or I would go and get her food myself.

Almost every day, I was going to the store or restaurant and getting Nicole something she could eat. It was a constant battle and I found myself in the same situation as we were with the first Hospice. I had nurses not wanting to bathe Nicole, so I would. Many times, she was turned on her side with force and she would start crying and then I would rip into them. I was so tired of the nurses being lazy that I would bathe and hand-feed her because she couldn't use her arms any more. I was washing her hair and making sure, when she was awake, to give her something to drink. I would read to her and always had her tablet by her bed so she could watch movies.

Months had passed, and I would not leave the Hospice House for long periods of time because many of the nurses would treat the people dying with disrespect, or would try and figure out how they could euthanize them. Every day, people are euthanized and neglected of their basic human rights, and if I wasn't there, they probably would have killed Nicole long before she passed away. I will say this: my Father in Heaven showed me the evil that lies right in front of the world to see, and what goes on in the House with the Dove is evil cloaked in mercy.

Once, I had one of the nurses ask me, 'Why do you use the Holy water every night and in the morning, and put the sign of the cross above the doors and windows?' I explained to her that 'The Devil is everywhere, even in this House. I use these to fight the Devil and to protect Nicole.' Moreover, I explained to her, 'my wife found faith when we were together and, even now, she loves and adores our Father in Heaven. But the Devil's goal is to try and break her faith, and I am Nicole's watcher, as she always told me, and I am not about to let that happen.' The nurse laughed and said, 'The Devil isn't real.' I replied by telling her, 'How can the Devil not be real when the motto of this house is, *Angels Are Everywhere*? One cannot believe in angels and not the Devil and, if you believe that, then your thought process is skewed.' The nurse walked away and didn't say a word. During my stay in the Hospice House, Heather and I were in the office twice a week because the nursing staff didn't feel appreciated, or they would get upset because I would feed Nicole and wasn't trying to rush her death by using too much morphine.

Heather asked the director one time if she was concerned that her staff was trying to administer more morphine than needed. Furthermore, in one of our meetings, she told the director, 'We know that Nicole has had a gradual increase over time, because of her increased levels of pain, but the term *morphine out* is ridiculous.' I told Ruby if her staff would do their job, and give compassion to those in need, then Heather and I wouldn't need to be in her office. I also told her that murder is a sin and, even when it is masked by the name Hospice, it is still murder. Ruby said she would find out and talk with her staff, but Heather and I never heard back from her.

Again, I found myself having to watch those who took an oath to do no harm. Once, I recall that the director and social worker for Hospice said that people only live in their house for five to seven days before they die. I understand now why that is, and why people die so soon after their diagnoses. I personally watched over thirty people die during my time there. Some people would walk up to me and say, 'Today is the day my loved one dies.' I would ask them how they knew, and they would say the Hospice staff is giving their loved one thirty milligrams of morphine every hour, on the hour, whether they wanted it or not. I was blown away.

I never left Nicole's side, despite being told by the Hospice pastor I should just leave her and let the nurses take care of her. The pastor told me, 'She could be gone in two days if I just left her alone.' I told him, 'I can't wait for you to meet my Father in Heaven' and just walked away. The House with the Dove is filled with lies. I lived there for seven months and four days, right alongside Nicole, and I watched the abuses and neglect to the young and old who were dying. Euthanasia happens, every day, behind the glass. I wasn't the only one who had seen their practices and how murder is carried out."

Bridgett interjected, "Aaron, how was Nicole possibly enduring all of this for so long?"

"I hand-fed her every day, bathed her, sat with her, and did everything I could. The Hospice nurses were worthless, for the most part, due to my interference with their murdering of my wife. Don't get me wrong: there was one nurse and staff member that were kind, but the few certainly did not outweigh the many. Nicole first lost the use of her hands, then her arms, and then her legs. The cancer ate through her left side, from her breast line down to her hip – eight inches long by three and a half inches wide by two to three inches into her stomach area. The doctor of Hospice at that point said, 'In fifteen years he had never seen a cancer be so aggressive,' adding that 'the cancer made her flesh fall off as if it was being burned off in layers.' Soon thereafter, Nicole had a stroke and couldn't eat or drink at all, so I swabbed her mouth for sixteen days. I didn't sleep and when I did, it wasn't sleep."

Bridgett, with tears running down her face, asked, "Aaron, how much longer was it after that before Nicole passed away?"

"Her time was coming soon. Before she had her stroke and could still talk, I remember she asked me to tell her about our place in Heaven. I told her that we have a cabin in the woods. There is a river in the back of the cabin and the trees are all around us, with lilies and rose bushes in full bloom. We have a loft and all of our friends in Heaven are with us always. She smiled and said, 'I love you, Aaron' and told her that I loved her, too. As Nicole smiled, she said, 'Shhh, honey, we must be quiet.' I asked her why and she replied, 'Our babies are sleeping upstairs, and I am finally with them. I can finally be a mother to my babies. I will give the children a hug from you and me.' I asked Nicole if the children were Mattie and Amber, and she smiled and said, 'Yes, Mathew John and Amber Rose.' I told her I would be quiet and, with a smile, she said 'Honey, our Father is proud of you and soon you will be with me and our children.' When she had her stroke and the pain had increased, we started giving her more morphine and fentanyl, but her pain was still there. The seizures were not stopping, and I was once again at a crossroads. I sat down with Heather and the Hospice staff and was told if we didn't increase the pain medications, Nicole would feel immeasurable pain, but if I allowed the morphine, fentanyl and ketamine to be increased, she would go to sleep within ten hours. Every day I hurt and cry knowing I made the decision to increase the pain medications and she would go to sleep. But, at that point I knew I had too, because I loved her, and I did not want her in pain. In doing so, even though it alleviated her suffering, I became no better than the ones who euthanized every day. Therefore, her death is on my hands."

With tears streaming down his face, Johnathon manages to utter, "It's not your fault, Aaron. You cannot keep carrying that burden."

"Johnathon, every day I know her death is my fault and I cannot forgive myself, nor will I ever. But I know this: the Devil made me watch as He tried to break her faith by making her suffer. Lucifer put Nicole and me in that situation and I will find him in the afterlife. I will not rest until I stand in front of Him with my sword in hand. With every breath I take each day, with every step I take, I am getting closer to the reckoning that is deserved. I will come with my shield of faith, my armor, my Lord God, and my sword will mete out the Devil's judgement.

It was October 09, 2018, at 10:55 p.m. when my wife left and went to Heaven. The morning Nicole passed away, I remember one of the Hospice nurses who came onto her shift walked up to me and said, 'So, Nicole *went cold* last night, didn't she?' I went through the roof and told her she was the most cold-hearted bitch I had ever seen, and that she shouldn't be so happy, because one day God will have his judgement on her."

"Aaron, there is no doubt that the Devil was present throughout your and Nicole's life together. He took everything away from you and her and, in the end, you both are separated from one another. But, I also know that Nicole lives within your heart and soul…"

As Johnathon speaks to Aaron, Bridgett runs into the cabin, sobbing. Johnathon tells her to come back, but she cries, 'No, just leave me alone for a while!"

"Aaron, is there another reason why you feel Nicole's death was your fault?"

"Yes, Johnathon, there is. Through the years I often quoted lines to Nicole from the movie *Rocky V*, spoken by Burgess Meredith and Sylvester Stallone. They go like this:

Ah, come here Nicole. My God, you're ready, aren't you? The Devil won't know what hit him. You're going to roll over him like a bulldozer. You know, my love; I know how you feel about this fight that's coming up. Cause I was lost once, too. And I'll tell you something. Well, if you weren't here, I probably wouldn't be alive today. The fact that you're here and doing as well as you're doing gives me - what do you call it - motivation? Huh? To stay alive, because I think that people die sometimes when they don't want to live no more, and nature is smarter than people think. Little by little, we lose our friends, we lose everything. We keep losing and losing till we say, you know, 'Oh what the hell am I living around here for? I got no reason to go on.' But with you Nicole, I got a reason to go on. And I'm going to stay alive and I will watch you make good and I'll never leave you until that happens. Cause, when I leave you, you'll not only know how to fight, you'll be able to take care of yourself outside the ring, too, is that okay? It's okay. Now I got a little gift for you. Aaron, you don't have to. No, wait a minute. Hey, look at that. See that? This is the favorite thing that I have on this Earth. And my Father in Heaven gave me this cross and now I am giving it to you Nicole and it, it's going to be like a, like an angel on your shoulder, see? If you ever get hurt and you feel that you're going down, this little angel is going to whisper in your ear. It's going to say, 'Get up, Nicole, because I love you.'

When I left Nicole, her heart broke while I was gone, and I know in my heart, as I sit here, crying, talking to you, Johnathan, that Nicole was losing hope for my returning home. And when she got sick, it was already too late. The Devil had snuck in and created her disease. It wasn't enough that I checked in on her. Nicole needed me all the time. I believe, with all my heart and soul, that she lost her motivation to stay alive. I know how people die when they lose their motivation to live. I was Nicole's rock and I failed her because I became weak."

"Aaron, when you left her, you had fallen. There were many things in your life, and hers, that you both were trying to understand, and enduring the war over Nicole's soul was not something many people could see, much less understand, or know how to help her with. I am not saying your ways were excusable, but, as you have said, the Devil is subtle and enticing. He has ways of drawing out those who are hurting, and are lost, into a realm of destruction."

"Yes, Johnathon, that is all true. But then the Devil found a way around the seal placed by the angels and God. Instead of coming through Nicole, as he and his demons had done for decades, Lucifer came at her with force and made me watch what he did to her for fourteen months. Every day I tried fighting him, but he took the final thing in this world I cherished with all my heart. If I hadn't have left Nicole, she might still be alive. I failed my Lord in Heaven and I failed my wife. And, by the time I re-found that love – like I used to love Nicole – it was too late. She was gone."

"Aaron, that is a heavy burden to place on your shoulders. You did fight the Devil and you won, but you also had to lose. You taught Nicole faith, love and understanding. You came back after you crossed the line and not many men would have left their home, jobs, and life to move back and take care of their ex-wife. You *did* find that love again and you gave her the greatest gift ever, which was your love. The Devil came that night in the apartment, because he despised your work of faith and he knew Nicole belonged to her Father in Heaven. Please listen to my words. Our Father found his lost sheep and, when she came home, He cried out, 'Rejoice, rejoice, for I have found the lost sheep through Aaron's hands!' Nicole is home, now, and she doesn't have to take medications, fight the Devil, or hurt from the pain any more. I know you hurt, Aaron, and I know your tears, as we speak, flood the rivers, but believe me when I say that your wife is with her biological father, her babies Mattie and Amber, and she walks with our Lord Jesus as she had done before – only now it's forever."

"Johnathon, Heather always said I was there when it mattered the most. She also told me I was like this knight in shining armor that rode in on a white horse from the north to help Nicole."

"She was right, Aaron, and whether you believe it or not, you saved her and you came full circle in your life. Sometimes, you must lose in order to win and, yes, you lost Nicole in the flesh, but you won because she is in Heaven and at peace. Now, give me a hug and then let's find Bridgett."

"Okay, Johnathon. And thank you for your thoughtful words but I refuse to accept that I was a knight in shining armor, and I never will."

As they hug each other, Aaron stands up from the rocking chairs and looks over at the angel water fountain. He sees the baby fawn, staring. Turning towards the cabin door, they walk back in and find Bridgett on the floor in front of the fireplace in the sitting room.

Johnathon asks, "Bridgett, are you okay?"

"Yes, I am better now. I just can't believe mom went through so much in her life, from the beginning to the end."

"I know, but she is home now, and you know that she no longer feels any pain or threats from the Devil," Johnathon said, trying to soothe her.

"Aaron, I must know, did her daughters come to see her in the end?"

"No, Bridgett, they did not."

"I didn't think they would. Was there a funeral?"

"At the time, I couldn't afford one, so Nicole was cremated.

Her ashes were buried in Calvary."

"Will you be buried next to mom, Aaron?"

"I will be, Bridgett, and she and I have a black granite, heart-shaped headstone with the parable of the lost sheep inscribed on the back, with a porcelain picture of her and me holding each other. I also had another headstone made that matches our headstone, with two hearts for her two babies, Mattie and Amber. Because her two babies were taken away from this world, I wanted them to finally have a resting place with their mother. I put lanterns above each monument to light up the darkness of night."

Bridgett and Johnathon begin to cry and hug their father.

Chapter Forty-Five

In the Wind

"I will tell you that, when I laid Nicole to rest, Heather was there with me. I put her ashes in a vault with a picture of us together, as well as one of Nicole and Heather, with a red rose. Heather visits her resting place often, and I go see her at least twice a day."

Bridgett and Johnathon both tell Aaron they love him and he whispers back, 'I love you both, too." As the day moves on there is a silence upon the cabin, many tears are shed, and Aaron has this feeling in his gut that time is precious.

As evening approaches, Bridgett asks, "Aaron, will you play us a song on the piano?"

"I would be proud to play for you and Johnathon."

"What are you going to play for us?"

"Johnathon, it's a song called "*If I Could Be Where You Are* by the artist Enya."

Aaron begins to play, gently pressing against the ivory keys. He turns his head and looks at Johnathon and Bridgett, who are both crying as they listen to the melody being played. They hold each other as the song continues. Aaron, feeling their love, strikes the last key, closes the fallboard and stands tall.

Bridgett, still wiping her tears, says, "That was beautiful. May I ask one more favor?"

"You may, but what do you mean one last favor?"

"It was just a question. Can we sit in the living room tonight for a while?"

"I don't mind at all, Bridgett. Why change things up now?"

They all walk to the living room and sit comfortably.

"Aaron, you will always be remembered in Heaven."

"I hope so, Johnathon."

The night has set in and the fireplace is lively with flames. There is calmness in the air that can't be explained. As Aaron talks with Bridgett and Johnathon in the living room, he is startled and turns his head quickly to the loft. He swears he hears babies crying. Turning back, he asks them if they heard the crying, but they are no longer there. He calls out for them, but there is no answer.

He can hear the babies again, and he heads upstairs quickly. To his sheer amazement, he finds two cribs – one with a little boy and one with a little girl, both lying there in baby clothes. He walks over to the cribs and picks them up and holds them in his arms. Mystified, he thinks to himself, how can this possibly be? The babies stop crying and smile at Aaron. He cries, thinking about Mattie, Amber, and his son that left so long ago. Rocking back and forth in the rocker, he closes his eyes for a brief second to understand what is going on and, when he opens his eyes back up, the little babies are gone. On the mattress in the loft, he sees a letter with his name on the envelope, next to the pine wooden box that is now uncovered from underneath the pillow and quilt. He stands and reaches for the letter and the pine wooden box, and then sits back down. Afraid to open the letter, he sits for a moment to collect his thoughts. He builds up the courage and slowly pulls the letter out of the envelope. He opens it and begins reading:

Dear Aaron:

The time we spent together was very special to Johnathon and me, and we both love you as our father. You gave us a gift of knowing all these years that we were loved. Johnathon and I have been alone for so many years in Heaven and now we are with our mother. You see, Aaron, our real names are "Mattie," Mathew John, and Amber Rose. We wanted to hear from you what our mother went through in life, and you gave us that gift through the hands of our Father in Heaven. Mattie and I asked mom if it was okay and she said we could. If it weren't for you, mom wouldn't be in Heaven today, and that is why Mattie and I call you dad. I know you don't like to be told you saved our mother, but you did, and Mattie and I love you for always caring. The time we spent together in the cabin gave us the time to know you. Mom told Mattie and me all about you, and now I understand why mom is sad most of the time in Heaven without you by her side. It's like half of her soul is with you and half of your soul is with her.

We can't thank you enough for honoring us on Earth and in Heaven. Every day we prayed for a miracle from Jesus and we received one when we met you. Our hearts are saddened, as moms' heart is sad, and we wish you were here with us now, together as a family in Heaven, but I know you made promises to mom, and I know you will find her family and honor her as you have honored Mattie and me. We love you as our dad and always will, forever. I am sorry we had to leave the cabin, but mom called, and we had to return home. Dad, I know this must be hard for you, and I have seen you shed many tears just as you are crying now, but don't let the sadness blind the miracle of what you and mom did through the years. You taught mom how to love our Lord, and Mattie and I know that, without you helping her, mom would never have been found. But, just like the lost sheep that was found by the shepherd, she now has an everlasting home in the kingdom of Heaven. Remember, dad, we are only a heartbeat away and, when you find mom's sisters and brother to pass on Mom's legacy, the sun will shine brighter than ever before and Heaven will sing praise. I must go now, Dad, and

Mattie sends his love.

P. S.

I love you, Dad. We all love you. And please open the box

Amber Rose and "Mattie," Mathew John

Emotions flood from within Aaron and his tears are heavy. Holding the letter to his heart, he whispers, "Thank you, Father in Heaven, for blessing me with the gift of knowing Nicole's babies and for Nicole. Setting the letter down in his lap, he reaches for the box and opens the lid slowly. He pulls out the picture that was made by the sketch artist so many years ago and remembers every moment they shared together. With tears running down his face, he reaches for the envelope and opens it with care. It reads:

My dear husband:

I love you and always will. I know now that Heaven is a place where happiness and joy are everywhere, but I miss you every day and I am sad without you. I call your name and I know you can hear me because I hear you call for me, too. I walk with our Lord daily and he feels my sadness. I ask our Lord Jesus, "When can my husband come to be with me?" and He keeps telling me, "Soon." I cry most days, my love, and Mattie and Amber comfort me during those times. I want you to know that you were my protector and our Lord Jesus gave you the strength and courage to fight every day. I was hard on you, my love, for many years, and I also know the Devil took almost everything from you and me. We weren't perfect, and we both faltered in life, but without you I wouldn't be in Heaven and our Father wouldn't have found his lost sheep. My darling husband, you are one of God's true heavenly warriors. I long for you to come home and be at my side again, and at our Father's side, but until that day comes, I will always love and be with you.

Looking down from Heaven, I will smile, but still be sad. Your son, Anthony, is always with me, as well, and he looks just like you. Thank you, my love, for saving me from the Devil. I know guilt rules your life and weighs heavy on your shoulders, because you blame yourself for my going home to Heaven, but you shouldn't feel that way. My husband, no man could have fought harder than you fought, and I am proud of you, my love. I see you at my resting place every day and the monuments are beautiful. I know now that my legacy will continue and people will remember who I was, in life, and what I endured. All those years, I never fully understood what love was until I met you. So, I thank you and I will see you again. I must go for now, but remember, half of my soul is with you on Earth and half of your soul is with me in Heaven. I will watch from above, always, and there is a book called 'A Love Story' you should pick up off of the chest and read, my husband.

P.S.

You were right. A man and woman do not need a piece of paper to show they are married.

With all my love, and Eskimo kisses, I will see you again,

Nicole

Aaron's heart is overwhelmed, both in great sadness and overwhelming joy. His thoughts are scattered, as the unexplainable gifts he has been given are a miracle from Heaven. He holds both letters in his right hand, stands, and picks up the book called *A Love Story* off of the chest. He sits back down and holds the book against his chest, scared to open it and find out what's inside. But his heart tells him not to fear the unknown and to embrace the love. He slowly opens the front cover and, on the inside, he sees the dedication page, which is to him, with the following words inlaid below a picture and an inscription: *Dedicated to my husband, Aaron, God's true warrior and angel. Written by Nicole.* Slowly, Aaron turns the page and reads the preface:

The journey has been long, and our hearts are one.
With faith, love and understanding, this is *A Love Story*. We
sit on the grains of sand under the moonlit sky, embracing the
moment. The clouds glow in the night and the wind is subtle.
The ocean tides are calming, and the stars sparkle flawlessly.
I found my love in the midst of darkness and, now, he is my
guiding light. His touch is of an angel and my touch is of
happiness. Together forever, we said, and love is our hope.
I think to myself, this can't be real, but it is, and I love him.
After all these years of hardship and pain, one man took me
aside and rescued me from this world. His hands begin to softly
caress my body. His lips gently press against my neck and my
body rushes with a feeling of desire. His hand slides to my
thigh and I feel every part of my body melt in the sand as he
feels my flesh against his flesh.

Aaron stops reading and now knows that Nicole is writing a
new story – one of him and her together forever in Heaven. He puts the
letters back in the envelopes and lays them inside the pages of Nicole's
book. He stands and walks to the window in the loft and looks out,
staring at the angel marble statue. The night is lonely without Mattie
and Amber, his children, and the cabin is empty. He knows in his heart
that it is time for him to return home. He opens the window to feel the
night air as he holds his gifts.

Behind him, a voice speaks softly, "Dad..." Startled, Aaron
turns around and sees Trenton standing there. "I only have a few
moments, but I want you to know, like Mattie and Amber, that I,
Trenton, am your son, Anthony. I love you, Dad, and I miss you so
much. Now, stand with me and look upon the angel that loved me as
her own."

They turn and the marble angel statue burns bright, even
though there is no moon shining in the sky. Aaron calls out, "My wife,
I love you."

Nicole appears from the angel statue and smiles. Aaron hears
the words, "I love you, Aaron."

"Dad, mom is beautiful, isn't she?"

"Yes, she is, son."

Nicole, hovering above them, descends to where Aaron stands. They embrace each other and he whispers in her ear, "Please don't go."

Nicole whispers back, "I am always with you, my love."

Behind her, Aaron sees the mute swans as they transform into Heaven's angels. He looks up into the sky, which lights up inexplicably, and sees the eagle turn into Amy, Nicole's guardian angel, and the white-feathered owl transforms into St. John. Slowly, the light fades, and Nicole and all who were with her are gone. Anthony whispers, "Goodbye, Dad, until we meet again, and I love you."

Aaron falls to the bed with his gifts, crying and overwhelmed. He wraps the quilt around him and, emotionally exhausted, falls asleep deep within its warmth. When morning arrives, he awakens, for the first time in a long time, alone. As he opens his eyes, he painfully realizes that he is no longer at the cabin, and it seems his fear has now become reality. He sees the ruins of what once was and has returned home as the others have. He sits on the side of his bed, reaches for a cigarette and lights it with tears running down his cheek. He takes a drag and thinks to himself, why did the war have to happen? And why did I have to leave?

He raises his head and, looking around, notices the pine wooden box – open, with the letters, the picture of him and Nicole, and the book called *A Love Story* on the bed. As Aaron sees the gifts from his wife and children, his mind wonders how the gifts came to be with him in the ruins. A lady's voice echoes through the temple ruins, "With faith, no explanation is necessary." Filled with emotion, he grabs his gifts and whispers, "I love you all" and kisses the letters and the book. He stands and places the gifts in his rucksack, knowing that his loves, his wife and family, are with him in his heart.

Chapter Forty-Six
Into the Unknown

*F*eeling my cleaved and wounded body, I slowly dress and reach for my black cowboy hat. I put on my worn cowboy boots and make my way outside of the temple ruins and check on my horse, "Faithful." The sky is grey, and the wind is subtle. My white horse looks at me, knowing we have one more journey to fulfill. I saddle her with all that remains and my gifts from above. I mount my horse, holding onto the reins as we begin to ride away from what I once knew as my home. Slowly, I ride to Nicole's resting place, where she and Mattie and Amber are recognized and remembered. I look back with sadness one more time at the ruins of where our lives once thrived with joy, peace and love. Slowly, Faithful and I arrive, and I dismount her and stand before my wife and children.

Kneeling upon the green grass, I feel the love in the air, even though the day is cloudy. The wind blows softly in the trees. "My wife, I love you, and 'Faithful' and I must go to find your family. I want you to know that, no matter what, I will always carry your picture with me in my heart, body and soul. I must pass on your legacy to your sisters and brother, so they know your story and can have some closure. I will not fail you again, nor will I give up until I find them. I love you all. I will see you again, my love, and I will return one day."

I walk up to Faithful, pat her on the neck, grab the horn, put my foot into the stirrup and mount my only companion. Holding the reins once again, Faithful and I look to the west and begin riding into the unknown, with my Lord and the love of all in Heaven guiding each step.

Author's Notes

Through the thirteen years Christina and I battled the Devil and his demons, it was by the hand of our Lord in Heaven that we prevailed in the end. But it was not without much hardship, pain and suffering. Many angels died and suffered their own losses, and many demons were destroyed. In the final battle, Lucifer tried breaking Christina's faith in the year of our Lord, 2018, by making her suffer. I stood by her side one last time, protecting her day and night. In the end, when I again found that love I once had, it was too late. I knew then I must lose in this life, and see my wife pass away, in order to defeat the Devil. Christina left this Earth holding the cross I gave her many years ago and with her faith intact.

Below is the list of the names Christina and I encountered over the years. I say this to all: Heaven and Hell are real, and all who came forth were from different realms beyond what we see in our daily lives. When an archangel dies in battle, God puts the angels in a special place. However, with blessings, an archangel can be given Graces, just as one who has lived in Hell can be graced with forgiveness and be pulled to Heaven.

In the Temple of Heaven in the Layer of the Highest: Our Lord Jesus Christ, Our God of Abraham, Most Holy Mother Mary, St. Joseph, and St. Job.

The Disciples: St. Matthew, St. Mark, St. Isaiah, St. John, St. Luke, and St. Samuel.

The Three Heavenly Women Angels: They came in the end of the war over Christina's soul and took up the cross around my neck, which became the one of the three seals. These three angels came again, right before Christina passed away.

Our Lord God in Heaven's Highest Angels who Aided in the Battle: St. Michael, St. Uriel, St. Gabriel, St. Amintiel, St. Raphael, and St. Ramiel.

Archangels Serving Heaven: Nicole, Julie, Doug, Ernie, Savanna, Al, Bo, Joe, Luke, April, Bill, Ed, Eddy, Edward, Keith, Kyle, Lance, Ron, Rita, Maurice, Joyce, Billy, Janette, Jack, Pam, Brandon, Aric, White Feather, Ralph, and Grey Eagle.

Christina's Guardian Angel: Amy, who was there in the

beginning and the end.

Heaven's Children: Mattie, Amber, John Paul, Justin, Lucas James, Samuel Allan, Dan, Bridgett, Marcus, Christina, Trenton, Joshua, Johnathon, Anthony, Gilbert, Isaac, and Heather.

Names of the Demons: Lucifer, Lucifer's Disciples, Diablo, James, Jackal, Leo, Leon, Ramon, Ramon Jr, Salone, Jade, Baal, Daniel, Judas, Amos, Karin, Judith, Lilith, Belial, Vince, and Michael.

The Messengers of Hell: Came as one…

Those that Came into the House: They called themselves Legion.

Note: Toward the end of the thirteen-year war over Christina's soul, our Lord God granted graces upon some of those in Hell, who had seen their wicked ways and repented. Among those names were Leon, Ramon, Ramon Jr. Salone, Jade, Leo and George. These souls were judged and brought to Heaven by the most Holy. My eyes have seen with the faith that blows in the wind, touching every man woman and child upon the Earth. And, with faith, no explanation is necessary.

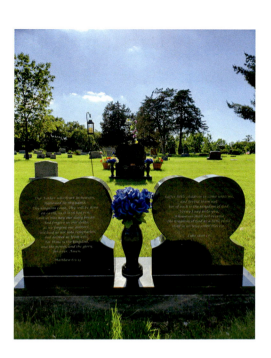